RETHINKING TOURISM
AND ECOTRAVEL

RETHINKING TOURISM AND ECOTRAVEL

Second Edition

Deborah McLaren

Kumarian
Press, Inc.

Rethinking Tourism and Ecotravel

Published 2003 in the United States of America by Kumarian Press, Inc.
1294 Blue Hills Avenue, Bloomfield, CT 06002 USA.

Copyright © 1998, 2003 Deborah McLaren. All rights reserved.
First edition 1998
Second edition 2003

No part of this book may be reproduced or transmitted in any form or by any means, electronic or mechanical, including photocopy, recording, or information storage and retrieval system, without prior permission of the publisher.

Production, design, indexing, and proofreading by ediType, Yorktown Heights, N.Y.
The text of this book is set in 10.5/13 Electra.
The display type is La Bamba.

Printed in Canada on acid-free paper by Transcontinental Printing.
Text printed with vegetable oil–based ink.

∞ The paper used in this publication meets the minimum requirements of the American National Standard for Information Sciences–Permanence of Paper for Printed Library Materials, ANSI Z39.48-1984.

Library of Congress Cataloging-in-Publication Data

McLaren, Deborah, 1959-
    Rethinking tourism and ecotravel/Deborah McLaren.– 2nd ed.
        p.   cm.
    Includes bibliographical references and index.
    ISBN 1-56549-169-6 (pbk. : alk. paper)
        1. Ecotourism.   I. Title.
G156.5.E26.M46 2003
338.4′791 – dc21

                                            2003004069

---

11 10 09 08 07 06 05 04 03   10 9 8 7 6 5 4 3 2 1   First Printing 2003

Contents

Acknowledgments

The revised copy of this book would not be possible without the wisdom, prayers, and encouragement of many people, including my editor, Guy Bentham, production manager Adriana Rojas, and everyone at Kumarian Press. Special thanks to Cynthia Harrison and Sally Weleczki-Cmiel, the most dedicated researchers and book organizers I've ever worked with! And to Chris Beck, Virginia Hadsell, Ron Mader, Crescencio Resendiz Hernandez, Luis Vivanco, David Barkin, Norbert Hohl, Charles de Burlo, Nina Rao, Anita Pleumarom, Medora Woods, Martha Honey, Kaleo Patterson, Dave Lacy, Rob Ramer, Indigenous Tourism Rights International Advisory Council members, Indigenous and Native groups, and the growing Indigenous and responsible tourism movements.

Thanks to Clay Hubbs, editor of *Transitions Abroad* magazine. I'm also indebted to Clay Butler for the use of his insightful cartoons, UNICEF for publication usage, Tourism Concern for the use of some of their publications and photographs, photographer Eric Lawrie, photographer Jim Duff, the Burma Campaign for use of their postcard, Greenpeace for their photos, and to everyone who contributed to this updated version of the book.

Thank you, Creator.

Prologue

A Personal Journey

My reasons for supporting change in the tourism industry came about through personal experience. I began to think about taking a vacation to Jamaica many years ago. I had heard about the island all my life and looked forward to going there. As a child, I had watched home movies of my missionary grandfather working in Jamaica. I particularly remember a film where twenty or so people were dancing outside under some trees; what most struck me were the spirit and joyousness the people projected.

My interest in Jamaica and Jamaican culture continued to take various turns over the years. During the early 1970s, when I was growing up in a small town in northeastern Oklahoma, some of my friends started a band and began singing the reggae songs of Bob Marley. Living in an economically depressed rural area and grappling with social and cultural issues of my own, I could identify with the meaning and message of struggle. More than a decade later, with some experience behind me and enough money to make the trip, I went to Jamaica to look, idealistically, for a chance to better understand the meaning of the revolutionary spirit. What I found was very different from what I had imagined. I had not realized the depth of struggle against racism and oppression, the sheer poverty that many Jamaicans live with every day, the historical oppression and hardships the culture had experienced. I had simply glossed over much of it. I bought into the dream that I could go to Jamaica as a package-deal tourist and have a profound experience with local people.

In fact I did have a profound experience, but not the type for which I was searching. The plane landed at Montego Bay, and I was immediately besieged by hawkers and hustlers, self-styled entrepreneurs in an economic situation born directly out of the business of tourism. I didn't even have time to look around as I downed my welcome-to-Jamaica shot of rum because I was so preoccupied with the hustlers:

"Like a beer for the ride, mon?" "Need some ganga, girl?" "You need a mon like John to show you around."

I stayed in a hotel arranged as part of a package deal with an airline. The resort was advertised as set in a "historical plantation in Old Jamaica"; its fences and golf course recalled a colonialist plantation, strong symbols of a time that never seemed to pass for some. It was a beautiful beach resort surrounded by imported comforts from home, while local people were banned from the beach and lived in a makeshift service village across the road. A sign near the fence at the end of the hotel beach said it all: "No Locals Allowed." The T-shirts and bikinis in the souvenir shop were imported from the United States; the restaurant's food was shipped in from Florida.

I didn't have much opportunity to meet local people on the "old plantation." Most were too busy working in their service jobs. One morning, determined to see a more genuine side of the island, I crossed the main road to take the local bus into Montego Bay. The guards at the gates of the hotel eyed me suspiciously. Some older women waiting for the bus cast an amused glance in my direction. A dilapidated school bus pulled up, and I boarded, along with the older women and a young man holding a live chicken. A hand-painted sign over the driver's seat reflected a contemporary social issue for Jamaicans: "Let us stay sober on our journey." My whole experience that day was one of hustlers, drug dealers, and more hustlers. I was unable to walk around without an offer for a "guide," to buy some "smoke," or to inspect a wood-carving shop. It was off-season, the tourism-dependent economy was in its downswing, and people were desperate. Shopkeepers even sent scouts out into the streets to round up tourists to bring back to their shops.

One evening I went to Montego Bay to hear some reggae music. After a considerable search, I finally found a small club for locals. As we listened to the music, a bus load of tourists rushed in and immediately began to complain to the deejay about the music. Soon Michael Jackson, Madonna, and Whitney Houston began to croon over the speakers while the tourists danced. After an hour or so, the tourists left and the American pop tunes were put to rest until the next round of tourists descended on the club. "The tourists," explained the deejay, "they like American music." The revolutionary songs of Bob Marley had no place in a carefree holiday market that depends upon providing pleasure for wealthy foreigners.

Throughout the rest of my stay in Jamaica, I tried to meet some local people without being accosted by entrepreneurs. But I was taken to other all-inclusive resorts around the island and to "destinations" like Dunns River Falls, where I climbed the waterfalls with other tourists and didn't see one local Jamaican on vacation. Instead, I saw the social discrepancies that distanced tourists from the local population. I noticed the way the residents reacted to me as a wealthy tourist with money to burn. I noticed the creation of a fantasy tourism culture that by no means represented the real culture of Jamaica. I noticed the almost entirely British and American management at the hotels. I noticed the dying reefs just off the beaches, polluted from unregulated waste from the resorts; the high price of black coral, disappearing quickly because of the excessive demand by tourists; the stench from piles of accumulated garbage behind the beautiful, artificial resorts; pristine lands being converted into more tourist accommodations; and fences that blocked the local people from the beach.

On my last day in Jamaica, I walked down the road to a horse stable where I met Joseph, a guide. While we rode around the hillside through villages conspicuously different from the hotel paradises I had been a part of, Joseph related some of his story. He had grown up in Jamaica and spent four years as a worker on cruise and fishing boats traveling throughout the Caribbean and to ports in Europe. Joseph was interested in people. In fact he said this interest motivated him to work on the boats and explained why he was currently employed as a guide at the stables. He wanted to see the world, especially the United States, where, Joseph said, "people have more opportunities...do not have to live in poverty. In the United States, people have good jobs and a good way of life that is better than here in Jamaica." He told me he was devastated when he was laid off from his job on a cruise ship just before it was scheduled to go to the United States. He had looked forward to the trip for years, and his disappointment was still visible. His interest in the United States had nonetheless continued to grow since then. As we rode our horses through a shantytown, Joseph made a remark about his missed opportunity that struck me. "Oh well," he said, "I will prepare myself so that I will understand more when I go there."

My time with Joseph is one of my best memories of the trip: it was a human connection, even if the unequal guide-tourist relationship prevented a real friendship from developing and even if we both had stereotyped views of each other. The very nature of tourism created in each of us idealized images of each other's culture: my perception of Jamaica was one of happy revolutionaries; his perception of the United

States was one of wealthy vacationers with no responsibilities at home. The tourism industry enforced and encouraged the distance between tourists and locals and reinforced a negative self-image for Joseph. It offered no mechanisms for fostering friendships with locals or gaining insight into local cultures, and I was hampered in my own attempts. I wanted to tell Joseph that the United States wasn't the utopia he thought it was, but who was I to talk? Since then I have thought about Joseph's wise words many times. I decided to prepare myself for the realities of whatever culture I might visit and to find ways to represent myself more realistically.

Over the years I have continued to learn from my experience in Jamaica. I was not able to contact much real Jamaican culture because of the culture that tourism had imposed. Why did it seem as though tourism controlled Jamaica and Jamaica had no control over tourism? I am disturbed by my own projections of a culture and people that exist only as a commodity, cooked up and dished out by the travel industry and the media. How did this happen? Did the colonial-plantation-cum-resort where I stayed represent a larger, more controversial phenomenon, something still being perpetrated?

My participation as a tourist propelled me into a process of critical analysis and a conscious effort to support change within the tourism industry. From this perspective, my goal is to demonstrate how traditional tourism, especially in countries in the global South (so-called developing countries in the Southern Hemisphere), basically follows a consumption-oriented Western model. The overwhelming growth of tourism has been destructive to both ecology and people in host countries. In fact, for that reason I helped found the Rethinking Tourism Project, which recently became Indigenous Tourism Rights International. The purpose of Tourism Rights is to assist in education and networking among Indigenous and rural communities in order to understand the long-term pros and cons of tourism development, and therefore be in a position to make informed choices about development.

A desperate need exists for information and tools to create change. I've learned to look past immediate tourism issues for root causes — to world economics, the media and technologies, development models, corporate control, the continuation of colonization, racism, and other forms of injustice. My exploration of tourism issues has been difficult, alarming, and wonderful and has led me to look for ways to change, challenge, and sometimes completely denounce the industry.

This book focuses on the global tourism industry and the recent boom in ecotravel. Tourism is inherently about our earth. Vacations at lakeside camps, at ski resorts, and in national parks reflect the need for human beings to spend time in nature. The global tourism industry obviously has an enormous impact on the environment and in most cases sells nature as part of the tourist product. We cannot simply buy into the ecojargon. What we need is an overview of tourism that acknowledges that "green" travel, or ecotravel, is a mere part of the larger impact of the industry and that we urgently need to look at the broad issues related to tourism's impacts upon the earth.

Traditional tourism is experiencing increasing resistance. Some of it has simply been to "greenwash" tourism and promote it as a sustainable development strategy or as "cultural heritage" that enshrines past culture and negates current culture. Since the 1970s, however, local people have joined with ecumenical groups, Indigenous Peoples, women's groups, grassroots groups, environmentalists, and even tourists to challenge and denounce the negative impacts of global tourism and seek alternatives in an international "responsible tourism" movement. Growing numbers of organizations outside of but reliant upon the travel industry are also rethinking their roles in tourism and creating strategies for change. Some of these groups are organizing solidarity tours to pressure governments and support each other at the grassroots level; others are linking with each other on social justice issues.

Thousands of communities around the world are attempting some form of tourism development. Many people in communities where abrupt transformations are taking place have little information about the forces changing their lives. What is apparent, though, is that most of these communities are going through almost entirely the same process: fairly well-defined cycles of expectation and disappointment. Yet tourism continues to grow haphazardly, often to the detriment of local people, communities, and the environment, with little long-term, integrated planning.

The Westernized model of unlimited economic growth has driven multinational aid and financial institutions since the 1940s, yet poverty has increased, arable lands are shrinking and threatened, and the socioeconomic situation of most of the world is worse than ever. World leaders are now organizing international meetings to determine what to do about preserving our global commons, the air we breathe and the water we drink, natural elements that cross borders — and that we all depend upon to survive. While interest is growing in other cultures, backlashes against ethnic groups are also occurring. Our capacity to learn and to work for change has never been more promising, yet the issues and solutions are dauntingly complex. In trying to protect our precious natural resources, we must look at both energy-consumptive high technologies and localized, less consumptive strategies.

The effects of travel and tourism development are usually studied in bits and pieces. For instance, environmentalists typically scrutinize the negative effects of tourism development upon natural resources and focus primarily on conservation issues. Economists concentrate upon business, employment, trade, and financial issues. Anthropologists document changing tribal cultures, some on the verge of vanishing. In the United States, we tend to study the global South as a separate entity, although we have recently come to learn that its survival is directly tied to the survival of the industrialized nations of the North. We must begin to explore the overlapping issues of tourism development and its effects upon the earth and society through a more integrated approach. Tourists are becoming increasingly concerned about the impact of their travel and the control of the giant tourism industry, and they are looking for information and tools to assist them in becoming more responsible travelers and bringing about change within the industry.

But should we work to change tourism, or should we stop traveling altogether? Concepts for alternative tourism as well as for alternatives to tourism reflect the growing awareness of the importance of cultural preservation, ecological protection, and decentralized political and economic decision making. These factors are critical, especially as the era of exploitive free trade and globalization of the economy intensifies. In the struggle to return control of tourism to the local community, we must increasingly scrutinize our motives for traveling, decide whether we have the "right" as consumers to buy other cultures and environments, and support responsible tourism. We must analyze "green" strategies such as ecotourism and sustainable tourism to determine whether we are simply being "greenwashed." In an age when the media dominates and shapes our views of the world, we must utilize tourism as a means to communicate with one another. In fact, we have no better way to understand the global crisis that we face than through people-to-people communication. Through firsthand, one-on-one meetings with people we encounter in our travels, we discover universal themes of human culture. We become more aware that no matter where we live, we are all confronting similar situations. Even nature travel is in many ways a reconnection between postindustrialized society and Mother Earth.

The issue of growth in the travel industry — how much, how fast, what kind — is crucial to the future of communities, local lifestyles and cultures, and the natural environment. A variety of instabilities and inequities are associated with the expansion of tourism. If the social costs of infinite growth (human consequences of ecological pollution, centralized concentration of power, inequitable income distribution) are as high as they appear to be, our current social systems cannot support such growth indefinitely. Tourism remains a passive luxury for thousands of travelers. This situation must change.

This book excludes large sectors of the travel industry, such as business travel and conferences and travel to most urban and developed areas. It focuses instead on tourism that affects areas where planned "development" has had a short history. I do not adequately address in this book many tourism subjects, such as how specific corporations are involved in tourism, how tourism can be linked to organized crime, or state policies on tourism.

I present here a starting point for rethinking a phenomenal industry, the largest in the world. This book is an invitation to undertake tourism-related studies and actions on issues such as agriculture, technologies, exploitation of women and children, and the role of transnational corporations. I look forward to future works that will engage these issues from other points of view and with different emphases. The purpose of my book is to encourage further investigation and action on the part of the reader.

Where will tourists be traveling in the next century? Will there be any places left to "discover"? Or will our search for unspoiled environments and cultures be in vain, as they become replaced by manufactured cultures on reconstructed islands of paradise? If the megamall, theme park, and cruise ship are any indication of our future, "supertourists," who can afford it, may pay to visit the last pristine places on the planet, to view the history of the Indigenous Peoples and organic agriculture, admire what used to be rain forests, and watch "virtual" cultural entertainment. Perhaps they will visit private, enclosed biospheres or even the moon. Of course, there will be plenty of souvenirs for them to buy.

One

An Overview of Tourism

Human beings have migrated across the planet for millennia. Plate tectonics, feet, and horses made for slow travel compared to the jet planes, trains, and automobiles we now use. No doubt our ancestors would be surprised at the infinite options we modern travelers enjoy. The earliest hunters and gatherers and nomads traveled in search of land and wildlife to sustain themselves; they were aware of the fragility of the earth and moved with the seasons. Travel that stemmed from basic survival was, of course, very different from the travel we undertake today. Only during the past few decades have higher incomes and paid holidays in the global North allowed great numbers of people to travel purely for pleasure and recreation.

Tourism began in part as an offshoot of religious pilgrimages and colonization. Vikings traveled across vast seas for natural resources. Traders traveled throughout Europe, North Africa, and the Middle East in search of spices and other goods. During the seventeenth century, young elites took "grand tours" through Europe to expand their educational and cultural horizons; the most privileged took two to three years to see the world. Civil and secular authorities traveled to participate in events the church deemed historical or went on special missions accompanied by large entourages that often included cooks, attendants, guides, and porters. Religious pilgrimages made on horseback and in coaches during the Enlightenment stimulated the growth of inns. Around the turn of the nineteenth century, Europeans journeyed to view scenery and other cultures.

Authors such as Somerset Maugham and Joseph Conrad wrote romantic accounts of the Far East and the heart of Africa. Travel heroes like Hemingway recounted their journeys to the lands of "savages," to hunt game, and their sea voyages in search of paradise. These conquering and self-indulgent adventurers brought along servants to make the trips comfortable. Few people could afford these exotic ventures into the wild, but some of these conquering ideals live on and constitute eco- and ethnocentrism that underlies much of modern tourism.

Naturalists such as Alexander von Humboldt and later Charles Darwin studied wildlife and plant species in exotic places and contributed greatly to an interest in travel. In the United States around the turn of the century, John Muir began to write about his wanderings overland through the southern states and journeys to Alaska and India. His trips made him an impassioned conservationist, and his work continues to inspire and mobilize people to preserve the natural world. Also about that time, a chain of national parks and other protected areas was created, partly in response to the fear that industrialization would consume them and partly to set aside unique lands to be shared by all citizens. Also in the twentieth century, anthropologists like Margaret Mead drew global attention to Indigenous societies. Nature and cultural travel have continued to play an important role in conflicts between conservationists and economists and the public and private sectors.

The views of land and place held by travelers and hosts, colonizers and original inhabitants, have varied widely, and the compulsion of newcomers to take control of their "discoveries" and the resources and people they find there is striking. The conquest of paradise, colonization, and "discovery" were historic rationalizations to take over new lands. Today most land, even what is perceived as "open" land, is not understood to be part of an intricate system of land use and maintenance, with residents using the resources for survival rather than importing goods. These areas, often multiple-use lands, and our global commons are threatened by increasing development and exploitation of natural resources.

The Emergence of Modern Tourism

The transition from a rural to an industrial society encouraged the growth of modern tourism. Before World War II, travel for pleasure was the province of the very rich. Since then, improved standards of living in the Northern Hemisphere and the availability of transportation have allowed more people to indulge. Modern tourism began in large part with the rise of the automobile industry and expanded road and highway systems.

Early jet travel was generally confined to the United States and Europe, but by the 1960s improvements in aircraft technology opened up the world to visitors. The development of commercial jet airlines enabled fast international travel, and the tourism industry exploded. Today airports in nearly every country in the world can accommodate jumbo jets full of tourists seeking new and unspoiled destinations.

Travel to "exotic" places is increasingly popular. Travelers are searching out the most remote places as well as the most unusual cultures. Ethnic tourism — involving visits to villages and homes to observe social customs and traditional occupations such as fishing and farming, see (and purchase) native arts, and watch local ceremonies — is one of the fastest-growing segments of the consumer travel market. New forms of environmental tourism are often related to ethnic tourism, marketing exotic cultures and areas where few have traveled.

These specialized segments of tourism are often excluded from analyses of the tourism industry. In economic terms, exotic cultures and unspoiled environments have become tourism's commodities. Although Indigenous populations and pristine environments are tourist attractions and important players in the industry, until recently they were rarely considered in tourism research, planning, development, and economics. Some debate takes place over using monetary economics for measuring gains and losses in the business of tourism. Tourism researchers are calling culture and environment the supply side of tourism.

Tourism doesn't just package and sell products and services, such as transportation, accommodations, food, and a good time. The tourist industry also sells beaches, mountains, and other natural sites, as well as cultures and people. The problem is that tourist businesses often do not own what they sell. Businesses in the industry purchase at inappropriately low prices, acquire free of charge, or simply expropriate these resources as part of their product. For example, when a developer builds a resort near a national park, part of the developer's product becomes the use of the park and all its natural attractions.

Tourism is often in direct conflict and competition with local people and communities, for it markets and develops natural resources the locals need. Because tourism requires an enormous amount of land, water, and energy, residents must fight the tourism industry and governments for land and water rights. Development of areas around the periphery of a protected area also threatens wildlife in the entire bioregion.

Deborah McLaren, Sikkim, India

Traditional architecture in the Himalayas uses materials natural to the area that are flexible and able to withstand frequent earthquakes.

Deborah McLaren, Sikkim, India

With rapidly expanding tourism development, multistoried concrete structures are dangerously built and degrade fragile mountain environments.

As tourism boosts demand for land, the cost of livable space increases, local people are displaced, and less space is available for sustainable lifestyles. Developers are notorious for filling in swamps, mangroves, and coral reefs, causing a chain reaction that hurts fishing, reduces the supply of fresh water for irrigation, and shrinks the land base. Local people are increasingly confined to infertile lands and degraded environments in nearby service cities. Ultimately, developers re-create the environment and culture on top of the real thing. These manufactured environments and cultures peddle the fiction that the tourism corporations care for the tourists who have earned the "right" to this short-term, expensive fantasy.

Tourism as Big Business

In a shrinking world of improved travel facilities and computer linkages, a network of group travel and mass tourism continues to grow. The World Tourism Organization (WTO) claims that tourism is currently the world's largest industry. With annual revenues of almost $3 trillion, its economic impact is second only to that of the weapons industry.

By 2001, the U.S. Department of Commerce reported that

- tourism generated $174 billion in direct payroll income;

- the tourism industry employed 7.8 million people directly and 11.5 million indirectly, accounting for more than 19 million U.S. jobs — which is one of every seven people employed in the civilian labor force;

- America's 1 billion domestic travelers spend $584.3 billion, providing $100 billion in tax revenues for local, state, and federal governments.[1]

According to the UNESCO *Courier,*

If the World Tourism Organization's forecasts are on target, international tourist arrivals will climb from the present 625 million a year to 1.6 billion in 2020. By this date, travelers will spend over US$2 trillion (against US$445 billion today), making tourism the world's leading industry.... Despite this growth forecast, tourism is and will remain the privilege of a few: WTO forecasts that only 7% of the world population will travel abroad by 2020 — that's double the 1996 figure (3.5%).[2]

Tourism is larger than almost any single item in world trade and is growing at least 8 to 10 percent per year.[3] The travel industry has become a vast and complex enterprise that includes transportation (airlines, airports, trains, cruise lines, automobiles, and rental car agencies); hotels, resorts, and vacation villages; the food industry; travel agencies and operators; and recreational and cultural promoters such as trekking and adventure agencies. The travel industry also includes related tourism services such as trailer parks, campgrounds, and amusement and recreation parks, with their wholesale and retail shops (eating and drinking establishments and some apparel and accessory stores). Tourism is big business, and it is largely controlled by big business. International corporations are involved not only in transportation and accommodations, but in motivating us to travel, feeding and entertaining us while we are on vacation, making travel arrangements for us, providing us with "travel" money and insurance, plying us with souvenirs, and even outfitting us for our trips. According to a 1996 study, top tourism "holding" companies were Pepsi Company, which owns Pizza Hut, Taco Bell, and Kentucky Fried Chicken, at $5.55 billion in annual sales; Marriott at $4.9 billion; McDonald's Corporation at $4 billion; and Disney (hotels and theme parks) at $605 million.[4] These are *big* businesses.

International financial institutions are integrated into the global tourism industry. American Express, for example, combines financial and travel services for business and leisure services and controls a major share of the world market for traveler's checks. With deregulation of global financial systems, travelers have benefited from improvements in the speed and convenience of financial activities. We use our credit and automatic teller machine (ATM) cards around the world, particularly in the tourist sector. In a matter of seconds, we can obtain cash almost anywhere. These transactions are remarkable not only because they take place in remote sites but also because of the images they promote. A current television advertisement shows a young boy in an unspecified developing country leading a lost American couple through a desert village to an ATM. Another ad for MasterCard announces that it is now "uniting the world." These images are intended to illustrate how innovative, convenient, and caring the travel industry is.

Tourism is a mighty force in free trade agreements such as the General Agreement on Trade in Services (GATS), which promotes privatization and free trade and undermines the power of governments to protect and control their labor markets and resources. Economists tell us that "GATS will contribute to the worldwide development of tourism. It will also constrain — and should over time eliminate — government discrimination toward foreign service companies."[5] The key to liberalization, they say, is market access — granting foreign service suppliers access to domestic markets, including services — and "national treatment" — where countries are obliged to treat foreign tourist services suppliers in the same way they do domestic suppliers.

In reality, these corporations are breaking economic barriers that would regulate them, giving them more control of world markets and allowing them to ignore restrictions to protect workers and the environment. They have no allegiance to any particular country; if they are in trouble in the United States because they have violated labor laws, for example, they can simply move to Mexico.

The multilateral development banks are investing heavily in tourism development around the global South as part of the foreign aid business. According to a report from the International Finance Corporation (IFC) and the World Bank, by 1994 the IFC had "approved close to $600 million in over a hundred tourism projects. The tourism portfolio has grown at an average annual rate of over 23% over the past five years. [As of June 1994], the committed portfolio was $434 million in 66 projects."[6]

Other international "players" in global tourism include intergovernmental organizations such as the World Health Organization (WHO), the Global Environment Facility (GEF), the World Bank and regional banks such as the Inter-American Development Bank (IDB), the World Intellectual Property Organization (WIPO), Commission for Sustainable Development (CSD), World Summit on Sustainable Development (WSSD), the Organization of American States (OAS), the Organization for Economic Cooperation and Development (OECD), the World Travel and Trade Council (WTTC), the Pacific Asia Travel Association (PATA), the World Trade Organization (WTO), and United Nations programs such as the United Nations Environmental Program (UNEP), the United Nations Educational, Scientific, and Cultural Organization (UNESCO), the UN's Convention on Biological Diversity (CBD), the UN Economic and Social Council (ECOSOC), and the United Nations Development Program (UNDP). The World Tourism Organization, located in Madrid, is a council of chief executive officers of private-sector companies involved in tourism. Their primary mandate is to affect government policy and business. The World Ecotourism Summit, held in Quebec in May

2002, was hosted by the World Tourism Organization (WTO/OMT), Tourisme Quebec (TQ), the Canadian Tourism Commission (CTC), and UNEP.

The tourism industry also comprises businesses that originate outside of the organized economy, forming what is called the "open air" economy of tourism. These meager, insecure, and illegal operations often spring up as poor people migrate to tourist sites to look for work. Because many of these jobs, such as selling drinks and fruit or running errands, are performed by children, the industry cannot account for them in its data. Many of these small operations are run by women and children pushed out by the giants in the industry.[7]

Tourism and Globalization

A traveler can decide today to go to the North Pole and be there by tomorrow. Global infrastructures such as transportation and communications and global policies for free trade have created a situation where people and businesses in the global North can easily access natural resources and cultures in the global South. Until 1999, when thousands of people around the world began organizing against it (e.g., the Battle in Seattle), globalization was not regarded as a danger to local economies and cultural diversity. In fact, politicians and the media tout globalization as the path to greater wealth and success. Although globalization may be the most primary transformation of the world's political and economic structures since the industrial revolution, its implications have yet to be fully understood or debated.

Most of the economic restructuring is in the interest of big business, not in the interest of the public. Under the banner of free trade, corporations have come to shape our lives through the consumer products we buy (including technologies), the media that feed us information, even the educational system that trains us. Politicians chant the mantra of privatization and globalization. What does that mean for individuals? According to Martin Khor, president of the non-governmental organization (NGO) Third World Network, globalization is a leading threat to local communities, particularly in the global South:

> Before colonial rule and the infusion of Western systems, people in the Third World lived in relatively self-sufficient communities.... The modes of production and style of life were largely in harmony with the natural environment. Colonial rule ... changed

PAVE THE PLANET

ONE ASPHALT, ONE PEOPLE

Sidewalk Bubblegum ©1993 Clay Butler

the social and economic structures of Third World societies. The new structures, consumption styles, and technological systems became so ingrained in Third World economies that even after the attainment of political independence, the importation of Western values, products, technologies and capital continued and expanded.... Third World governments were loaned billions of dollars to finance expensive infrastructure projects.... They were also supported by foundations, research institutions, and scientists in the industrialized countries that carried out research on new agricultural technologies that would "modernize" the Third World — that is, that would create conditions whereby the Third World would become dependent on the transnational companies for technology and inputs.[8]

The development of vast infrastructures such as roads and other transportation routes goes hand in hand with tourism development. As more tourists seek out hard-to-reach "frontier" destinations, those areas become popularized, and soon private industry takes over. Once an area is targeted for tourism development, the process begins with road building and displacement of the local population. Communication systems go in, as do energy-intensive and pollutive accommodations for visitors. The roads and communications in turn provide other industries with easy access to cheap labor and natural resources. This cycle of development is occurring at alarming rates in small communities and villages throughout the world; many of these areas are considered the most important biologically diverse regions of the planet. At the same time, roads built into places like the Amazon to serve primarily as transportation routes for extractive industries such as oil, logging, and mining inevitably become new corridors for colonists, including tourists.

Tourism increases local reliance upon a global economy, leaking many economic profits outside of the community back to the companies and countries that control most of the travel infrastructure. At the same time, tourism decreases dependence on local resources, as technologies, food, and health services are imported. Local people may also be pushed out or sell out, and local prices for commodities and services rise, as do taxes.

Any number of groups and individuals are concerned about the negative impacts of economic centralization via free trade and regional agreements such as the General Agreement on Tariffs and Trade (GATT) and the European Union. These organizations point out that the promotion of greater economic units and the expanded transport infrastructures they require result in urbanization in the global North and South alike, placing greater pressures on wilderness areas and destroying family farms and rural communities around the world. Proponents of free trade promise that all trading partners will be better off and that the practice will usher in a new era of global cooperation and prosperity, but according to a report by the International Society for Ecology and Culture:

> The reality is far different. Increased levels of world trade will lead to a widening of the gap between rich and poor, to further environmental decline, and to the enrichment of corporations at the expense of people in both the North and South. Small farmers and shopkeepers will be driven under by producers and marketers whose activities are undertaken at an ever larger scale, and many

local economies will simply not survive. Rural communities will be hardest hit, intensifying the trend toward urbanization. These "free trade" agreements are fundamentally anti-democratic. The ease with which corporations will be able to transcend national boundaries — to move wherever environmental and health standards are the weakest and wages lowest — will strip voters and even governments of their power to curb corporate excess.... In the new global economy, production everywhere will be focused on the needs of a single, Western monoculture, while Indigenous cultures and diverse location-specific adaptations will be steadily erased. Local self-sufficiency will become an ever more distant memory.[9]

Since September 11, 2001, the threat of global terrorism has been a key factor in government relationships and the tightening of restrictions for travelers. That day's events and aftermath have had an enormous impact on the airline industry and government support.

Tourism plays an increasingly important role in international relations. Links exist between tourist flow and regional integration, governments, military, and economic aid. "Most nations have several policies toward foreign tourists that are based not only on anticipated length of stay, but also on the degree of international cooperation existing between the two countries."[10]

Tourism is big business for governments and private enterprise alike. Any country with still-pristine areas of forests, beaches, mountains, and parklands or with ethnic tribes and other unique rural cultures has something to market in the global economy. Some of the largest corporations in the world are designing and carrying out policies that open up borders and allow them to operate in areas once restricted to individual country corporations. The tourist industry's entrance into and operations in China, the Middle East, the former Soviet Union, parts of the African continent, and countries with human rights abuses show that government and big business can work together despite trade restrictions and political differences. Corporations have become dominant governing institutions, often exceeding governments in size and power. As David Korten states, "Increasingly, it is the corporate interest more than the human interest that defines the policy agendas of states and international bodies, although this reality and its implications have gone largely unnoticed and unaddressed."[11] Nowhere is this more true than within travel and tourism.

Governmental instruments and international organizations that help shape international tourism policy encourage the growth and involvement of transnational corporations because they provide quick money and expanded trade and services. In supporting and increasing the power of such corporations, governments are ignoring the numerous inequalities, exploitation, and dislocations they foster. Countries create lax trade environments to attract the tourism industry, lifting restrictions that are applied to other industries and offering many incentives. As Alexander Goldsmith explains:

> Free trade zones [FTZs] are regions that have been fiscally or juridically redefined by their "host country" to give them a comparative advantage over neighboring regions and countries in luring transnational corporate activity. Most FTZs share the following characteristics: lax social, environmental, and employment regulations; a ready source of cheap labor; and fiscal and financial incentives that can take a huge variety of forms, although they generally consist of the lifting of customs duties, the removal of foreign exchange controls, tax holidays, and free land or reduced rents.[12]

The travel industry benefits greatly from these FTZs, sometimes even performing what may be considered "advance work" in doing away with free trade barriers for other industries.

Tales of Tourism, Globalization, and Anti-Globalization
Luis A. Vivanco

Not long ago, I received a joke through email, one of those whose origins and author are unknown, but it is worth recounting because it provides an unlikely and humorous perspective on the current organization of the world.

Once upon a time there was a shepherd tending his sheep by the edge of a country road. A brand new Land Rover screeches to a halt next to him. The driver, a young man dressed in a Brioni suit, Cerruti shoes, Ray-Ban sunglasses, and a Jovial Swiss watch, gets out and asks the shepherd, "If I guess how many sheep you have, will you give me one of them?" The shepherd looks at the young man and then looks at the sprawling field of sheep and says, "OK." The young man parks the

SUV, connects his notebook computer and wireless modem, enters a NASA website, scans the ground using his GPS, opens a database and sixty Excel tables filled with algorithms, then prints a 150-page report on his portable printer. He then turns to the shepherd and says, "You have exactly 1,586 sheep here." The shepherd answers, "That's correct, you can have your sheep." The young man takes one of the animals and puts it in the back of his vehicle.

The shepherd looks at him and asks, "Now, if I guess your profession, will you pay me back in kind?" The young man answers, "Sure." The shepherd says, "You're a consultant." The young man is astonished: "Exactly! How did you know?" "Very simple," the shepherd answers. "First, you came here without being called. Second, you charged me a fee to tell me something I already knew. And third, you really do not understand anything about my business, and I'd really like to have my dog back!"

For some, I suspect the humor of this situation rides on its David-and-Goliath quality, being a story of an earthy "local yokel" outwitting the urban elite. But for others, particularly people not accustomed to questioning the inevitable spread of modern technologies and McLuhan's cliché of "the global village," the humor of this story lies in its absurdity, the fact that the world simply does not work this way. Modernization and globalization are facts of life, and rural peoples' backwardness is more often the rightful object of jokes, not the progressive ways of the cosmopolitan businessman.

Since the end of the Cold War, "globalization" has come into vogue as a way to explain how the world is changing and why our shepherd above is, or will soon become, a relic of history. In the nearest it comes to a technical definition, globalization refers to a specific set of political and economic policies that advocate the expansion of capitalist free markets, the reduction or elimination of trade barriers and regulations, political democratization, and the decentralization of state institutions to reduce public-sector deficits. Sometimes called the "Washington Consensus" because of the aggressive way the United States and its closest allies promote them, these policies are enshrined in international trade treaties and organizations like the North American Free Trade Agreement, the International Monetary Fund, the World Trade Organization, and the World Bank.

But globalization often implies much more: the expansion of modernizing economic, political, and cultural forces into the farthest reaches of the globe to create a single world system based on Western values. Indeed, globalization can be seen as the latest triumphant story of *West-meets-Rest* relations, drawing from the same universalistic wellspring that produced ideals that others should live by, like civilization, progress, modernization, and development. The ubiquity of Western-style consumer products and transnational corporations—

Coca-Cola, Hollywood, CNN, etc. — and ever-increasing flows of information and capital seem to confirm that the world is being radically restructured along these lines.

For globalists, the "local" is still a relevant factor, though. For some, especially U.S. leaders after 9/11, the "local" is an anticosmopolitan place, where anti-Westernism and terrorism are bred. But attention to the local can also be profitable, as seen in the marketers' pursuit of "glocalization." For example, French McDonald's restaurants recently switched from using the American icon of Ronald McDonald to using the French icon, Asterix, to sell hamburgers. Both perspectives encourage even greater globalization, the former to justify a war economy and its pursuit of geopolitical interests, and the latter by using local symbols as a smokescreen to sell a product imagined, produced, and transported from elsewhere.

Because of its reach and scale, tourism is naturally identified as a vehicle for globalization. It has been eagerly adopted by governments and development agencies as a strategy for countries to generate income to service their foreign debts. But large transnational corporations often dominate the business landscape (hotels, airlines, travel agencies, etc.), leading to massive "leakage" (outflows of foreign exchange generated by tourism) of as high as 75 percent, predatory practices, and anticompetitive behavior that can undermine local ability to maintain basic quality standards and infrastructure. The World Tourism Organization, the industry's main representative and lobbyist, is one of the world's major proponents of the liberalization of tourism services, pushing for the reduction or elimination of trade barriers and labor and environmental regulations in international trade agreements. Tourism is also at the forefront of globalization in a cultural sense, providing the "shock troops" of middle-class values and tastes, and encouraging the abandonment of language and traditional ways of life for those who want to enjoy the economic benefits of tourism.

But as we have seen most dramatically in places like Chiapas with the Zapatistas and in anti-WTO protests, environmentalists, labor groups, ecumenical groups, grassroots communities, and Indigenous People have vigorously challenged the Washington Consensus's vision of globalization. These diverse groups are not united by a single ideology of how the world should work. They do, however, share a common rejection of the negative impacts of transnational free market capitalism on natural landscapes, livelihoods, and traditional cultures, and an assumption that people at the local level have the inherent right to shape their own destinies.

Tourism has been drawn into these antiglobalization debates and conflicts, most recently with the UN's declaration of 2002 as the International

Year of Ecotourism (IYE). The UN declaration is testimony to ecotourism's much-touted status as a positive form of globalization, because it uses market mechanisms to conserve natural landscapes and encourage local economic development (see chapter 5).[13] Like the business consultant in the joke above, tourism consultants and academics are showing up (often uninvited) in rural villages throughout the Global South, with promises of progress-and-conservation-through-ecotourism. But Indigenous People, who often inhabit the nondegraded lands targeted by ecotourism developers, have been especially critical of the IYE, and in response have been organizing counter-conferences and information-sharing coalitions like the Indigenous Tourism Network. Their main arguments are that much of what passes as ecotourism provides little or no local economic (and therefore ecological) benefits because of leakage; leads to eviction from traditional lands; becomes a vehicle for bioprospecting and biopiracy on Indigenous lands (the illegal collection of plants and other objects); forces the transformation of landscapes and cultures into consumer products; and undermines Indigenous self-determination because these peoples are often excluded from the design of projects.

The goal of these coalitions and conferences has not been the outright rejection of tourists and tourism, but affirmation of the diverse ways Indigenous communities can engage in tourism to support their cultural traditions and self-determination. A central theme is the inherent right of local people to accept, reject, and control tourism development on their own terms, through their own community mechanisms and traditions of collective ownership (see chapter 5).[14] Does this activism suggest that shepherds are one-upping cosmopolitan businesspeople? We have yet to really know. But at the very least, the values of pluralism and convivial intercultural dialogue that shape these organizing efforts represent a challenge to the globalist and free-market aspirations of ecotourism's promoters. Perhaps even more important, these values are forcing open a space within the global tourism industry where concern over cultural and ecological survival are not just objects to sell in a marketplace of products and services imagined and produced by transnational corporations.

International and National
Tourism Regulations and Policies

International agreements and national policies both regulate tourism in the United States. For about twenty years, perhaps the best-known international pacts concerning tourism were the 1975 Helsinki Accord, which deals with the rights of people to migrate freely and of governments to increase tourism, and the Accord of Mutual Understanding and Cooperation in Sports, which discourages boycotts of the Olympic Games for political reasons.[15] The 1980 Manila Declaration and the Acapulco Charter did not provide much beyond vague guidelines that "tourism resources should be managed and conserved" and "international cooperation, both financial and technological, should be encouraged." Initially, almost all tourism agreements focus on the expansion and promotion of trade. Tourism is rarely recognized within the context of environmental and labor issues, although responsible tourism organizations and women's groups have pushed a plan demanding that countries observe the United Nations Convention on the Rights of the Child on behalf of children who are prostituted, enslaved, and trafficked internationally through tourism. However, the United Nations is beginning to design policies that include tourism and biodiversity protection, and the World Tourism Organization released guidelines about social and environmental responsibilities of the tourism industry. Worldwide pressure from NGOs, Indigenous Peoples, and communities are responsible for pushing tourism issues to the forefront.

A boom in international interest in sustainable tourism and ecotourism began in earnest in 1999, when the Commission for Sustainable Development (CSD-7) focused on sustainable tourism. The CSD's coordinating body, the Economic and Social Council (ECOSOC) — which coordinates the work of the fourteen UN specialized agencies — proclaimed 2002 as the "International Year of Ecotourism." This year was important because it was also the year for the World Summit on Sustainable Development (WSSD), a ten-year follow-up to the Earth Summit held in 1992. Since 1999, many international policy fora and treaties have focused on sustainable tourism or ecotourism policies.

The WSSD was held in Johannesburg, South Africa, in August 2002. Preparatory meetings, particularly the fourth and final preparatory meeting held in Bali, Indonesia, were helpful, according to intergovernmental agencies, and a disaster according to non-governmental organizations (NGOs) and Indigenous Peoples. Informal discussions between countries aimed at bridging the remaining differences in the outcome document for the World Summit on Sustainable Development. Summit officials were hopeful that the behind-the-scene efforts would pave the way for success. However, NGOs and Indigenous Peoples had little hope that their input and voices would be heard, because they have had little impact on the economic and development-driven process. Time will tell whether the process delivered meaningful public voice and policy-making.

The first World Ecotourism Summit (WES) was held in Quebec in May 2002. Over eleven hundred delegates, from 133 different countries, wrapped up the summit with the Quebec Declaration on Ecotourism, a new tool for the international development of this type of tourism, officially tabled at the WSSD. The bulk of the delegates were from the tourist industry, tourism councils, and ministries. According to the local coordinators and participant NGOs, preparatory meetings for the WES in India, Thailand, Peru, and elsewhere proved conflictive. Concern arose that UNEP and WES coordinators' agenda and presentations did not allow for meaningful public input, and in fact, local participation and concerns were sometimes marginalized. In Peru, some participants walked out of the meetings. In Thailand, Indigenous Peoples organized a meeting outside of the formal process, created their own declaration of concerns to present at the meetings, and were later lambasted by UN officials for voicing criticism. Hardly participatory, but the process continues to move through the mainstream development process with little conflict resolution.

In fact, when the United Nations proclaimed 2002 as an International Year of Ecotourism, many NGOs who had been monitoring tourism impacts went on the alert. In October 2001, an international coalition of environmental, human rights, and Indigenous Peoples groups — organized through the Third World Network in Malaysia — launched a call for a fundamental reassessment of the UN International Year of Ecotourism 2002. This coalition also denounced the lack of transparency and failure to meaningfully involve Indigenous Peoples and Southern organizations in ongoing preparations. Unfortunately, little changed during 2002 to rectify the situation, and development-as-usual continues.

The Tourism Policy and Export Promotion Act of 1992 set the stage for the direction of U.S. tourism policy; it targeted untapped markets and lesser-known destinations. The State Department has the primary role in establishing bilateral tourism agreements with nations. A 1993 Commerce Department report describes tourism as "embedded in...agreements designed and negotiated for broad trade and investment reasons.... Under these agreements, U.S. companies are generally guaranteed national treatment for establishing themselves in the other country for advertising and selling in the other market."[16] Numerous congressional hearings have focused on activities such as marketing tourism and using tourism to boost rural economic development. Although tourism is an intrinsic part of international trade policy, fewer formal government tourism offices are now in operation, as global corporations take over their function. According to the State Department, "In 1995, the U.S. government decided to withdraw from organizations such as the World Tourism Organization, and private tourism companies such as Disney and Visa have become affiliate members instead."[17] In 1996, the USTTA was abolished because of severe budget cutbacks. U.S. tourism policymakers and industry developers now belong to the Office of Tourism Industries, within the International Trade Administration's Trade Development Office. U.S. tourism has thus become part of the process of global trade liberalization.

Tourism and Development

Tourism is the preeminent salesperson for Western development, the process of planned change to raise the standard of living through technological advances and economic growth, substituting a monoculture and a single economic system for regional diversity and self-reliance. Tourism creates enclaves of Western society and development in rural and Indigenous communities that further new technologies, economic growth and free trade, and capitalist values and consumer culture. This model causes many problems. As Helena Norberg-Hodge suggests, "Today's conquistadors are 'development,' advertising, the media and tourism.... [This] spread of the industrial monoculture is a tragedy of many dimensions. With the destruction of each culture, we are erasing centuries of accumulated knowledge, and as diverse ethnic groups feel their identity threatened, conflict and social breakdown almost inheritably follow."[18]

In host communities, tourism forms part of the total Western package of media, music, and technologies delivered to the global South. According to policy analysts Richard Barnet and John Cavanagh, these consumerized cultural products offer consumers "the illusion of being connected to cultural currents sweeping across the world, but this has little to do with the creation of a new global identification with the welfare of the whole human species and with the planet itself.... So far, commodity consciousness is the only awareness that has been stimulated."[19] The United Nations, multilateral institutions, international aid agencies, and governments are now promoting "sustainable tourism," or "clean" development, discovering important new places to "protect." On the surface, many of the ideas appear to be credible, suggesting the long-term preservation of cultural heritage sites, national parks, and other destinations. Yet this protection is offered by investors who focus on the returns a site can bring, travel companies such as hoteliers and airlines who are selling rooms and flights, and governments looking for foreign exchange and infrastructure development. This form of development, too, comes into direct conflict with the way residents have used and cared for the land for centuries. Paul Gonsalves, a former Asia director of the Ecumenical Coalition on Third World Tourism (ECTWT), explains:

> Culture has repeatedly been viewed by the tourism industry in the limited sense of built heritage (historical buildings, architectural styles, archaeological sites, etc.) and cultural expression (dance, music, arts and crafts) — tending towards monumentalizing culture. This takes place to the complete exclusion of the reality of which it is a part... everyday customs and mores, familial and social relationships, the annual cycle of planting, tending and harvesting.... Such an interpretation is at best ethnocentric and fragmentary, at worst a display of cultural insensitivity and naïveté.... Tourism has accentuated cross-cultural stereotypes, led to mutual distrust, and accelerated cultural change (read "Westernization").... Faced with threats from "development" projects such as dams, resettlement projects... agro-industry, displacement from traditional lands... [Indigenous Peoples] have clung to their culture as a basic source of identity.... Ironically, ethnic culture has frequently been used to promote the uniqueness of a tourism destination. Sadly, behind this transformation of culture into entertainment lies all too often a history of enslavement, enforced poverty and genocide. The commoditization of culture for the sake of earning tourist dollars is bad enough: it is reprehensible when it does so at the expense of a people's misery.[20]

Tourism is seen as a way to propel regional economic growth in countries, a panacea for development, especially in the global South: Tourism promises jobs, economic growth, and infrastructure development. Chayant Pholphoke of Life Travels in Bangkok says that "the intent of Buddhism is to achieve nirvana. However, in Thailand, tourism is supposed to achieve the same." In Cancún, Mexico, "the government explicitly decided to use tourism as a way of stimulating economic development in diverse regions of the country. While no one would point to Cancún as a desirable model of tourism development, its transformation from a fishing village with 426 residents to a major tourism center" with a permanent population of nearly 500,000 in 2002 and serving 2.3 million tourists a year (as well as accounting for 25 percent of all Mexican tourism revenues) is "a dramatic example of the potential for tourism to serve as a development growth pole."[21]

Understanding the negative impacts of a logging company that displaces Indigenous cultures by cutting down trees or a refinery that pollutes its surroundings is easy. Tourism is another ball game. Although many of its impacts are the same as those of other industries, tourism's enormous corporate power and long-term influence are not clearly recognized or are simply glossed over or rationalized. Tourism appears to fit into "cultural heritage" and "sustainable development" strategies because a corporation would presumably share an interest in its communities' values and have a stake in its future. In fact, tourism is rapidly gobbling the world's remaining natural resources and displacing people from their homes. As tourists, we consider travel an inherent, economic right. Yet we are supporting the loss of jobs, subsidizing corporations, and cooperating with governments known for human rights abuses. Tourists and locals must become active citizens and make clear the connection between the corporate path of globalization and the multitude of injustices taking place under the guise of a vacation.

At the same time, however, we see staunch resistance to tourism and its negative effects at the local level. From Indigenous Peoples who organized separately at the WES preparatory meetings, to the global campaign that called for a fundamental reassessment of the International Year of Ecotourism, to the International Forum on Indigenous Tourism, to numerous activities taking place in communities themselves, a global campaign is growing against the top-down tourism development process that governments and industry are promoting.

Two

The Promises of Tourism

"Welcome to paradise! It's a place where you can relax, have fun, be waited upon." Travel promotions play on these fantasies, offering us an opportunity to purchase experiences we would not get at home, to remove us from our everyday lives and responsibilities.

Welcome to paradise — while it lasts. As villages and tribal cultures become commodified and turned into megaresorts and shopping malls, some travel agents are marketing threatened areas as places to see before they are gone. The ads gloss over the economic, environmental, and social problems in the destinations they describe, much as the tourists' sites have fenced out the same realities in the host communities.

The Media: Spin Doctors and Dream Weavers

The tourism industry has powerful marketing and advertising. As media critic Marshall McLuhan said, "The ads are by far the best part of any magazine or newspaper. More pain and thought, more wit and art, go into the making of an ad than into any prose feature of press or magazine. Ads are news. What is wrong with them is that they are always good news."[1]

In 1993 Pratap Rughani, an editor at *New Internationalist* magazine, devoted an entire issue to tourism. He wrote:

Starting through dozens of tourist brochures I began to feel nauseous. The more I looked the less I seemed to see. Like most TV news coverage of the Third World I was being offered images of the South that process eighty percent of the world's population into a quick cliche. The transformation is the opposite of "famine pornography" — this time it's fantasy-island escape. There are endless brown and black people smiling and saying, "I want to be your friend."... Travel today is a commodity supporting

21

a vast industry. Considering the scope and economic importance of tourism there's remarkably little analysis. Meanwhile the brochures breed. . . . The gap opening up between this fantasy land and tourism's real impact made me feel that brochures are in some sense obscene — "if not vomitorial" as [another editor] put it.[2]

Tourism's corporate advertisers and marketers weave magical dreams, illusions of paradise in the same countries that other factions of the media and foreign aid and development authorities consider destitute. Tourists purchase these illusions, expecting a dream and sometimes finding a nightmare. Some of this reaction can be attributed to culture shock and the need to adjust to an entirely different environment. Yet most of the response comes from a lack of preparation and a belief in tourism industry propaganda. The perceptions of tourism and goals of the tourism industry often conflict with those of the host communities, governments, even tourists themselves. In the stressful, industrialized consumer culture, the overworked and underpaid laborers are encouraged to "get away from it all." Corporations promote cultural homogenization at the same time they market modern resorts in exotic locales. Travel agents present destinations as safe locations offering a multitude of fantasy elements. They may go as far as subtly encouraging sexual permissiveness and freedom from conventional morals. Marketers rarely provide information that could dispel some of the unrealistic expectations tourists hold and create greater understanding between hosts and guests. Tourists who prepare themselves for the cultural, political, economic, and environmental realities of their host destinations before they travel experience fewer problems adapting to a temporary change in lifestyle.

The travel industry supports biased journalism. Travel journalists benefit greatly by reporting only positive stories with little critical analysis; they would not only lose their reputation but also a job for taking a critical view of the industry. A magazine editor who represents a major travel industry newspaper once called me to write for a "green" tourism magazine the lead story on environmental travel trends. He said he believed I could provide insightful criticism about ecotravel. I wrote the piece and provided supporting resource materials. Just before press time, the editor called to say the magazine had decided the feature would not be included. Although I can't prove it, I'm sure the corporate sponsors were uncomfortable with a feature story that was not completely supportive of "green" travel. Because I challenged some of the greenwashing tactics of the ecotourism industry, what I reported (and supported) was suppressed. A tremendous amount of misinformation and greenwashing takes place in marketing paradise.

Encountering Nature and Other Cultures ("Savage Paradise!")

Some of the last places on earth that have not been heavily touristed are Indigenous homelands. Marketing trends point toward the Amazon, the Himalayas, the hills of northern Thailand, tribal areas in Africa, and aboriginal areas of Canada and Australia. Travel advertisements market the residents of such destinations as people who are warm, smiling, friendly, unthreatening, and who are servile and welcoming, there for the tourist's pleasure. Travel advertising says, "Come and meet the happy people, even as their paradise vanishes." This type of marketing promotes glib, racist caricatures. *Cultural Survival Quarterly* illustrated this exploitation in a cover photo: several male tourists, smiling sheepishly, cameras dangling from their necks, wear tribal garb over their Western clothes as they participate in a funeral.[3]

Consumers from the "developed" world seek solace in cultures, environments, and even the religions of disappearing cultures. Aeroperu has catered to this market by advertising itself as "the new world airline" in new-age magazines. One ad claimed, "We know you're searching. For experiences. For answers. For visions of Nature's deepest secrets. We can help fulfill your request. We'll bring you close to your dream." Shelley Attix, a tourism researcher, found through survey that most new-age tour companies are owned and operated by individuals influenced by the focus on personal growth, self-actualization, spiritual philosophies, and Eastern religions introduced to America's consciousness during the 1960s. Many undertake journeys with small groups only once or twice a year, but according to Attix, "As these spiritual trips become more like 'mass tourism,' they become less personal and harder to undertake properly."[4]

Tourism markets cultures — hula girls, wandering tribesmen, Asian mountain folk, and Native Americans. Some critics of tourism suggest that when we travel, we buy a product that includes people. Tourism offers an exciting chance (for those who can afford it) to buy or become, if only for a little while, a part of another culture. Indigenous rights and responsible tourism alternatives are issues that have been marginalized in economic or environmental evaluations of tourism development, although local peoples, activists, and others are starting to influence tourism developers, tourists, and politicians.

Royal Treatment ("A Charming Plantation")

Travel anywhere, at any time, and you will find glaring examples of the imbalance between so-called hosts and guests. I was traveling through the Himalayas with some local travel operators who are friends of mine when we ran into a caravan of travelers with the same company. One of the guides ran over to our van and told us they had been forced to stay up all night with a German couple who was drinking excessively. One of the pair, a middle-aged woman, had announced that she was a professional dancer and had spent the entire night making the young guides learn dances. The guides made sure the tourists were comfortable, fed, and entertained, then got up at dawn to prepare breakfast, pack everything away, and shoulder the packs, while cheerfully assisting the stumbling, aggravated tourists through another day of hangovers. This unequal treatment is one of the major selling points of tourism. Tourists are led to expect that goods and services — even human ones — are available for a nominal price, particularly in developing countries.

On a beach in Thailand, I watched as an elderly European male tourist pulled behind him a petrified young girl. This child looked no more than twelve or thirteen years old. Unfortunately, there was little anyone could do to rescue her in a country that promotes the exploitation of women and children in order to cater to sex tourists. In bars in Hong Kong and Taipei, young women dance provocatively while tourists drink and laugh. Often, the tourists arrange for the dancers to go back to their hotels with them. In the Amazon, renegade tour guides contract out to tourists, offering to take them into the wilds of the rain forest to "go native." Tourists follow these guides into Indigenous villages, demand to stay with local families, eat their food, and expect the locals to entertain them. Only then do they make a token payment. They then simply move on to the next village. The tourists are the wandering elite, demanding royal treatment, excitement, and service from people who may not want to be part of the "travel experience."

Myth: Your Dollars Help Local Communities ("No More Whining on Paradise Island")

Many tourists, unique ambassadors in the development scheme of tourism, believe their mere presence constitutes an investment in "less-developed" host destinations. In 1990 I undertook an attitudinal survey of tourists on Bali as part of my graduate research.[5] Several respondents felt that they positively contributed to the economy and served to teach the Balinese about the "outside world"; other respondents were concerned that their presence increased prices for the local people and helped to fuel the commercialism of Bali.

Investors claim that locals receive many economic benefits for land. Once tourism takes hold, however, the price of commercial land rises to international levels, pricing local buyers out of the market. This cycle makes it easy to displace people, especially when investors buy huge areas from governments or from one local landowner at a low price. An example is the real estate and asset accumulation activity of the United States, Britain, Japan, Hong Kong, and to a lesser extent rapidly "advancing" countries like Taiwan. Investment capital from these nations buys prime real estate in the global South. Hotels are relatively "safe" investments during periods of inflation because price increases are easily passed on to the customer. International corporations and developers race to enter the hotel industry for its promise of enriching balance sheets with appreciating assets and immediate payback.

Many of the economic arguments used to justify existing tourism are based upon the multiplier effect. This theory says that tourist expenditures ripple throughout the local economy, through transactions from laborers to local markets, benefiting the whole community. In fact, though, because of "leakages," little of the money from tourism appears to remain in the community, particularly when a corporate chain is involved — international hotels where transportation, food, drinks, and other products are purchased outside the country and brought in only for the tourists. According to a 1990s study of economic distribution in Tangkoko Dua Saudra, Indonesia, the benefit distribution was 47 percent to the major tour company, 44 percent to hotels, and only 7 percent to guides, of which the head reserve guard received 20 percent. Guides and food are usually brought in from the provincial capital, so few benefits are retained at the village level.[6] In cases where leakages are up to 80 or 90 percent, only ten cents of each dollar goes into the community. This formula can be a recipe for disaster with respect to the international balance of payments for a small, underdeveloped country.

Concern is increasing about blocking these leakages and promoting local and regional goods and services to supply the tourism sector. Polly Puttallo explains:

> The other side of the economic coin to leakages is known as "linkages." These are the ways in which the tourist industry utilizes locally produced goods and services rather than exporting them. Maximizing the linkages minimizes the leakages of foreign exchange. This process also lessens the dependence of tourism on outside factors while stimulating local economies and "people development" and encouraging a greater sense of self-determination.[7]

Because the economic multiplier from a tourist enclave tends to be minimal, the economic payoff would be greater if the tourist resort were domestically owned. As a report on tourism development in Belize points out:

> criticism may also arise due to the perceived socioeconomic costs of the venture. A large tourist project may have a significant impact on labor, causing workers to migrate away from traditional forms of labor. This works against a stated government policy of developing rural areas. Furthermore, the impact may only be among the unskilled labor force and freeze the socioeconomic strata.... Other traditional criticisms of tourism stem from a sociocultural basis. Many Belizeans fear that their country could become a "nation of busboys and waiters."[8]

Tourism is an unsustainable form of development because its instability can worsen a country's economic situation. Tourism is a seasonal, fluctuating business that can rise and fall quickly as a result of political changes, natural disasters (such as hurricanes), the whims of tourists, and reliance on the global economy. According to the World Wildlife Fund, "Tourism can falter when exchange rates fluctuate. How the dollar stands up to the yen, deutschmark, British pound or Mexican peso, can dramatically affect the purchasing power of consumers, hence what type of foreign vacation they 'purchase.' If the dollar is weak against the pound but strong related to the peso, the tourism industry is quick to channel summer trips away from Britain and into Mexico."[9]

Trends in Exploitation
("You Don't Have to Be Columbus to 'Discover' the Caribbean")

The tourism industry follows a well-trudged corporate path that exploits people and resources around the world in the name of economic growth. Two alarming trends are greenwashing and corporate support of countries with controversial human rights records. Greenwashing not only paints products, services, and destinations as ecofriendly but often is a screen for corporations that are actually causing great harm to the environment. The travel industry furthers human rights abuses when it collaborates with oppressive governments in the race for the almighty tourist dollar. One finds it difficult to imagine that tourists who are willing to shell out thousands of dollars to visit a specific country would wittingly support such atrocities. Responsible tourism and educational travel organizations are beginning to give tourists more complete information about destination communities. Some provide overviews of the country and cross-cultural training for tourists before they travel. Others offer volunteer opportunities for travelers interested in social, environmental, and economic justice. While most mainstream travel advertising continues to perpetuate misinformation, the movement to provide accurate information may push conventional marketing to do a better job. However, the individual traveler has the responsibility to push for the truth.

The trend toward greenwashing has its roots in anti-environmental industries. Any number of industries advertise their commitment to a clean and healthy environment. Chemical, oil, and transportation companies have designed campaigns to present polluting industries as environmental advocates. Although these companies may not be perceived as part of the tourism industry, oil and transportation are of course part of global travel. The growing popularity of pro-environmental values has been one reason these polluting industries have taken to greening up their images. The emergence of green consumerism around the 1990 Earth Day celebrations had a tremendous impact on marketing, with many old products re-created as ecofriendly, earth-saving, and biodegradable. Many of the ads for products such as biodegradable trash bags and diapers were found to contain misleading and deceptive information; the products simply were not better for the environment. But the ads still succeed.

Hotels and resorts are awarding themselves green merit points for recycling or reducing their use of plastics even as they continue to consume enormous amounts of energy, chemicals, and pesticides, particularly in the global South. Some of the greenest hotels in North America are the worst polluters in other countries, often operating without waste systems and using chemicals that are illegal in the United States. Some travel organizations donate funds to environmental protection and local health and community development programs, shifting the focus away from the environmental regulations they violate and to short-term support for local people and projects.

In 1995 the Foundation for Clean Air Progress (FCAP) was formed to represent transportation, energy, manufacturing, and agricultural groups, industries that support core operations and services for the global tourism industry. The purpose of FCAP is to lobby *against* the Clean Air Act. Burson-Martsteller was the public relations company representing FCAP. They were also representing the National Smokers Alliance and its tobacco clients.[10] While making money through tourism in one area, transportation and other companies may be looking for economic gains through the destruction of protected wilderness in another.

Human Rights Abuses ("A Carefree Life!")

Advertisements that promote tours to Burma (Myanmar) and other places with blatant human rights abuses clearly misrepresent the situation. One tour ad says, "There's much in Burma to capture the imagination and win the heart. A thousand pagodas studding a vast plain by the muddy Irrawaddy; the reverence in the face of a child climbing the steps of the glittering Shwedagon; the delicate ballet of an Intha fisherman leg-rowing his slim vessel; and the warmth and grace of a long-suffering people. One understands how Kipling, Orwell, and many GIs building the Burma Road fell in love with this golden land." The ecotour company then notes, "We work only with the private sector in Burma. As for shaping politics, we think that the value of the two-way information flow that occurs in travel outweighs any economic benefits derived by the Burmese junta." The company goes on to advertise "The Land of the Golden Pagoda . . . Archaeology, River Travel, Buddhist Culture, Remote Traditional Villages, Ethnic Minorities, Day Hikes. Very untouristed." The reality is that the "two-way information

Sidewalk Bubblegum © 1996 Clay Butler

flow" between tourists and these locals rarely takes place. A trend is in place toward "shielding" tourists: group travel is monitored by a government, the travelers given propaganda and misinformation by both the government and the tour company and escorted through their trip so they do not meet the people who are being displaced and abused.

Fortunately, the U.S. government banned all new investment in the country in 1997. Free Burma Coalition activists worked hard for the investment ban, and the boycotts seem to work. For example, the Burma Forum Los Angeles, part of the Free Burma Coalition, organized a boycott of Best Western in June 2000. The hotel almost immediately terminated operations.

As the tourism industry follows travelers into remote areas, it can become a support mechanism for oppressive governments, dictators, and notorious human rights abusers. Pressure from human rights groups has helped in persuading some companies to stop working in areas with active human rights abuses. For example, Holiday Inn Worldwide, owned by the British brewing company Bass PLC, was the cornerstone of the Chinese policy of only allowing group tours into the country.[11] The London-based Free Tibet Campaign (formerly the Tibet Support Group) claimed that Holiday Inn

> [had] become the key to developing the exact type of tourism the Chinese authorities desire. Tour groups have to stay at government-approved hotels, usually the Holiday Inn, which explains the estimates that the revenue from this hotel alone stands at 75 percent of all foreign exchange entering Tibet. Not only [were] the Chinese able to extract considerably higher amounts of foreign exchange from expensive group tours, but [could] tightly control their itineraries, contact with Tibetans and movements more closely.... Holiday Inn [was] also subject to the volatile fluctuations of tourist numbers during the demonstrations. For example, in June 1993, after the anti-Chinese protests earlier in the year and the arrest of tour guide Gendun Rinchen, the occupancy rate fell to only 24 percent. The Holiday Inn, therefore, [had] a vested interest in promoting the situation as "normal" alongside the Chinese authorities, despite what may [have been] happening in reality.[12]

"In 1997, Holiday Inn withdrew from Tibet," Paul Golding of the Free Tibet Campaign told me recently. "The hotel itself is still being used (now the Lhasa Hotel) and is run by the Chinese authorities. Many Western tour groups stay there, and it is a prime venue for business conferences. It is still the most expensive and lucrative hotel in Tibet. The hotel continues to be referred to as the former Holiday Inn by the Chinese authorities."

> Holiday Inn gave no reason for their withdrawal, however Free Tibet Campaign believes the decision has been influenced by its international boycott of the hotel group, launched in 1993. The announcement [came] only a few months after organisations in the USA joined the boycott of both Holiday Inn and its parent company Bass PLC. Protests [were] held at Bass PLC Annual General Meetings, outside Holiday Inn hotels in the UK and the USA and at international travel industry fairs. Meetings were held with Holiday Inn and Bass officials in London and Atlanta throughout the campaign to discuss concerns.... US groups, the

Milarepa Fund and Students for a Free Tibet, joined the campaign in 1997. "This is a great campaign victory for the Tibet movement internationally," said Alison Reynolds of Free Tibet Campaign. "We will continue to do all we can to ensure that the Chinese do not profit financially from their illegal occupation of Tibet, and we congratulate Holiday Inn on their decision."[13]

Some of the largest tour corporations with the most cheerful images, those you would believe have the best interests of children at heart, are blatant examples of labor exploitation. The National Labor Committee (NLC) claims that Disney exploits workers in countries in the global South. Child workers are often underpaid, working long shifts in unsafe conditions. In a memo, *Setting the Record Straight/The Real Disney*, that was sent to Disney executives, NLC wrote:

> On December 17, 1996, an NBC *Dateline* undercover investigation aired which delivered another almost fatal blow to Disney's claim to set high human rights standards for its offshore contractors, which are then, supposedly, rigorously monitored. In what *Dateline* called "the story you haven't heard — children making toys for children, for your children," its investigators revealed children "many as young as 13 years old" toiling long hours behind the "barbed wire and prison-like walls of toy factories" in Indonesia and China.... [Some underage workers making the toys] were paid just 21 cents per hour, which is already well below subsistence levels.... Another impression which struck the *Dateline* team — especially in factories outside of Jakarta — was how isolated and vulnerable the young workers were. Who could they turn to for help?... China's Xiangjiang Province — where Disney is a major producer — shocked several of the *Dateline* team who felt as if they had somehow stumbled into the middle ages. "Here, all-night factories churn out one of every two toys sold in America. Here more than a million migrant female workers eat, sleep and work in factory compounds for just over a dollar a day." *That's 13 cents an hour.* [emphasis in original][14]

The handful of chief executives running the multinational corporations and the tourists blindly buying their products are far removed from the realities of the people who work for them. The economic gap between the CEOs of travel corporations and people in host communities is as wide as, if not wider than, those in any other industry.

Governments Chasing Tourism Rainbows
("A British Colonial Beach Resort")

The tourism industry relies heavily on the cooperation, attentiveness, and performance of governments, while governments rely heavily on the economic benefits of tourism. Governments are responsible for providing safety from both political and natural forces and a modern infrastructure, the most expensive part of which may be an international airport. Many airports built in the global South since the 1980s have been financed largely by foreign governments and international aid agencies, though the host countries bear the cost of maintaining them. Expensive roads, sewers, electricity, communications, and medical facilities are also part of the tourism industry's requirements. These amenities rarely benefit locals, who may live in poverty alongside the Western-style accommodations. Yet the locals have to finance the facilities, including the special tourist police, and rely upon a seasonal tourist economy and a fickle industry.

Economic competition has created conflicts at many levels. Governments compete with one another for the travel industry's business, offering foreign investors capital cost incentives (free land, provision of infrastructure, allowances for duty-free importation of building materials, equipment), operating incentives (tax holidays, tax credits on interest payments, accelerated depreciation allowances), and investment guarantees (for repatriation of invested capital, profits, dividends, interest and expatriate salaries, availability of foreign exchange, and exchange rates). Many governments overlook environmental guidelines and accountability as well. Increased economic competition has created internal conflicts within communities, as individuals and families vie with one another for economic benefits or struggle to maintain their lands and protect the environment.

Thousands of "lessons learned" are from communities that have received few benefits from tourism. Yet communities, governments, and investors continue with haphazard planning and growth despite the costs. A report from the U.S. Agency for International Development (USAID) discusses this worldwide phenomenon:

> Many African governments have national tourist boards that promote tourism in their countries through external marketing and public relations. In some countries, they also have responsibility for establishing standards for ground operators. Tourist boards

are not noted for their concern for the environmental impact of tourism. Rarely do their marketing plans consider the impact large numbers of tourists may have on the tourist attractions they are marketing. Their mandate is simply to attract tourists, and for the most part, the more arrivals the better. Clearly their marketing efforts are not well coordinated with planning and resource management ministries of governments.[15]

To assume that tourism development does not have strong political implications would be naive. Government commitment and investment can rarely be justified by economic advantages. According to Asian tourism analyst Linda Richter, "Socialist nations see in tourism a means of improving the international press while rightist regimes tend to encourage luxury tourism and convey a sense of capitalism rather than of more ascetic virtues."[16]

The Power of Corporations
("We Unite the World")

Countries in the global South are not the only ones affected politically by tourism. In the United States, especially in Alaska and Hawaii, Indigenous People must confront the political repercussions of the rapid growth of tourism.

➤►((◐))◄◄

A Hawaiian Indigenous Perspective
on Corporate Tourism
Kaleo Patterson

From our experiences and our history with tourism, to turn the other cheek, to ignore the tide of visitors, and to refuse to sell the crafts and the flower leis is not enough. Inevitability and very quickly, others will take our place in the venture of tourism; any other brown-skinned or well-tanned replacement will do. A time will come when our most sacred of words and traditions, cherished dreams and ideas, become common property to the world — all because tourism has no real purpose but to make money. This desire is so strong that the development of tourism in a place like Hawaii is like a tsunami, washing away all that is real and once was and leaving behind something new and foreign. When all that sustained a people in the past is gone, we shall one day look and sadly see that nothing is left and that we have lost everything.

With total abandonment, the political resolve in Hawaii was easily seduced by tourism. The history of Hawaii is a history of uncontrollable ignorant tourism development supported in great part by Hawaiian politics. Tourism's partnership with the political intelligence of Hawaii eventually contributed to the early demise of a once dominant agriculturally based economy focused on sugar and pineapple. Hawaii is now controlled by a dominant tourism industry economy. Although the Indigenous Kanaka Maoli people (Native Hawaiian) resisted tourism development on every island, resistance is not enough. So we have been very active in the political arena as well. The Indigenous People of any community must act to prevent the idea from becoming reality. In order to do this, Indigenous People must strategize offensively first of all to protect our lands, culture, and traditions. Second, every breathing moment of every day must offer a plan and action to offensively protect the Indigenous way of life. To respond to the constant threats of tourism is difficult in itself, but to not respond offensively is death.

Kaleo Patterson's words may seem extreme, but in reality, his experience reflects a long history of struggling over transnational corporations' control of Native Hawaiian homelands. It helps explain how Native Hawaiians are approaching these struggles today, through the strength of their own spirituality. Corporate greed is a concept far from the values of most traditional and rural cultures. From the Amazon to the Arctic, tribal people value their lands for the common good. But subsistence lifestyles and traditional economies are considered inefficient and outdated in a culture that promotes economic growth, free trade, consumerism, consumptive technologies, and exploitation of natural resources. Global economic practices are completely at odds with subsistence economies. "Because the products of subsistence activities are not controlled by market conditions and commercial profits, nor are they subject to government taxes, it is impossible to say how much these products cost or what they're worth. This feature of the subsistence economy leads bureaucrats to dismiss its importance and makes governments unwilling to strengthen it."[17]

In his book *In the Absence of the Sacred: The Failure of Technology and the Survival of Indian Nations*, Jerry Mander argues that "corporate-controlled fantasies" promote manufactured culture and destinations. The message they hope to convey is that the corporations are working in our best interests and are responsible for creating our fantasy futures. Mander warns that the trend toward remaking communities into repackaged forms of themselves and re-creating environments that belong somewhere else is symptomatic of our society's disconnection from the earth and nature. Our tendency to consume these created fantasies, the manufactured environment and culture, will result in "disorientation and madness . . . and the obsessive need to attempt to re-create nature and life."[18] The disconnection from nature contributes to the loss of a sense of stewardship for the land. The commodification of cultures and environments dilutes any sense of responsibility for the earth and distances us from social and environmental injustices. Tourists are well-trained superconsumers who have become so removed from reality, from nature, that purchasing stuffed animals that represent endangered species or T-shirts that feature a rain forest design has replaced true action to stop illegal wildlife trafficking or prevent clear-cutting. By paying for a replicated version of a threatened part of nature, the consumer is perpetrating the fantasy that he or she has somehow contributed to its preservation.

Globalization and Monocultures ("A Place Filled with Warm Friendly People")

Respect for local tastes and cultural differences greatly complicate global marketing campaigns. Corporate marketers promote the globalized consumer culture in order to publicize their names and sell their products with the same advertisements around the world. Tourists are "trained" to seek out names they recognize. Franchises and other corporate cultural "clones" appeal to consumers because they are familiar. On the one hand, tourism advertising creates exotic fantasies; on the other, it turns cultures into replicated, Westernized tourist enclaves. Travel corporations often make locals dress in uniforms so that everyone looks the same. Accommodations are basically the same, and the food is the same. Everything is Westernized. The world's diverse languages are not needed in an English-speaking destination. The entertainment industry, the media, and other corporations have been the source of cultural cloning that tourism brings into local communities. The transnational sounds and images choke off traditional music and arts and create a homogenized culture that reflects Western corporate values and priorities.

Tourist corridors throughout the United States have followed the same development path. The corporate takeover is evident along the major roads from New York to Vermont. Locally owned, mom-and-pop gas stations, restaurants, and shops have been replaced by Exxon, Denny's, and Wal-Mart. As public funds are used to finance infrastructure in rural areas, these corporations follow along, colonizing the communities along the transport routes to tour destinations. These corporations put Mom and Pop out of business, and ultimately locals become service employees rather than business owners.

Tourism's Truths and Realities ("El Conquistador: The Ultimate Resort!")

Author Jamaica Kincaid has captured the dominant philosophy of the tourism industry. "[You] needn't let that slightly funny feeling you have from time to time about exploitation, oppression, domination develop into full-fledged unease, discomfort; you could ruin your holiday."[19] Some tourists are becoming much more savvy consumers and are taking their local concerns and activism along with them on holidays. In the long run, the corporations that choose to greenwash, misinform, and promote vanishing cultures are undercutting their own viability and credibility. Sponsoring misinformation campaigns via marketing information and the majority of travel journalism is fraudulent and undermines basic democracy. Supporting corporations that exploit women, children, workers, and the environment ultimately threatens us all.

Changes are coming not because tourism advertising and marketing are becoming more conscientious and less exploitative, but because people are demanding it. As one Native Hawaiian responsible tourism group states, "Crass commercialism, massive overdevelopment and institutionalized racism limit [the tourist's] ability to connect with the 'paradise' promised by tourism advertising. We demand ethical business practices from the tourism industry.... Our material poverty is not 'exotic,' certainly not to us. Images used in advertising should be fair and honest and represent our realities."[20]

As Pratap Rughani says, "If we can discard these manufactured dreams we're more likely to be able to change the tourism industry from below. Travel is a strong human urge. For me it's about hope. It's the prospect of cross-cultural communication; an exploration of self and other."[21] Travel can educate tourists about other places and peoples; it can also help them better understand their own culture and society. In an age where we are overwhelmed with images, symbols, information, and misinformation, travel can be an important way for us to communicate directly with one another. No computer, travel brochure, or television ad can ever replace that. To do that, locals must participate not as objects or dependents on tourism for their economies but as shapers of their own cultures with the right to maintain their own privacy and limits.

Three

Guests and Hosts:
Disillusioned with Paradise

The terms "hosts" and "guests" are used broadly throughout the travel industry to imply a congenial invitation between people of roughly equal stature. In reality, "hosts" are local people who often have little say about their role. "Guests" are actually consumers with the economic power to purchase "rights" and "services"; they are not invited by local people.

A honeymooning British couple in Bali expressed their displeasure when they found themselves at an isolated hotel on an artificial beach along with crowds of similar foreign tourists. The honeymooners had paid almost seven thousand dollars for what they expected to be two weeks in paradise. Their lack of planning not only left them disappointed in their own accommodations but kept them at a distance from any real Balinese culture. As they explained to me, "The hotel is nice, the food is good, but it's all quite contrived. We are far away from anything interesting. We feel we are prisoners of our hotel. When we want to go to another beach, we have to take the expensive cabbies provided by our hotel. Since we've already paid for all of our food and lodging at our hotel, we can't afford to visit anywhere else. We had no idea that everywhere we go we'd be attacked by people trying to sell us things. You think they really have it that bad here to have to be so aggressive? Bali seems like it would be quite a nice place for these people to make a living."

That tourists can afford to travel to a "host" community and buy the most expensive accommodations and food creates not only an imbalanced relationship but also an imbalanced perception. The tourist's everyday reality of work and responsibilities is not apparent to a person in a rural community on the other side of the world. The local who sees a carefree vacationer with an incredible amount of money is not likely to think of the tourist as a worker. And it is the rare tourist who wants to engage the locals in serious discussions about issues such as poverty, homelessness, and violence. Even if someone wanted to, the inherent inequality of the situation would create an artificiality and distance. Locals have no context in which to understand that guests must pay substantially more for shelter, food, and other necessities in their home countries. Locals have a hard time grasping that one reason the tourists are in the destination community is that it provides an unusual, short-term break from the tourists' real world.

An important paradox is inherent in tourism. The underlying contradiction is that it must lure consumers away from home by implying that a tour is a rare chance to visit unique peoples and environments. But once tourists start invading, a version of the original culture of the destination is co-opted by the tourist industry and supplants the more complex, organic original. This development model reflects the colonialism that is still firmly in place in Western thought.

The consumer culture that tourism brings with it often promotes what Helena Norberg-Hodge calls the "psychological pressure to modernize,"[1] as locals begin to feel inadequate compared to the tourist consumer culture and psychologically compelled to reject what they see as their own poor culture. The tourist consumer culture creates a homogenization of culture, or a consumer monoculture.

The Business of Selling Paradise: Commodifying Cultures

On Koh Samui, Thailand, developers protect choice beachfront property by building high walls along an access road. Directly across the road, isolated from the seaside resorts, is a service village built in a mosquito-infested swamp and piled high with mountains of tourist trash. Tourists' clothing, laundered by the locals, hangs like flags from lines strung up around the swamp. The village is somewhat obstructed by trees so that tourists quickly driving past on their way to paradise are not confronted with the dismal living conditions of the locals. As the destination site grows, so does the service city, with the rapid migration of people looking for jobs that require few skills.

A steady increase of tourists puts pressure on the urban infrastructure, particularly existing transport networks. An expanding tourist population means increased competition with local people for the use of the infrastructure (transportation, potable water). The stress created by these problems further alienates local people. Tourism is often seasonal, which can also strain both infrastructure and the local citizens' stamina. In crowded tourist communities on the island of Koh Samui, small trucks are the only means of local transportation. At the height of the tourist season, as many as thirty-five people with assorted luggage, livestock, and groceries are crushed into the fourteen-passenger trucks. A tourist can later recall this brief, frustrating experience with humor. For the people of Koh Samui, such a ride is a permanent feature of daily life.

Local People:
Performing for the Tourist Dollar

Yet local people do not present *themselves* realistically either. Governments in the global South try to sweep aside evidence of problems such as violence and pollution that might make guests uncomfortable. Local people must compete for tourist dollars and sometimes exploit each other or their cultures and environments for short-term economic benefits, which is especially evident when locals market their history, ceremonies, religion, and culture.

Many local people are simply identifying and selling any community resources they think tourists might buy, sometimes fabricating performances and ceremonies they believe tourists will pay to see. In doing so they are prostituting their identities and manufacturing themselves as tourist attractions. Some are genuinely looking for ways to improve their economic situations. Others believe that allowing tourists into their villages is acceptable if restrictions and limitations are in place regarding behavior and photography. Some want money. Others genuinely want to teach spiritual lessons. Yet not all of these individual activities are community-sanctioned, and some have caused conflicts between families and communities. For example, in the United States, several individuals offer participation in religious ceremonies such as visits to sweat lodges and vision quests, believing that non-Natives will benefit from a greater respect for the earth and sensing that these seekers are desperately in need of spirituality. According to Native elders and leaders who are organizing to protect their spiritual beliefs from co-optation, Indian people do not "sell" their spirituality; they consider the idea extremely sacrilegious. Traditional Native American spiritual practices do not include conversion of non-Native peoples.

Prominent Native organizations consider this practice to be one of the worst problems facing First Nations People today.

While some Native groups have taken measures to oppose the exploitation of Indigenous culture and spirituality, consumers present a growing demand, believing they have the basic right to buy anything as long as they have the means to do so. The Indigenous/non-Indigenous relationship may continue to be one of exploitation, no matter how well intended, because of global economic forces, multinational corporations, and technological development aimed to complete the eradication of Indigenous knowledge and livelihoods. According to some Native teachers, corporate practices ensure that not one wildlife reserve, wilderness, or Indigenous culture will survive in the global market economy.

A case in Ecuador illustrates how misperceptions by both tourists and locals persist. An ecotourism program in the community of Rio Blanco promotes small-scale development and community control of resources and decision making. The project, which is operated communally by member families, expected about three hundred visitors in 1996. Rio Blanco was founded in the early 1970s by Quichua migrants from the Andean foothills and relies mainly on cash-crop farming. David Schaller, who did extensive research in the Amazon, reported:

> Community members rarely spend time in the primary forest, although tourists spend most of their time there with few believing commercial agriculture is the mainstay of the community's economy. Tourists also reported being confused and upset by the cultural program which they felt was not authentic. Not all community members indicated a connection between tourism development and forest preservation. While many community members reported they would rather increase tourism than agriculture, nearly half intended to clear more forest for cultivation.[2]

Tourists visiting Rio Blanco clearly have preconceived ideas about Indigenous Peoples living in the rain forest. They fail to see that the community is agrarian and does not rely on or have knowledge of forest resources. Rio Blanco depends on outside economic factors: export agriculture and manufactured cultural tourism. Neither tourists nor locals understand the global forces transforming their lives, and no mechanism seems to exist for educating either hosts or guests to evaluate

Eric Lawrie

Traditional activities in commonly used open space become tourist "experiences" that make locals uncomfortable. Tourists sometimes profit by photographing open-space activities and selling the photos to be used as postcards or books.

their own roles in the circumstances that are bringing about disillusion on all sides.

A journalist wrote about his vacation to a reservation in Arizona, where he stayed in a tepee, learned some handicrafts, and visited pow-wows and casinos. He referred to traditional clothing as "costumes." He had hoped he would camp within an Indian community so he could observe daily life, but his tepee site was far from any village. Although the tour operator had arranged for him to stay on the Fort McDowell Indian Reservation, he had no contact with its tribal members, instead visiting other reservations. Even so, he ended the article by stating he was sure he'd "learned a lot about the Indians."[3] Bernadine Boyd, vice president of the Fort McDowell Tribal Council told me, "We don't live in tepees here — maybe he was reading very old literature. We're a small reservation with only twenty-four hundred acres. If someone wants to get to know us, they could do that by contacting our offices."

The article is typical of how mainstream media present First Nations. Clearly the writer did not consider that certain tribes might not want him on their lands or may have restrictions regarding tourists. Although he was curious about why he did not spend time on the reservations, he never looked into it. He had hoped to be in a traditional village in order to observe the lifestyles of the community. Had the journalist actually realized his dreams, he might have been surprised to find himself in low-income housing listening to barking dogs all night.

Many tourists seem unaware that simply being observed by someone can be uncomfortable and disruptive. Most tourists would feel strange if visitors to their community took photographs of them walking down the street or buying milk at the neighborhood market. Such behavior is even stranger in a community that values open space (communally shared outdoor areas such as yards, rivers and lakes, or forests) for daily activities, work, and relationships. Although the journalist touched upon the loss of land and culture, he did not delve into the issues, nor did he mention poverty and unemployment, both of which are rampant on reservations.

Keeping Cultures Locked in the Past

Many travelers have preconceived, myopic notions about other cultures. Travel journalism that idealizes Indigenous Peoples creates high expectations, and tourists (as well as journalists) are usually disappointed with the realities: people who wear Western clothing, own their own businesses, and deal with tough social issues. Idealizing cultures keeps them locked in the past, sometimes creates conflicts between hosts and guests, and undermines all attempts to understand the realities of modern Indigenous Peoples.

Dharamsala, India, is the home-in-exile for the Dalai Lama and a Tibetan refugee community. The village is full of travelers from the global North seeking spiritual enlightenment or simply passing through on their way to the Himalayas. The Buddhist temple is a center for the community; every day Tibetans gather there for spiritual teaching, upkeep of the temples, and other tasks that have brought them together for hundreds of years. Children cry, locals in the back rows chat and make jokes, while others hustle about preparing things. Several times during my visits, I heard the angry comments of visitors that "these Tibetans are disrespectful at their own ceremonies." The tourist's idealization of the sacredness of the ceremony conflicted with the practicality of the Tibetans, whose temples are integrated into their daily routines. Some visitors are unaware that this is truly Tibetan religion. Tjokorde Raka Kerthyasa, a Balinese artist, explained to me that "the ceremonies in Bali (and probably all religious ceremonies in the world) are not commercial performances. They are part of our daily life. Because our ceremonies are unique and appear so spectacular, visitors from all over the world come to visit and witness them. This can have a negative impact during the ceremonies, as intrusive distractions can create difficulties and misunderstanding for both the Balinese and the visitors." Tourist demands for "authenticity" may indeed prompt locals to alter their practices to ensure that tourists are satisfied and continue to come and spend money.

I have heard travelers declare that Indigenous and other ethnic people were not "real" because they wore Western clothes or were trained in both Western and traditional ways. They fail to consider that people living in tourist destinations are dealing with the onslaught of tourists, consumerism, and exploitation of their cultures.

Elusive "Authenticity"

Tourism is artificial in many ways. "Authenticity" is elusive when one is part of a travel elite, an alien invader with no common history, no shared responsibilities, no ties whatsoever to the local people and culture. Moreover, local people rarely have an opportunity to learn who the tourists really are. Tourism sets up a one-sided view of travelers and creates a "tourist" personality that encourages irresponsible and even unethical conduct. Tourism is a magnifying lens of consumer culture; the focus is constantly on spending money. Because tourists often believe they "help" local communities, they have established a paternalistic attitude toward the locals. "Authenticity" can hardly be found in such a fabricated and unequal guest-host situation.

Tourism could provide a chance for visitors to discuss with locals issues that affect them: consumerism, employment and unemployment, homelessness, widespread psychological ills, isolationism, environmental blight, urbanization, drugs, racism, women's issues, education, stress, the lack of extended families and community support, violence, the gap between rich and poor. Few opportunities arise to talk about how the world is on a course of overconsumption that is eroding the planet's natural resources and displacing millions. But more important is the potential to exchange through listening and learning. Travel can counter the myths and harmful activities of the global North while supporting local efforts and creating useful cross-border organizing with those in the global South who share similar concerns. Travel could also be a way to work together toward the common good of the planet.

The Economic Power to Buy: Shopping for Culture

Few tourists have escaped a welcome lei, a smiling greeting committee of native women bearing necklaces and drinks, a welcome-to-Jamaica shot of rum, or other such cultural concoctions. Yet manufactured culture goes beyond the initial welcome to include almost all tourist experiences — dining, excursions, and entertainment. Millions of tourists routinely experience their entire vacations through the lens of counterfeit culture.

Tjokorde Raka Kerthyasa told me, "Some tourists and visitors who know nothing (or do not want to know) about the meaning and purpose of our customs and religious practices attend ceremonies just for the sake of taking pictures to prove they have been on a holiday." In the small Balinese arts village of Ubud, dances are performed for tourists, but their evolution has been unusual. Rather than being manufactured and approved by the tourism industry, the performances are the work of the community. Members of the community, many of whom have gained international recognition, perform dances and music in the courtyard of the Ubud Palace. Kerthyasa argues that the tourist performances can reinforce local culture: "More (young) people are willing to learn techniques from the old masters." Community members, especially family and friends of the performers, watch along with the tourists. Balinese children see their parents weave hypnotic visual and musical compositions. Although these performances, too, are contrived, they are an accepted form of traditional ceremonies and dances that the community has decided to share with tourists. Yet those who oppose this form of tourism suggest that the pressure not to change may prevent normal progress, even if it serves to benefit the local people.

Purchasing the "Other"

Tour agents sell the "Other" — ethnic cultures that are not part of the dominant, Eurocentric consumer culture. Writer and professor bell hooks, who speaks widely on issues of race, class, and gender, believes the market offers a commodity culture that exploits conventional thinking about race and gender. According to hooks, the current wave of "imperialist nostalgia," where people mourn the passing of what they themselves have transformed and destroyed,

> takes the form of reenacting and re-ritualizing in different ways the imperialistic colonizing journey as narrative fantasy of power and desire of seduction by the Other.... The desire to make contact with those bodies deemed Other, with no apparent will to dominate, assuages the guilt of the past, even takes the form of a defiant gesture where one denies accountability and historical connection. Most importantly, it establishes a contemporary narrative where the suffering imposed by structures of domination on those designated Other is deflected by an emphasis on seduction and longing where the desire is not to make the Other over in one's image, but to become the Other.[4]

In our homogeneous society, the longing for the primitive is expressed in tourists' projections of another culture. The tourism industry exploits destination cultures as exotic, bohemian, mystical, culturally rich, glorified societies. As hooks says, "Masses of young people dissatisfied by U.S. imperialism ... afflicted by the post-modern malaise of alienation, no sense of grounding, no redemptive identity, can be manipulated by cultural strategies that offer Otherness as appeasement, particularly through commodification."[5] Travel to rural and Indigenous cultures is increasing at a rate never seen before as the world becomes globalized and we lose our cultural identities and ties with community.

In our capitalistic society, individual power lies in economic strength, not in who we are or what we contribute as a whole to our communities. This characterization offers the central difference between Western societies and those societies where individuals think of themselves as part of their larger community and tradition. Industrialization has fostered human isolation. People feel lonely and detached even within cities filled with millions of people. Westerners are indeed prime customers for cultural purchases because we are living examples of commodities ourselves. How much we make, what we can afford to buy and do, the level of education we can pay for, and our monetary assets classify us and constitute our individuality. As imperialism persists throughout our own society we, the modern colonialists of the new tourism frontier, culturally isolated consumers that we are, seek out opportunities to purchase a fleeting, exciting, intense encounter with the Other. But many Indigenous Peoples claim tourism is just a form of cultural voyeurism, allowing the curious to glimpse Native cultures.

As hooks explains, simply by expressing the desire for "intimate" contact with other cultures, foreigners do not remove the politics of racial domination. She encourages us to recognize that purchasing an experience with another culture is a form of racism and that "mutual recognition of racism, its impact both on those who are dominated and those who dominate, is the only standpoint that makes possible an encounter between races that is not based on denial and fantasy."[6]

Macabre Forms of Tourism

One of the most disturbing phenomena in Bali is the commercialization of cremation ceremonies. After a water ritual at a village stream, private rites are performed. The people then proceed through the village together, bearing the body to the cremation site in a huge bull built out of wood and paper and beautifully decorated. Women dressed in colorful, hand-dyed skirts carry sculpted fruit offerings.

A death is big news on Bali, and many tour operators sell tickets to the cremation ceremonies. Signs in front of the tour offices urge, "Don't Leave the Island Until You See the Big Cremation — Get Tickets Here." Once a death is announced, local agents contract minivans and buses to deliver tourists to the destination village. Since ceremonies take place in public areas with village participation, locals can do little to keep tourists from joining the procession to the cremation site. Local people are crowded out by aggressive tourists who want photos. Fences, in fact, must be built around the cremation sites to keep the tourists out of the immediate area. Along the fence tourists crowd shoulder to shoulder, pointing their cameras at the burning funeral pyre. They are careful not to get any other tourists in their photographs. Their photos are calculated to show friends back home that they were one of the special few to see such an exotic religious ceremony — although as many as two hundred tourists may be on hand. A British tourist who witnessed the activities at a ceremony remarked, "It was an amazing experience, but I felt bad for the local people carrying the body when two motorcycles joined the procession. These tourists rode up wearing only their swim suits, waving bottles of beer and having a great time. I was embarrassed to be there."

Deborah McLaren, Bali, Indonesia

We offer you

**Don't leave bali
Before you see
a big cremation**

on : 19-4-91
depart : 11.00. am
price : 10.000 Rp

please book here !

PT NOMINASI
CHANDRA
WISATA.

Herick

Even death and funeral rites have become commodified for tourism in Bali, where enterprising businesses begin arranging tourist vans and selling tickets as soon as they hear someone is dying.

Some locals view tourists as a possible means of help, while others react with pain to having their suffering photographed and documented. The *Wall Street Journal* reported that as of 1998, Westerners by the thousands visit Papua New Guinea for safaris. For about ten thousand dollars per person, they go to tribal war zones to gawk at humans marketed as warring cannibals:

Visitors jet in and out of villages, snap a few photos, and are back at their resorts in time for a five-course dinner. . . . Critics call it one of the most macabre forms of tourism today. Though casualties in the tribal skirmishes are rare, the battles can be brutal and bloody — something that human-rights groups say shouldn't be exploited for tourism. "It's voyeuristic," says Barbara Gehrels, a manager at Survival International, a London-based group that monitors tourism of Indigenous peoples. Paul Taylor, who heads the Asia history program at the Smithsonian Institution, says it is worse. "You're subsidizing warfare," he says. "You're almost encouraging it."[7]

Not all tourists visiting these areas know about the cannibal tours and are appalled to learn about it. Tour operators argue that "tribal tourism isn't exploiting anyone, in part because the tribes are accepting money. 'We want the people to maintain their culture,' [a tour operator] says, 'That's what sells Papua New Guinea.'"[8] Tour operators to Irian Jaya, Indonesia, where tourists participate in funeral processions, also claim the income keeps the locals happy and the tourists coming. Yet the local people are concerned about the loss of cultural artifacts, burial gifts, and icons, which the tourists take home as souvenirs. One visibly shaken woman told me, "They took my mother's image [a wood carving]; they have stolen her soul."

Tourists continue to flock to see the macabre. A large number of places associated with war, genocide, assassination, and other tragic events have become significant tourist destinations. Professor John Lennon and his associate, Professor Malcolm Foley, at the Moffat Centre at Glasgow Caledonian University have labeled this phenomenon *dark tourism*[9] and look at possible reasons that tourists visit these attractions — for remembrance, education, or entertainment. From the death camps of Poland to the death site of an American president, their work demonstrates the sometimes disturbing reality. Dark tourism sites present governments and other authorities with moral and ethical dilemmas, where recent tragic history often confronts the dynamic of commercial development and exploitation.

Elvis Batiks: Manufactured Tourism Culture

Radical resistance to manufactured tourism is present in many Indigenous societies that have become tourist destinations. In Hawaii, where tourism is the dominant industry, the commodification of island culture has been so complete that the image that probably comes to mind when you think of the atoll is smiling, friendly women in grass skirts that cater to relaxing tourists.

Haunani Kay Trask is a Native Hawaiian activist who is keenly aware of the cultural costs tourism imposes through commodification and remanufacturing. Trask charges that an entire Indigenous culture has been successfully commodified, the culture deformed to the point of prostitution. Prostitution in this context "refer(s) to the entire institution which defines a woman ... as an object of degraded and victimized sexual value for use and exchange through the medium of money."[10] Trask describes how *haoles*, or white tourists, have stereotyped and commodified Hawaii:

The commodification of Hawaiian culture includes a marketing of Native values and practices, on *haole* terms. (After all, a prostitute is only as good as her income-producing talents.) These talents, in terms, are the "hula," the generosity, "aloha" of our people, the "u'i" or youthful beauty of our men and women, and the continuing allure of our lands and waters. Tourism converts all of these into profits. Hula dancers wear clown-like makeup, don costumes from a mix of Polynesian cultures and behave in a smutty manner, rather than in a powerfully erotic manner. The distance between the smutty and the erotic is precisely the difference between western culture and Hawaiian culture. In the hotel version of the hula, the sacredness of the dance has disappeared, and been replaced with an ornamental hoax.... Needless to say, Hawaiians don't participate (in manufactured tourism), and didn't participate in such things before the advent of *haoles* in the islands.[11]

Tourists often do not comprehend that other people live in a place, that they are born, grow up, and die there; that it is their home. Perhaps it is the anonymous nature of tourism — the lack of obligation, the likelihood tourists will never visit the community again — combined with the self-righteousness of purchasing power that allows tourists to deny their part in the exploitation and to participate in activities they would consider repulsive at home. For example, tourists have a reputation for wearing inappropriate clothing. Travel advertising encourages tourists to be free and easy in their dress as much as everything else. One famous photograph shows two Muslim women on a beach, even their heads completely covered, curiously glancing at a bikini-clad tourist in repose on the sand. The image of the contrast between women of two cultures is striking. Yet the tourist has the economic clout to do as she pleases, even when it challenges every moral standard of the culture she visits.

Corporations have long been in the business of manufacturing traditional arts and crafts, clothing, and other cultural "artifacts," crowding out those made by traditional craftspeople. The goods are mass-produced, eliminating the local artist and using cheap labor outside of the country. Vases from China, T-shirts from the United States, and belts from Guatemala are typically found in souvenir shops in any country. Traditional arts and crafts are highly commercialized under the power of tourism. For instance, in Malaysia and Indonesia the fine art of batik, a dye and wax process that creates beautiful prints on natural fiber, is now mass-produced on synthetic materials in hundreds of factories throughout Southeast Asia, and traditional designs have been replaced by pop art and Elvis Presley. Traditional crafts like bamboo art and reed weaving are marketed in a wide range of new applications: as beer mugs, candle holders, and coffee and tea sets. Over the past few years, many Latin American Indigenous handicrafts have taken on the Guatemalan style of bright colors and simple patterns. In Otavalo, Ecuador, most of the products sold in Indian markets are faux Guatemalan. The Kunas of Panama recently began to sew cartoon characters into their hand-layered textile motifs, or *molés*, replacing traditional designs and animal figures. This activity may be simply a change in culture, but the change stems directly from tourist demand.

However, to counter the exploitation of traditional arts, local craftspeople in many destinations have organized cooperatives to ensure that they are not taken over by outside industry. Women artists throughout Java and Bali, for example, have joined handicraft cooperatives. Yet local businesspeople and artists show increasing concern as the doors of free trade swing open that these cooperatives are in competition with each other, which is the case in Otavalo, where weavers have destroyed competitors' looms.

Along the highways of the desert southwest in the United States, billboards beckon tourists to stop at "Real Indian Trading Posts." Kachina dolls and sacred pipes are sold alongside rubber tomahawks. In the Black Hills of the Dakotas, where a non-Native-owned tourism industry pulls in $1 million annually, tourists dress up like Indians to get their pictures taken beside an "Indian chief." More than 2.5 million tourists each year stop by to see Mount Rushmore and visit the local Indian population.[12] Few Indians have been able to adapt to the new conditions; they are viewed only as relics.

Tourism scholar Dean MacCannell says, "When an ethnic group begins to sell itself . . . as an ethnic attraction, it ceases to evolve naturally. The group members begin to think of themselves . . . as living representatives of an authentic way of life. Suddenly any change in life style is not a mere question of practical utility but a weighty question which has economic and political implications for the entire group."[13] Staged authenticity places tremendous constraints on a community. The demands of tourists frequently outweigh a community's own power and lifestyle. Concerning her own community, Haunani Kay Trask warns,

"Tourism deforms the culture so much that many young Hawaiian children grow up thinking that our culture is the *haole* interpretation of culture — to dance the hula is to dance for tourists . . . and if you smile real nice, some *haole* is going to take you out."[14] Any argument for rethinking tourism must be made by the community itself, as should the effort to balance economic interests with critical protection for its people and culture.

The Hopi Nation may be one of the last holdouts. Signs warn tourists not to take photographs or wander past designated areas. When Anne Coyner, an intern working on the Dine' (Navajo) reservation, traveled to Hopi with a Dine' friend to visit an acquaintance, they were stopped before they could enter the residential section of the village. A Hopi woman told her, "It may not seem like there are a lot of people around, but you would be surprised to learn how many eyes are watching." Each village makes its own decision about tourists, but the overarching sentiment is obvious with so many tourist warning signs appearing on the reservation. Ten of twelve villages have closed their kachina dances to the non-Native public. The Hopis enforce tourist guidelines, including dress codes and the confiscation of cameras and artist's sketches. Tourist inquiries to the tribal office receive the following reply: "Hiking and off-road travel is strictly prohibited because of the disregard for the sanctity of our sacred religious shrines by past visitors. The Hopi Tribe does not publish a schedule of traditional ceremonial activities as these are religious events that are not staged for the entertainment of tourists. Such publicity would be disrespectful of their very spiritual nature."[15] So far, the Hopis are determined to keep tourists at a distance and keep their culture intact; they have taken strong stands against all types of development that would influence their culture.

Political Disruption, Travel Boycotts, and Campaigns

The events of September 11 rocked the tourism industry to an overwhelming degree, causing multibillion-dollar airline industries to flounder and massive layoffs of tourism workers (airlines, hotels, resorts, etc.) around the world. These fluctuations in tourism severely affect small states, Indigenous communities, and rural communities that inordinately suffer from even a slight decline in expected income.

This fact calls into serious question the use of tourism as a sustainable development strategy with long-term, stable benefits. The World Travel and Tourism Council (WTTC) reports that

> the United States and Germany will be the two countries most affected by September 11, suffering decreases in travel and tourism demand of US$92.3 billion and US$24.7 billion respectively for years 2001 and 2002 combined.... WTTC estimates the impact of September 11 will cause a 7.4 percent decline in travel-and-tourism-related demand in years 2001 and 2002 combined, which will result in a total worldwide loss to employment of over 10 million jobs.[16]

According to a Canadian tourism report, "The terrorist attacks of September 11, 2001 have had profound effects on the tourism industry worldwide.... These impacts can be ascribed to both fear of travel and the economic fallout of the attacks."[17]

The effects of foreign tourism boycotts on governments and people are difficult to determine, although they are a powerful tool to make countries toe the line of economic liberalization. Because local economies become so dependent upon foreign ones, many of the immediate effects are on the local businesses, whether they are part of the open-air economy or the official economy. In the case of China, after tourism nose-dived in 1989 following the Tiananmen Square massacre, many Chinese activists believed that economic sanctions should be increased against the state but that tourism should continue. A Chinese living in the United States said, "We don't want China to be closed off from the rest of the world." The situation is a catch-22 for conscientious tourists: not to travel in China censures the Chinese government's actions while isolating China's people from outside contact.

Burmese solidarity campaigns around the world responded quite differently by calling a boycott of the "Visit Myanmar (Burma) 1997" campaign, sponsored by the country's repressive government. A representative of the Free Burma Coalition I spoke with warned, "Tourist dollars do not benefit the people of Burma; the tourism promotion is an effort by the government simply to gain currency while carrying out gross human rights abuses on its citizens." Over twenty Burma support groups around the world have warned tourists, the travel industry, and the media that visiting Burma under its brutal military regime supports human rights abuses and only furthers economic trade and political ties without solving injustice.

Glenys Kinnock, a member of the European Parliament, has long argued against travel to the military-run country. In a 2001 article published by *TimeAsia.com* she was quoted as follows:

> Holidays, of course, should be about fun and relaxation. But how many of us have ever questioned our right to travel and enjoy total freedom of movement? Probably not many.
>
> And yet this is a very real issue — you could say it's a matter of life and death — for those in a certain country who are asking us to make an ethical decision to stay away at present. They're not some radical, out-of-touch extremists; in fact, they form a democratically elected party that won 82 percent of the seats in a parliament that has never been allowed to convene. These people have made very clear policy decisions, specifically asking foreign visitors to stay away, until the brutal military junta that rules the country allows them to take up their rightful place in government. The country is Burma. And the party that has pleaded with tourists not to visit their country is the National League for Democracy, led by Aung San Suu Kyi, winner of the 1991 Nobel Peace Prize.[18]

Responsible tourism campaigns work, as illustrated by the Tourism Concern campaign against U.K. guidebook publishers to respect the wishes of the Burmese democracy and stop promoting and facilitating tourism to Burma through producing guidebooks to the country. *Rough Guide* was the only publisher who did not produce a guide on ethical grounds. "*Lonely Planet* was the focus of our high profile public and media campaign, run jointly with the Burma Campaign, UK....Although *Lonely Planet* were intractable in their opposition to our campaign and did not withdraw their guide, the campaign was hugely successful in raising the public profile of the campaign for democracy in Burma.... Two other major guidebook publishers announced they would not be producing future editions of their Burma guides."[19]

Tourism Concern has also initiated the Porters' Campaign. "A myth seems to have been created that porters are superhuman. The massive weights they carry, the cold and the high altitudes are nothing to them. They're different.... But this is madness. In fact, Nepalese porters suffer four times more accidents and illnesses than western trekkers. Making matters worse, there are many reports of porters being abandoned by tour groups when they fall ill. Porters have even been

Dr. Jim Duff, photographer, www.ippg.net

Nepalese porter wears only a plastic bag for protection in subzero conditions.

abandoned in life-threatening blizzards while trekkers were rescued by helicopter."[20] Porters around the world are beginning to organize for their rights. Tourism Concern believes that fair trade in tourism offers an opportunity for real change. Fair trade in tourism means a fair deal for everyone involved in the tourism chain, and includes tour operators addressing the working conditions of their porters. They are promoting guidelines for U.K. operators on porters' rights and working conditions. Some of the guidelines limit loads, pay fair wages, and provide adequate clothing for porters.

Expanding Corporate Influence on the Global Economy

Often international corporations hold a monopoly on an entire segment of the tourism industry. One example is hospitality firms, especially lodging corporations, which have entered into tourism through the hotel development business. Firms build hotels and then

Lorette Dorreboom/Greenpeace

New developments in paradise: tourism, McDonald's restaurants, and construction in Guam

sell them to investment groups, perhaps becoming involved as investors themselves, primarily to ensure that they will be able to secure the contract for the long-term management of that property. Most such firms thus become management contract organizations. They also continue their monopoly by franchising. They use others' capital to fuel growth and ensure cash flow. Cash-rich European and Asian transnationals, for instance, have been acquiring U.S. hotel company assets to demonstrate growth and aggressiveness in their capital markets. This pattern is not limited to the United States, however: it is occurring throughout the world. Seeing cash-rich firms from different nations pooling their resources to acquire assets in another nation is not unusual.

International corporations often undermine the efforts of local businesses. A study of the most visible members of the informal economy in Acapulco — street vendors — suggests that "street vendors are generally less informal than is...assumed. They have licenses, sell in broad daylight and have open relationships with formal sector suppliers....Domestic tourists buy from lower-priced street vendors in response to the higher prices charged by formal establishments. Paradoxically, hotel owners are those most opposed to allowing street vendors on the beach."[21]

"In India, since 1968 tourism has been an important ideological front, if not economically supported," tourism professor Nina Rao recently explained to me. During the third five-year government development plan, tourism was included in the budget. During that time, "India went through a foreign exchange crisis and was forced to take a World Bank loan. Now the situation is such that we have a more comfortable position on foreign exchange, but the argument has shifted to income and employment."

During the third five-year plan, the tourism minister announced a package of measures to increase the number of tourist arrivals from 1.5 million to 5 million in five years and to double the amount of hotel rooms in three years. But the tourism minister's projections did not disguise the transfer of power that he envisaged for the industry, from the public to the private sector, from blanket to intensive development of specific "routes" and "destinations" around the country. The National Action Plan (NAP) was designed to herald the arrival of resort tourism and attract the free-spending visitors whom India had never been able to draw.[22] However, Rao explains that "in 1975 the UNDP advised India to move away from cultural to vacation tourism and they identified Goa, and envisioned moving it away from hippie beaches to high spending resorts. They also selected Gulmarg in Kashmir for winter sports. These models were to be followed by other states.... In a recent PATA meeting though, it was suggested that India should go back to backpackers whose length of stay led to greater expenditures. This idea was rejected by both the government and industry."[23] According to *India Today*, by 1995, "the only beneficiaries of the NAP and its accompanying baggage have been the hoteliers, who have been building with enthusiasm, using loans guaranteed by the Tourism Finance Corporation (TFIC) and benefiting from tax breaks provided by the government."[24]

As of 2001, India offered more than a hundred thousand hotel rooms — with an average occupancy of 15 to 25 percent. Rao says that tourists are not occupying the upper category in the metropolitan areas. Despite this, "It was always a policy that the private sector should match the government in investment, which never happened, and the public sector Ashok chain grew to be the largest in India. Now most hotels are being privatized."

Fifteen special tourism areas (STAs) were designed with financial incentives to encourage private investment in hotels, infrastructure and other tourist facilities.

The sites were selected on the basis of consultations between hoteliers and tourism departments, both state and central. And here the problems began.... Had tourism officials solicited the views of the Ministry of Environment and Forests before conferring STA status on Orissa's Marine Drive, then considerable embarrassment and expense could have been spared. The result has been red faces in the state's Tourism Department and the unwelcome discovery that local sentiment cannot be ignored, even to the convenience of large hoteliers.... [Sixty hoteliers applied for permits to build and] the plan would entail the felling of a reserved forest, encroachment on the Balukhanda black buck sanctuary and the subsequent exposure of the coast's agriculture to the shifting sands and cycles that had prompted the British to plant the forest in the first place.[25]

People in fifty villages in the area learned about the expansive project and feared that the forest's destruction would turn their fertile land into sand and threaten their way of life. Local people further opposed "the culture of affluence." The state tourism minister, also a resort owner, applied for land in the proposed area to build his own hotel. "And so arose one of the nation's first tourism-related political movements, as *panchayat* [community] leaders mobilized thousands of locals . . . which resulted in a broad-based coalition which three times thwarted the attempts of Chief Minister Biju Patnaik to have the state's forests deregulated."[26]

In 1995 I visited India on an environmental fellowship that focused on private enterprise and biodiversity protection through ecotourism. I met with several state tourism ministers to discuss ecotourism development; all of them told me that tourism was not involved with any other governmental sectors and that they did not see a need for integrated planning. Although they had a tremendous interest in and expectations for increasing international tourism, these tourists represented a mere 10 percent of all tourists to some states. And most tourism ministers could not adequately track income from tourism, where it came from and where it went.

Moving to Equity

In the 1970s the World Bank claimed that tourism would be a beneficial opportunity for development in Cuzco, Peru. Twenty-five years later, local studies of the region reported that "tourism has not translated into an employment boom for the region. When you look at the number who are actually employed by the tourist industry...it really turns out to be just a few....Out of 280,000 economically active persons in the region, only 6,000 (slightly more than 2 percent) are directly or indirectly employed by the tourism industry."[27] Commercial enterprises such as high-rise hotels rarely use the local population as the management system. Foreigners usually fill mid- and upper management positions. Locals are employed mostly in service-level positions (as maids, waiters, bellhops, transportation help), and they have infrequent opportunities to advance into management positions. Only rarely, when they already have extensive education and language skills, are locals sent abroad for management training.

The tourism industry can be merciless. When increased economic growth is the leading factor for development, conflicts and competition develop between people, between communities, and even between nations. Political systems are under pressure to provide goods and services that tourism developers, international corporations, and even their own populations desire. Market forces are determining the shape of world economic activity in general and tourism in particular. The need exists to encourage efforts to establish decentralized, locally owned projects that will ensure tourism is socially and ecologically responsible. Another need just as great is to encourage responsible and responsive research and development to support these programs.

Tourism has become the new form of colonization over the poor of the world. Considering that international travel accounts for the exchange of more than $3 trillion a year, as one responsible tourism writer wrote, "it may be safely said that tourism exerts a greater, more pervasive influence on the countries and cultures of the world than any imperial power ever has....The sun never sets on the tourist empire."[28] Virginia Hadsell, founder of the Center for Responsible Tourism, recently told me that she believes there are some promising new developments.

> You must know the dark side of tourism! It grows. But there are encouraging pockets of responsible opportunities for travel that benefit both host and guest. Study tours that use locally owned and operated accommodations, where meeting residents with a common interest in a subject, or involvement in a common project, are personally rewarding for both. These experiences

are worth the search; they can stretch one's mind, warm one's heart, and open a whole new way of understanding the world and one's self.

People-to-people experiences that are equal, informed, and further understanding about common concerns — and joys — are the only way to avoid disillusion between "hosts" and "guests." Understand what you are "buying" when you travel, demand realistic information from the travel industry, learn about tourism's role in undermining local economies and cultures, and support local communities and responsible tourism organizations. Investigate and boycott irresponsible tourism industries. Take action against economic liberalization and privatizing the environment. Most important, work for change in the community where you live or the one that you visit on vacation each year.

Four

Tourism Development
in the Local Community

Imagine one morning you wake up and walk outside to pick up the newspaper. *Flash!* Aliens with cameras giggle and point at you while their children run through your yard, jump on your car, and scream for their photos to be taken. Down the street you notice a couple of hip young aliens returning from an early morning swim at the beach. They stop by your church on the corner, still in their skimpy, wet swimsuits as they wander in to watch your neighbors participate in services.

Click! Flash! The duck pond in the middle of the block has become an overnight attraction. Suddenly two hundred aliens gather around its small shores, trampling the flowers you helped plant there last spring. The ducks fly away. You walk down the street to the corner market to pick up some things for lunch only to find that the market is so full of aliens that you can't get through the aisles. On top of that, the aliens are willing to pay incredible prices for practically anything in the store. You can't afford to be here; quietly you slip away. What's wrong with this picture?

Tourism means turmoil for residents of tourist destinations. Social pressures — a changing local environment and economy, increasing numbers of tourists, and the effects of media and technologies brought in to support the development — build up very quickly and change lives and cultures forever. Many changes are obvious, while others are subtle. In some cases, communities have become human zoos. For example, hill tribespeople in northern Thailand and the Maasai in Kenya have herds of trekkers and caravans of camera-toting tourists seeking them out. The impacts on a small host community and culture create permanent negative change.

As an article in *New Frontiers* reports:

"TAT's [Tourism Authority of Thailand's] unbridled promotion of hilltribe tourism is part of a vicious cycle which, primed by

63

tourists' insatiable desire for the 'unspoiled,' can decimate a community," says anthropologist David Feingold, of the Ophidian Research Institute. "Tourists *discover* a village," Feingold says, "and the village community adapts to them." Yet that adaptation — modern accommodation, the relentless hawking of handicrafts and soft drinks, and the use of pat phrases in English, Hebrew, Japanese and French — is precisely what makes them less appealing to future visitors. "That village, which has adapted itself to tourism, then finds it difficult to return to their previous existence," he says. More often than not, they slide towards what Feingold calls the "bottom end" of the industry: peddling opium and child prostitution.[1]

Indigenous cultures are being devastated by an invasion. At this level, tourism creates its own universe, an artificial world with no place for the local population. The locals struggle just to survive. Given the almost total lack of government control, the absence of industry self-policing, and most important, the increased competition to make a profit, the tourist industry more than ever wields unprecedented power in communities.

Ladakh, fortressed above the Himalayas on the Tibetan Plateau, was virtually isolated from the West until the mid-1970s, when the Indian government, worried about border conflicts with China, built an airport and increased military presence there. Overnight the West invaded — tourists, media, technologies, pesticides, roads, and consumerism. Helena Norberg-Hodge observed the process from the beginning:

> I became aware that our [Western] culture looks infinitely more successful from the outside than we experience it on the inside. ...With no warning, people from another world descended on Ladakh. Each day many would spend as much as a hundred dollars, an amount roughly equivalent to someone spending fifty thousand dollars a day in America. ... Ladakhis did not realize that money played a completely different role for foreigners ... [in Ladakh basic needs were free of charge], that back home they needed it to survive, that food, clothing, and shelter all cost money — a lot of money. Compared to these strangers, they suddenly felt poor.[2]

The psychological pressures took on many forms of cultural rejection. Begging became an increasing problem. Some farmers began to call themselves "donkeys," indicating they were poor work animals next to the wealthy tourists. The tourists looked at the Ladakhis as if they were backward or primitive. When I visited Ladakh in 1990, hundreds of tourists from the Middle East were there to escape the Gulf War. Many of them told me they believed Ladakh was backward. An American woman who lived in Kuwait told me that "if the Ladakhis could understand that better resorts would attract better tourists, they might escape from this poverty."

Tourism promotes the same colonial tendencies that agricultural export companies, missionaries, and others perpetrated in earlier centuries. Colonizing is not new, but tourism development as a form of colonizing is new and growing at tremendous rates. Between 1950 and 1990, tourist arrivals grew from 7 million to 80 million in the Americas; from virtually nothing to almost 50 million in East Asia and the Pacific; and from less than a half million to 14 million in Africa.[3] The numbers are remarkable and the effects catastrophic.

Sociological Cycles of Tourism Development

Tourism's emergence in host communities follows a typical pattern. The first stage is euphoria, which is typified by the residents' race to trade everything they have (land, natural resources, autonomy, culture) for the "riches" of the global economy. Many local communities and governments are passionate in their belief that tourism is the path to all future development. The multinational tourism industry promises jobs, distinction, and outside support to the community or country.

Tourism researchers often refer to the second stage as apathy: locals begin to notice changes, such as restrictions of their traditional land use, and their initial excitement wanes as they realize few benefits. The tourism industry fashions an irresistible fantasy of jobs and money. Few communities have the knowledge or experience to see through the illusion, nor do they have the resources to plan for its problems. Tourism divides communities into those who believe it may provide some benefits and those who are opposed. The need arises at this critical moment for tools and information to help the residents analyze the situation, make informed choices, and develop strategic plans by looking at other models (including other communities that have resisted tourism or created alternatives). Yet development agencies, investors, and governments rarely provide this information, and locals seldom realize the economic and employment opportunities promised by this conventional path of development. Infrastructure for tourist use is subsidized by public funds, but the public rarely uses it. In fact, prices for public transportation often increase beyond the local public's means. The locals are displaced and priced out of an international real estate market. Prostitution, alcoholism, and venereal disease increase; traditional skills are forgotten; the beautiful landscape erodes.

As the infrastructure is built, competition between hosts and guests mount. In this third stage, hosts become antagonistic and blame their growing problems on tourists. Competition accelerates between locals and tourists for transportation, sanitation, food security, money, space and environment, and even cultural integrity. By the time the locals have experienced the full cycle of tourism, they are too debilitated to fight back. The new infrastructure makes the region more desirable for other industries besides tourism. The urbanization facilitates migration to the area and provides corporations with a pool of cheap labor. A system is created to train locals and migrants for service jobs in tourism or as low-skilled labor for other industries.

The stratification between rich and poor, tourist and local, is fueled by the new consumer culture. Locals invariably begin to regard themselves as "poor." When a community loses its self-reliance and depends on foreign corporations for wages, necessities like food and shelter become unaffordable. The globalization of the economy transforms the local and self-sufficient (tribal, farming, hunting) community into a consumer-oriented and dependent society. Convinced that internationally manufactured goods are superior, they reject their own, locally produced goods.

Now reliant upon an income in a monetary economy, the local cannot afford the things he once owned. He eventually drifts into the impoverished population of the service industry. In the past, as a subsistence farmer, he had agricultural skills, knew where his food came from, and was self-supporting. His family did not rely upon his income to ensure their shelter, and a fluctuating seasonal tourist market did not jeopardize his livelihood. Once considered a landowner or a farmer, he was an important member of his own community. As a bellhop or busboy, he contributes little to the community, his status declines in the new tourist society, and his descent into self-rejection begins. This pattern of economic gains and losses is not addressed in traditional accounts of tourism.

Economic Myths

Tourism is praised as a source of employment in host destinations, perceived as a highly labor-intensive industry that can offer employment to the semiskilled and unskilled. In regions with high unemployment, tourism is said to provide moderately quick relief. In some countries that are predominantly rural with semiskilled and unskilled labor, nearly all the management personnel must come from abroad. Positions like caterers and cooks tend to be filled by foreigners; expatriates may in fact even be needed to fill a portion of the unskilled staff in this labor-intensive business. The majority of locals are left with low-wage jobs. With few management training programs, no escape from a life of service jobs is available.

Despite their history of callous indifference to employees, international corporations are still encouraged by governments who buy into the same promises of job creation. Governments lavish money on beach resorts, although recent statistics show "beach resorts account for just seventeen percent of total jobs created, despite having received the greatest share of government support."[4] The hotel industry is heralded as a job source and may benefit from official programs, yet

> contrary to the usual claims, the hotel industry is not the main source of job creation in tourism — one of the key objectives of official tourism promotion programs [in this case, in Mexico] — since its share in total direct employment is under fourteen percent.... Jobs in surface transportation, travel agencies, and airlines account for ten percent of total direct employment, a relatively low figure. The greatest relative job creation is in services, restaurants and bars. These account for forty percent of the total direct employment.[5]

Tourism offers temporary, low-wage jobs without long-term commitment from the industry or benefit for the community. In most of the world, tourism is an unstable source of jobs, because it is inherently seasonal. Benefits common in North America or Europe are unheard of, and year-round employment is nonexistent. Even hazardous construction work offers no contracts, no insurance, no benefits. Many hotel and resort construction sites are labor camps, with entire families living in makeshift shanties.

A tourism activist in Hawaii relates what tourism developers promised and what really happened:

[The developer] promised 6,500 jobs when he was collecting permits to build. What he seems to be saying these days is something
not so promising. The tourist "industry" is the lowest paying
major industry in the state; most of it paying minimum wage.
And when there is a slump, you are sent home: "don't call us,
we'll call you." Often the lay-off is far too short a time to collect
unemployment, but long enough to consume any meager savings
one might have. Even these jobs will go to those with the skills
and education needed to function in the resort scene.[6]

Many hotels and restaurants in tourist sites are foreign-owned, so the
dollar spent by the tourist almost inevitably does not stay where it is
spent. A great deal of the cost of a vacation is transportation, the means
of which are overwhelmingly controlled by the countries from which
tourists come. Moreover, the growing tendency for the same company
to own a "chain" of travel businesses, or "corporate alliances," opens
up a further channel for ensuring that the minimum amount of money
is received by the host community or country. In many countries, determining the links in the "chain" is difficult. In the United States,
Disney's director of public affairs, Bill Warren, told me that "corporate
alliances are part of the package. We have alliances with all the major
hotel chains, any number of airlines, cab companies. . . . It literally gets
into the thousands."

Human Rights, Migration, and Displacement

Tourism development has fostered human rights abuses and supported
oppressive governments. In some cases the locals are seen as a nuisance
to tourists, and the military patrols areas to keep the local vendors away.
In countries with records of human rights abuses, the government has
displaced local people and sometimes even enslaved them as workers
to build hotels and other sites. Government tourism officials prevent
locals from having contact with tourists.

In addition, many people in destination communities around the
world are fighting for their own land rights. Usually the poorest and
most underrepresented and marginalized are simply fighting for their
right to have a place to live. Some atrocious examples were reported in
the media in 1996 when the president of the Philippines ordered entire

shantytowns torn down to "beautify" the area for international development meetings. Most fights over land rights are directly in conflict with governments and private investors.

The group Tourism Concern supports global campaigns to protest displacement of people caused by tourism in Burma, Indonesia, and Kenya. Burma, a country with an atrocious human rights record, "celebrated" 1996–97 as the Year of the Tourist to promote economic growth and investment in the country. However, many of Burma's tourist sites were constructed by forced "voluntary labor." In Pagan fifty-two hundred people who lived in villages among ancient pagodas were given two weeks to move and were allowed no compensation or anywhere to go. Now Pagan and its pagodas welcome tourists in peace and quiet while its people live on bare, parched earth with little shelter.

The island of Lombok in Indonesia has gained popularity with international tourists, and the Indonesian government is demolishing homes to make way for tourism development. "Hundreds of thousands of people in the Third World are facing malnutrition and starvation, not because of famine or war, but because they have lost access to the land and resources that could sustain them. It's happening because their governments are pursuing the tourist dollar, and need more room to develop the industry."[7]

Several tourist developments in Africa displaced the traditional population: peoples who had lived there for thousands of years, cultures that made a living on sparse lands and existed only because of access to the area's natural resources. The Sarova Shaba Hotel in Kenya was built for tourists in the Shaba National Reserve:

> A spring provides fresh water for the hotel, and, where it emerges through the rocks outside the lobby, it cascades over a series of waterfalls into a pool below, where fish swim and water lilies cover the surface. The bedrooms of the hotel are situated around the enormous swimming pool. This was once the watering-hole used by the local Samburu and provides the only pure water in the region.... The Samburu are now confined to arid land devoid of grass.... The plight of the Samburu is desperate. Their cattle are dying from drought conditions and loss of access to water, and now the people are faced with starvation.[8]

How about a golf vacation? What could possibly be a problem? Golfers might find it hard to believe that the construction of golf courses around the world has become a factor in displacement of people. According to Chee Yoke Ling, director of the World Anti-Golf Movement,

> Uncontrolled proliferation of golf courses world-wide is directly threatening people and natural resources. While the last few years have witnessed increased discussions on sustainable development, golf development is becoming one of the most unsustainable and damaging activities to people and the environment. The 25,000 golf courses world-wide cover an area as large as Belgium and the business of building them is one of the fastest growing land developments in the world. Golf developers in Third World countries pay golf architects like Jack Nicklaus US$1 million for designing a course, far more than the compensation paid to the people it displaces.[9]

The United States is not immune to this phenomenon, as Native Hawaiians have been displaced by the popularity of golf. "In 1986, Yasuo Yasodo, a Japanese national, bought the 1,200 acres that our homes were on for the last 30–50 years. We are Keiki O Ka'Aina (children of the land), yet we were evicted, our cattle stolen and killed, our houses bulldozed and our lives ruined just so a Japanese foreign national could build this lavish golf course complex. We are now gone from the land we loved, it is too late for us, but we plead with the Japanese government...do not let [these] investors come to Hawaii and terrorize us."[10] Ling reports that the Keiki O Ka'Aina plea has gone unheeded: "Japan's national airline, JAL, has recently obtained approval to build a huge resort with a 27-hole golf course, a restaurant, 100 units of private lodges and 1,440 luxury houses on 1,500 acres of agricultural land and 800 archaeological sites on the west coast of Hawaii. Traditional burial grounds are also included in the area.... Displacement even takes place for the ancestors of the local Hawaiian residents."[11]

How about a cruise? The staff always seemed happy on the Love Boat. According to the Cruise Lines International Association (CLIA) and the American Association of Port Authorities, "the size of the North American cruise market was 5.9 million passengers for 1999. ...The industry has 158 ships deployed in North America and that number is expected to rise 38% to 206 by 2004."[12] Many are registered in countries like Panama to avoid U.S. laws that protect cruise ship employees, "seafarers." The community of people from the global South who live and work on cruise ships often put up with squalid conditions and little pay. According to the Center for Seafarers' Rights, "500–700 workers are on each ship, typically from 30–40 different poor, under-developed nations, working and living side by side. Most workers have no written contract, work 12–14 hours a day, often get no day off for an entire year, live in cramped, unsanitary rooms deep in the bowels of the ship, are fed poorly and are only paid a few hundred dollars a month."[13]

So many cruise ships pay inadequate attention to safety standards that numerous fires have resulted in recent years, triggering an investigation by the National Transportation Safety Board. Responsible tourism organizations suggest investigating the living and working conditions of seafarers. This is difficult to do, since "guests" are not allowed to visit the living areas of employees. But "When approached with dignity and understanding they will often open up and let you know what life aboard the ship is really like. Most crew members will appreciate your genuine effort to get to know them as human beings."[14]

Loss of Traditional Culture

Tourism researcher and scholar Valene Smith writes that the seasonal nature of tourism "may leave hotels empty, carriers and tour operators idle, and employees jobless.... Individuals who are tied to tourism experience either 'feast or famine.' "[15] The local people do not often experience the "feast." Most of the accommodations at a tourist destination are owned by outsiders. The service-level jobs local people fill do not provide enough benefits ever to call them "feasts." Most of the millions of people who make up the world's tourism labor do not have job security, health care, or a minimum wage. Outside of countries in the global North, few countries have labor unions. In some countries, unions are created by the corporations and not the workers, effectively controlling any protests from labor.

But the local people are familiar with the "famine." Enticed by the promise of jobs that will allow them into a monetary economy, they often give up work on land and a subsistence lifestyle to become dependent upon a monetary economic lifestyle when they migrate to the service cities. Because of the seasonal nature of tourism, local workers make meager wages during the high season and virtually nothing during the off-season. This situation is clearly not feast-or-famine; instead, it is more "low-maintenance-or-famine." While in the Westernized view "subsistence" has negative connotations, to those from other cultures "subsistence" can mean success. Yet tourism displacement forces people from lands that offer a subsistence lifestyle.

Multiple problems arise from the clash between Western, technological cultures and traditional cultures. Like other large international corporations, corporations in tourism are rapidly replacing workers with computers, particularly in communications and financial services, doing away with phone operators and bank tellers, for example. Travel hospitality suppliers, travel agencies, air transportation, travel vendors, corporate travel managers, and megacorporations that provide travel technologies and integrators are areas that increasingly promote new technologies. Other technologies that support tourism, such as tools and machines used in water and sewage, construction, agriculture, and transportation, also downsize job opportunities for locals. Other, more subtle problems arise from the culture clash. Friction often comes about over the concept of time. Tourists from the high-tech world expect locals to move faster, sometimes ridiculing or in other ways degrading employees who may be ill trained for their jobs and may have only rudimentary skills in foreign languages. As time-saving technologies are introduced, life gets faster for both local people and tourists. Workers are exploited by tourists and the industry that consider their economic value only, not their time or the toll that introduced technologies have created. As Norberg-Hodge explains, the shift from traditional lifestyles to a technological world "represents a shift from ethical values that encourage an empathetic and compassionate relationship with all that lives toward a value-free 'objectivity' that has no ethical foundation."[16]

Norberg-Hodge questions the reasons for traditional Western development paths: "I believe that the most important breakdown of traditional societies is the *psychological* pressure to modernize."[17] Traditional societies were self-sufficient before "development" came along. Introduced development ideologies, technologies, and outside influences, such as tourists and the media, represent consumerism's most exaggerated features. "Development" undermines self-esteem and eventually becomes "essential." That people, especially the young, are blinded by the promise of capitalism when their exposure to Western culture is so narrow is easy to understand: they see only the media and movie stars or travelers who seem to be rich, unburdened by jobs or responsibilities. The "psychological pressures to modernize" and the promise of economic gain are potent rationalizations for tourism development.

All forms of development are based on economics.

The word "development" presupposes agents that engineer change: changes in the natural environment, changes in social structures, changes in production patterns, etc. These changes are supposed to generate improvements in the quality of life of the people involved.... The idea of development is very much a concept from the North. Its roots go back to at least the period of Enlightenment.... It was then that the early colonial powers started to establish administrative systems to rule and control huge regions in the South.[18]

The very language of development, terms like "First World," "Third World," and "less-developed countries," reinforce the Western biases about poverty. The U.S. Agency for International Development was established to "develop" the rest of the world in its own image, one that holds capitalism and economic growth as a central value. In addition, interconnected agencies and pacts such as the International Monetary Fund (IMF), the World Bank, and World Trade Organization (WTO) were established to form a structure to manipulate world trade. They are directing the world's development processes: liberalizing environmental, labor, and economic barriers and developing the world infrastructure in order to reach natural resources. The road to progress has had only one path, one that has proven ineffective and incongruous for most of humanity.

Transnational Corporations

Even in the United States, where international corporations are common, their effect is palpable. The wide reach of international corporations is shown in Hawaii, where families who acquired wealth through plantation agriculture now own tourism. These families are selling and leasing land to international corporations for hotel and resort development. Real estate prices escalate and locals rarely can afford to buy their own lands, although public support is required to provide services and infrastructure. The future of Hawaii is determined by international corporations that are interested only in investment, overseas corporate boards that base decisions on speculation and sometimes money laundering. Development is no longer grounded in community well-being nor used to promote local self-reliance and decision making.

The international corporations are becoming more influential, powerful, and political. They have a strong hold on the tourism industry, creating the "need" to go on vacation and for the development of destination communities. According to Matthew Rothschild,

> In today's world, the single most important economic actor is the [TNC]. A few hundred of these giant companies, based in the U.S., Europe and Japan, affect the lives of people all across the globe. They influence what we eat and wear, and at what price; how we make our living, and at what wage level; where we reside, and whether we — or they — own the land we live on. They poison our water, pollute our air and contaminate our food. They corrupt our governments and ally with those who deprive us of our rights. [International corporations] play such a role because they have enormous power, and because they are interested not in our well-being, but in the making of profit.[19]

Critics argue that developing countries form the majority of the world's population and should be free and equal participants in the shaping of world development. International corporations, however, maintain a hold over international relations. Although such global institutions as the United Nations exist to rectify conflict among nations, international corporations have historically rejected the decisions of international organizations that don't suit them. Many of these corporations also control the world's resources and wealth. These superpowers have vast economic and military clout and are ultimately able to control countries in the global South.

International corporation hotelier conglomerates frequently operate through consortium-type organizations, spreading control to additional companies rather than into the community. In many cases international corporations are franchises. Name recognition for a hotel chain or product is promoted by franchising, and the financial arrangements are attractive to both franchisee and franchiser. By forming global travel partnerships (affiliations among credit card companies, banks, transportation, travel agencies, hoteliers) and unfettered by the free trade laws of any nation, international corporations have solidified their dominance of world tourism. This situation, along with the amalgamation of frequent-user programs by hospitality and travel firms (for instance, frequent-flyer programs that merge with hotel and car rental programs), suggests that the marketing alliance effort will continue and that community control and benefits will be suppressed.

International corporations with few tourism development restrictions are responsible for problems of much of the infrastructure in destinations in the global South. Land planning and layout design by these global corporations often interfere with environment and local traditions. This type of development has not met with a favorable reaction in many communities. Tourism researcher Linda K. Richter has written that at "tropical paradise" destinations in Indonesia "some Balinese are fighting to retake some measure of control over the tourism industry before it pollutes the very culture so many others came to experience....Accommodations like the traditional *losmen* allow guests to stay in small-scale labor intensive accommodations that range in scale from modest hostels to luxury inns. These units are ecologically far more compatible with the environment than the high rise, high import, high energy five star hotels that the World Bank helped finance."[20]

Examples of international corporations' control in the United States abound. Seibu Alaska, a local unit of the giant Japanese Seibu Group, owns the Alyeska ski resort in Alaska and expanded it greatly:

> A world-class, all-season resort. The resort includes a 307-room Prince Hotel and a tramway to a high-end mountaintop restaurant. This world-class resort is positioned to accommodate a projected expansion of the international tourist market over the next decade.[21]

Effects of Tourism Development on Indigenous Peoples and Rural Communities

In many places around the world, the conflicts among international corporations, governments, tourists, and Indigenous Peoples are coming to a head. Any analysis of these problems must avoid lumping all Indigenous Peoples into one ethnic group with the same set of concerns. Rather, each group should be viewed within its own set of circumstances, concepts about land use and development, and most important, according to its own right to self-determination.

Eurocentric patterns of privatizing lands are at direct odds with Indigenous concepts of land, which include strong emphasis on managing for the common good and taking responsibility for the earth. Colonization, acculturation, and industrialization have a long history of affecting virtually every Indigenous group. Vine Deloria and Clifford Lytle write about the impact on Native Americans:

> Expansionist forces beyond the government's control inevitably destroyed the effort to keep the Indian and white communities apart. The increasing sophistication of American technology enabled settlement where none was thought possible so that, as the Indians were pushed farther west, they were replaced by a civilization that could not easily be dislodged, a civilization that was intimately linked to eastern industrial society.[22]

Tourism continues the same human, technological, and industrial invasion of Indigenous lands. Of Hawaii, tourism activist Kaleo Patterson says:

> I have seen the exploitation caused by an out-of-control global industry that has no understanding of its limits, nor responsibility or concern for the host population of a land. I can say with certainty that the majority of Hawaiians long for a better way of life, of simple respect and dignity, that today's tourism industry has systematically undermined. . . . At a place called Honokahua, a developer's excavations unearthed over 1,100 intact burial bundles, while local community groups protested in anger. It took mass demonstrations before the developer stopped. Tourism is not an Indigenous practice; nor has it been initiated by the native Hawaiian people. Rather, tourism promotion and development has been directly controlled by those who already control wealth and power, nationally and internationally. . . . While local elites and transnational corporations benefit from tourism, native Hawaiians remain the poorest, sickest and least educated of all peoples in Hawaii. Current trends show that tourism will never benefit us.[23]

The past few decades have seen an unprecedented force to be reckoned with as Indigenous Peoples organize around issues like land rights, civil rights, and intellectual property rights. They are powerful players in developing legal structures and policies prepared by the United Nations and the World Bank. They are becoming a solid force that TNCs in the timber and oil industries must recognize and work with. Indigenous Peoples are succeeding either in resisting tourism's negative impacts or formulating creative strategies to take it over on their own terms. While many Indigenous Peoples remain fairly isolated and do not have the experience and history required to understand and deal with tourism, new international strategies and alliance-building around the issues will establish connections between those who know tourism all too well and those who are new to it.

Many tribal people resent the purchase and practice of Native cultures and religions by outsiders. These sentiments are part of a growing movement. In the 1980s the American Indian Movement (AIM) issued resolutions condemning non-Native adoption of facets of Native spirituality. Certain writers, anthropologists, and others have been banned from Native lands because of their exploitation of the people and their religion. Native groups have issued a declaration of war against non-Native cultists, commercial profiteers, and self-styled new-age shamans.

In Talkeetna, "a hamlet in Mt. McKinley's shadow, residents have presented petitions and staged a rally to protest a large Denali National Park visitors center [that was] proposed for their tiny town."[24] As Chris Beck reports:

> Girdwood is a town of about 1500 people and a large number of seasonal residences, located a 40-mile drive south of Anchorage. The town sits on the uppermost fringes of Cook Inlet, in a striking, glacier-rimmed valley, and is home to Alaska's first and largest ski resort, Alyeska.
>
> Like many small Alaska towns, Girdwood is poised between a quiet, small town past and an uncertain future. For the last 20–30 years, Girdwood has been a small, tight-knit community, with a strong sense of the shared pleasures of the surrounding mountains, rivers and forests. In the early 1990s, a major hotel, tram and mid-mountain facility were built at the ski resort, by the Seibu Corporation. While leading to an expansion of the ski mountain, which locals mostly liked, this project was a major jolt to the community. With the construction of the hotel, residents began to take seriously claims that Girdwood was destined to become a "major world class four season resort" — a vision that had been floating in the area for years.
>
> Since that time, the town has worked to develop a range of plans to manage predicted growth. These include a comprehensive land use plan, a package of design standards, and master

plans for commercial areas and transportation. A controversial plan to develop a golf course, on land held by the Municipality of Anchorage, is currently being passionately debated.

The character of the future community remains unclear. The town's natural beauty and good access are likely to continue to create pressures for development. At the same time, Alaska is far enough from major markets that growth is slow. Girdwood is just another place where, depending on how growth is managed, the best of the past could be saved or lost.[25]

Here Come the Tourists!

"Give me the T-shirt," I watched a local woman say to the tourist. The small village in the Amazon was almost filled with beggars. It was hard to believe that the community began its ecotourism project in 1992 in order to protect natural resources. In a few short years, the villagers had lost interest in the land and became enchanted by things the tourists had. Their repeated "requests" annoyed tourists. Some locals were more skilled and playful in their requests, others up-front and demanding. "They have money and many things," said the woman asking for the T-shirt. "It's no problem for tourists."

Locals have no problem perceiving tourists as incredibly wealthy. The entire tourist experience revolves around money and purchases. The community itself is being purchased. Tourists are superconsumers who bring their foreign languages and communications, strange and inappropriate clothing, and cameras into the community. In the context of a brief visit, sometimes an overnight, few real friendships are formed between tourists and locals. Tourists are eager for adventure, or at least the perfect photo opportunity. If the tourist becomes upset in the midst of the excitement, the local usually pays the price. But these strange people sometimes give away token gifts to locals, even money. This act results in begging, which becomes increasingly widespread as locals begin to see themselves as "poor" and the tourists as "rich." The psychological pressure of viewing oneself as poor or backward can manifest itself in crimes not previously common in a community.

Indigenous Peoples in the Andes demand compensation for having their photographs taken, saying it's intrusive. A woman in Otavalo, Ecuador, explained to me: "We see ourselves and our children on post-cards and in books. We do not benefit from having our photos taken.

ISEC/The Ladakh Project

The tourists:
from the locals' perspective

A foreigner does. We demand part of the profits." In some Indigenous communities, photography is taboo because it is believed to cause physical or spiritual harm to the person who is photographed. In India young children have had limbs torn from their bodies to make them more pathetic and hence "better" beggars. Adults who commit this violence often have several children who work for them. Other forms of begging sometimes found amusing by tourists offend many locals. An Indigenous leader from Panama told me, "It breaks my heart to see the young boys swimming after coins the tourists throw in the water. We spent years acquiring our rights to these lands. Now with tourism, the people here do not care about the land anymore. They just want tourist dollars."

While tourists believe they can contribute to destination communities, locals don't always agree. Money spent by budget travelers — especially backpackers — may go into the local economy. They tend to stay in cheaper hotels and eat in cheaper restaurants owned by locals and so get closer to the local culture. These young vacationers like to distinguish themselves as "travelers," not "tourists." They live by budget travel guides and often flock to the same inexpensive areas of villages and cities. But in "frontiers" like Kathmandu, Goa, and Bangkok, where a backpacking subculture has existed since it became part of the "hippie" routes in the 1960s, such travelers have a reputation for stinginess and rude, hard bargaining. In Indonesia I met a British bicyclist who was cycling around the world. He was proud that he had spent virtually no money on his trip. He lived with families that took him in every night from the road and ate what was offered to him by people he met along his way. He had not worked in any of the places he had visited. He was extremely happy that he had just bargained a local merchant down from the equivalent of ten cents to a penny for four pieces of bread. I thought it was rather odd that he was taking advantage of everyone he met and wouldn't even pay a fair price to a poor baker.

Health Issues

Tourists are often concerned about infections and illnesses they might contract while on vacation to another country — with good cause, because as tourist destinations become more urbanized, disease increases. The fear of disease can lead to declines in tourism; both Thailand and Kenya have suffered drops in tourism with the rise of AIDS. Tourists avoid parts of Africa and Asia because of malaria. Globalization has created scares about diseases and bacterial infections spread by tourists, like cholera. Even the Ebola virus and SARS were believed to be transported by airplanes.

While most travelers are concerned only about their own health risks, they are responsible for the expansion of disease. Tourism carries diseases and bacteria to new areas. Travelers routinely bring home the diseases they have picked up; in the United States, virtually all of the 398 cases of malaria reported between August and December of 2000 were contracted overseas.[26] The HIV/AIDS virus has spread to Europe and the Americas as tourists return to their home countries from well-known sex destinations. However, the disease tourists leave behind during the trips is rarely accounted for. An estimated 90 percent of Indigenous Peoples in the Americas died after exposure to infectious diseases imported by Europeans, and over half the groups once present in the Americas have become extinct. Millions of people in tourist destinations face health risks from tourists. HIV/AIDS is such a problem in Thailand because of tourism that hundreds, perhaps thousands of women, men, and children are dying as a result. Other sexually transmitted diseases are on the rise. Increased prostitution, alcoholism and drug addiction, displacement, and toxic and polluted environments attributed to tourism development have further contributed to a variety of health problems.

Parts of Asia and South America are now popular with a particularly lethal visitor, the drug tourist. To "go native," they find jungle guides, seek shamans, and take hallucinogenic drugs. In northern Thailand the high demand for opium among tourists has trickled down to the population at large, and many hill tribespeople have become addicts who cater to tourist demand. Little or no treatment is available for local people who become addicted. Tourists return home after a few weeks, never seeing the chaos their thrills have caused.

In Peru drug-voyeur tourists are traveling into the Amazon and bringing health problems that threaten the local population. The Urarina people have remained relatively isolated because of the remoteness of their settlements and by choice. The very reclusiveness of Urarina has contributed in large part to their reputation and served to draw this new breed of tourist. While they resisted missionaries and the culture of the colonialists, according to infectious disease physician Ritchie Witzig:

> Incursions of "foreigners" (non-Urarinas) into Urarina traditional lands are currently from river traders, loggers, colonists, oil exploration teams, and recently "drug-voyeur" tourists. . . . In the past two years, two Americans have arranged "jungle ecology tours" that include a two-week trip up the Amazon and Maranon rivers, and recently the lower Chambira river. During the river tour, a "shaman" from Iquitos manufactures the sacred hallucinogenic ayahuasca (*Banisteriopsis caapi*) for the tourists to drink and "experience the jungle like natives." Finally, they arrive in Urarina villages to "look at the Indians" and take pictures. Right after a tour in the spring of 1995, most of the children in a village, which had been visited, came down with a respiratory ailment requiring antibiotics to recover. This infection was most likely supplied by these "drug-voyeur" tourists from overseas. The Urarina are alarmed at this invasion, especially as they know the

tour operators are armed with weapons and take drugs, effectively mocking the Urarina religious ceremonies. The affected villages organized to write a complaint to the Peruvian Ministries of the Interior and Tourism in Iquitos, and the American Embassy in Lima, demanding that the individuals responsible be barred from their lands.[27]

Witzig believes that "ecological destruction and introduced diseases will gradually decimate" the Urarina, who "will likely need political support from outside Peru or they will join the long line of extinct cultures and peoples left behind by the ongoing colonization of this continent."[28]

The general health of people in tourist destinations is declining, and locals are the least likely to be able to afford treatment. If doctors are available, they usually serve wealthier tourists who can pay them. The claim that tourism will bring with it better health services is a myth. Tourists and locals compete for access to health care. When people are displaced, their health may be at greater risk because they have to relocate to places where survival is more difficult. The strain of development that accompanies tourism also destroys the environment and creates poverty and urban health problems. The lack of proper water and sewage treatment and virtually no garbage control further threaten locals. Quick-fix serums and vaccines cannot cure the real dangers to health: environmental devastation, increased urbanization, and related social ills.

Women and Youth at Risk

Tourism and tourists harm women and youth in particular. As traditional cultures are turned into service cultures, women are most likely to be demeaned by the industry as prostitutes and hostesses. In some countries very young girls and boys are recruited to serve the demands of a growing global sex tourism industry and are exploited by tourist pedophiles.

The following is an excerpt from a letter sent to the German embassy in Bangkok:

For the duration of my stay in Bangkok, I would like to hire a Thai girl. Since I do not want to return to Germany with the clap [gonorrhea] or syphilis, I would like her to be examined by a dermatologist or in a clinic. I would, therefore, be very grateful if you could give me the address of a reliable doctor or clinic. Perhaps you could also inform me of the approximate cost of an examination. Or is there even an agency in Bangkok, which guarantees that its girls are healthy? Thank you very much in advance for your trouble.[29]

According to the Ecumenical Coalition on Third World Tourism (ECTWT), the most striking feature about this and numerous other letters sent to official German institutions in Bangkok is "not so much the brazenness of the request itself, than the unabashed way in which it is taken for granted, that the recreation value of a holiday resort can be reduced to a mere question of the quality of brothel services."[30] In some countries, prostitution tourism has become so rampant that it not only attracts the sex tourist but is drawing some travelers to the countries permanently to become sex-tour guides and experts. Referring to a well-known American engineer who moved to Thailand and started writing "prostitution guidebooks," the ECTWT warns that "when an engineer becomes a tour guide, when skilled doctors (of which Thailand has not enough) specialize in serving tourists, when business people become marriage brokers, it is obvious there is money in the sex trade. We can clearly see who profits from it, but the real question raised is what is the cost?"[31]

Tourism prostitution is legal in some Asian countries. Japanese travel agencies send participants to Taiwan and Thailand, although tours are also organized from Europe, the Middle East, and the United States. While restrictions supposedly are in place on the number of prostitutes in some countries, two to three times more illegal prostitutes are working in Taipei today than those who receive licenses. Governments simply look the other way, because prostitution tourism is a lucrative business. At almost any bookstore or newsstand in Hong Kong, visitors can purchase *The Businessman's Little Black Book*, which is advertised as a compendium of essential information for the business visitor. After a few quick pages outlining how to establish a business and obtain servants in Hong Kong, the book goes into a twenty-two-page section on nightlife, which begins, "Let's start with sex" and goes on to list how and where to approach Chinese women. Pages of colored photographs follow, with updated telephone numbers handwritten in.

Women are not the only ones exploited. Tens of thousands of boys and girls are made prostitutes for tourists to parts of Asia, Africa, and the Middle East. Sri Lanka and the Philippines attract the highest rates of pedophiles. "The majority of pedophiles come to Sri Lanka on the recommendation of one guide book or another. One such guide, referring to the Philippines, says 'Manila is the world's ultimate paradise for gays including pedophiles.' After discussing various places where plenty of young boys can be found, this guide suggests that a good way of procuring a partner is to 'hang around various schools as students are leaving' in order to presumably to pick them up as they walk home."[32] End Child Prostitution in Asian Tourism (ECPAT) estimates there are 80,000 child prostitutes in Thailand, 60,000 in the Philippines, 30–40,000 in India, and 15,000 in Sri Lanka.[33] Through ECPAT's efforts, more child sex offenders can now be prosecuted in their home countries.

More than 130 countries, 500 NGO representatives, and 1,000 concerned individuals and the media participated in the World Congress Against Commercial Sexual Exploitation of Children in 1996 in Stockholm. UNICEF, a chief participant, reported that more than 1 million children a year are forced into prostitution, sold for sexual purposes, or used in pornography, and many are trafficked across national borders. According to Broken Bud, a prostitution tourism watch organization in the United States, the reason for such high numbers of exploited children is that "their own families, driven to desperation by crushing poverty — often caused by the economic injustice of first world countries — sell them, yes, sell their children."[34]

Children are at risk from tourism in many ways. Children and youth go to tourist centers because they can beg, deliver drugs to tourists, prostitute themselves, or get the low-skill jobs typical of hotels and restaurants. Even young people who live with their families are attracted to the potential economic benefits and the lifestyles of the travelers. A traveler-youth culture has appeared in every city around the world. The young people, often out of poverty or desperation, are lured by the consumer culture and reject their own cultures as primitive compared to what they perceive to be the travelers' culture. The result is the youth are drawn away from their families, communities, and more traditional activities to spend time with tourists. They become isolated from their families and often have few options other than making a meager living from tourists.

Child labor is extremely common within the tourism industry. Young children work in hotels, restaurants, clubs, and bars, the open-air economy of the tourism industry that is not formally recognized. In Ecuador

I met a little boy who was ten years old and "managed" a hotel. He had been stolen from his mother in a market when he was three. Abandoned by a "foster" mother when he was nine, the boy had managed to find employment in the tourism sector. He worked for a family who owned a hotel. A brilliant artist, he had designed murals in the dining room and the artwork on the menus. He was up early and went to bed late. When problems arose in the middle of the night, he tended to the guests. The family paid him a meager salary and even deducted the costs of his art supplies. His monthly pay was so little he could not afford to buy a pair of pants. When a local church was asked to look into his welfare, the boy simply disappeared. Officials refused to pursue the matter.

Impacts on Ecology

Tourism development, even in "ecotourism" destinations, is often at odds with both ecological preservation and local use. The large numbers of tourists going to these places greatly exceed the carrying capacities — the amount of people a land can accommodate without ecological degradation. Most tourism destinations are energy intensive and highly pollutive and tend to be built in "cluster sites," such as a chain of hotels along a beach. This pattern of development diverts resources (energy, land, and water) away from the local population to accommodate the tourist sector. This activity also puts heavy stress on the environment, because tourist sites require reconstruction of the landscape and increased use of petroleum products and toxics such as chemicals, fertilizers, and pesticides. These cluster sites greatly disturb natural human patterns of living and are at odds with wildlife and the natural world.

The ecological damage from tourism leads to battles between locals and the tourism industry for dwindling natural resources. A tourism researcher in Thailand explains how villagers must compete with tourists for the use of water in Phuket, Thailand:

A single local village only needs one half cubic meter of fresh water per day. This amount is not enough for one guest staying in a hotel. More fresh water is needed for showers, toilets, baths, swimming pools and golf courses, as well. The fresh water use for ten big hotels in Phuket — about 100,000 cubic meters per

Deborah McLaren, Ecuador

Hermes, a child laborer in the tourism industry in Ecuador, is missing after tourists inquired about his welfare.

day — equals the water used by the whole local Phuket population. In the dry season, when the underground water supplies dry up, many big hotels have to buy fresh water from the mainland, leaving the locals to find their own.[35]

An article in the *Bangkok Post* notes that "the government is seeking to overcome acute water shortages in three major resort islands — Phuket, Ko Chang in Trat and Ko Samui in Surat Thani — to avert tourism repercussions.... The government recently established the National Tap Water Policy Office to deal with problems."[36]

The most popular trekking routes in Nepal attract more than 60,000 visitors a year to the Annapurna Mountains. The ensuing demand for fuel, especially local firewood, has had enormous consequences. Each of the 60,000 visitors spends a minimum of seven nights in the area — a total of 420,000 person/nights where fuel is needed for cooking, showers, and heat. According to Nepali government figures, a single trekker uses twice the amount of wood a local household member would require. This demand is obviously much more than the local area can provide. With the threat to survival so great, can host destinations afford tourism? Can the benefits that they gain economically offset the other demands — in this case, depletion of the natural resources — that a community must endure at the hands of mass tourism development?

Some politicians have turned their attention to environmental issues, and tourism is proposed as a way to gain economic benefits and protect the environment. Costa Rica has an extensive system of national parks and reserves designed to protect the many ecosystems that attract tourists. That this model of ecotourism really works is doubtful. "The politicians talk a lot about a new ecological order, but they don't do anything concrete," says Guillermo Canessa, executive director of the Costa Rican Association for the Conservation of Nature (ASCONA). "The country gets an award from the American Association of Travel Agents, but meanwhile we're watching our forests disappear, and the reforestation incentives are mostly benefiting big businesses."[37] In fact the parks lack sufficient funding to upgrade visitor facilities or manage the land in the face of increasing pressure from loggers, hunters, colonists, and spiraling numbers of tourists. And neither the foreign tourists who are flocking to the nation's protected areas nor the tour companies that bring them there are contributing to their maintenance.

New Community Realities

An example of one town that decided the costs of tourism were too great is Hanalei, a small community on the island of Kauai, Hawaii, where residents are at odds with hordes of tourists. Local boat owners began taking tourists around their coastline to view the fabulous natural sea caves and waterfalls. But according to tourism activist James Stark:

> The tour boat business has become an environmental nightmare.
> ...Just over ten years ago, a local resident purchased a boat and began taking a handful of tourists on trips down the Na Pali Coast....Other family-run operations started up. Initially, the small business integrated well into the community, providing a reasonable income for some residents of Hanalei and ...not interfer[ing] with the quality of life within the community. However, soon outside entrepreneurs realizing the financial potential of the rafting tours in the area began to set up operations in Hanalei. Now, the small community's main street is lined with 27 tour boats ...carrying up to 1,400 tourists seven days a week.[38]

Business relationships between locals and outsiders have soured in Hanalei. The tour boats have taken over traditionally public space, which local Hawaiian families can no longer use. The new tour guides are not from the area and cannot provide tourists with accurate in-formation. The influx of gas- and oil-powered boats has increased the environmental damage to the fragile coastline and sea caves in the area.

Once outsiders become "insiders" and part of the community, the original inhabitants lose control over their lives. Businesses owned by outsiders have enormous political influence on policies and decision making. Since the purpose of companies is to increase tourism and profits, their goal is to garner bigger shares of the tourist market. The cycle is never-ending. Those fighting globalization believe citizens of the global South and North must form "chains," alliances built from experience. Solid support for regional trade and local self-reliance are crucial to the success of this effort. Small, local, responsible businesses need support in their battles against large corporations that consume enormous amounts of resources. These reforms would help to stem the tide of migration, lessen competition, and reduce environmental destruction.

Locals and tourists must recognize the great potential for utilizing the tourism industry as a tool for organizing, for establishing links between diverse sectors of people who are interested in being more than just tourists or just welcoming, smiling locals. This approach is not simply to encourage alternative tourism but actively to work against an exploitative global industry. As responsible tourism networks increase, opportunities arise for locals to gain outside support and information that can help them in their own communities and create international pressure. These networks are established and operated by people and organizations that are rethinking tourism, promoting responsibility, and linking with like-minded locals and tourists.

Some residents recently became fed up with irresponsible cruise ships at their Caribbean port that filled the area with snorkelers who were damaging the reefs and threatening the local fishing economy, trashing the city, and leaving at sunset. The cruise passengers didn't even eat in the town; the cruise ship was a mobile resort that simply floated away without any sense of obligation to the community. A request for support was sent out over the Internet. "Help!" the mes-sage said, "We have tried to talk to the cruise ship managers but they won't meet with us. We need the names of the top people at the company headquarters in Miami." Quickly responses came in: "I'll get that information and put pressure on them here," said one from the United States. Another suggestion was to organize international pressure on the company's stockholders. Within a few minutes, word of their plight had spread not only through North America and the Caribbean but to Europe and Asia. Consumer activists, environmentalists, and multinational watchdogs were informed. NGOs throughout the region, concerned tourists, students, and researchers who read alternative tourism bulletin boards were alerted. More suggestions poured in. International antitourism strategies were formed virtually overnight. Depending on the response from the cruise lines, an international campaign may form, which could certainly be of interest to the media. While unlikely to solve overall problems with the cruise lines or with tourism in that particular community, this incident is an example of people-to-people organizing and may encourage individuals to undertake a wider analysis of the problems with tourism.

Five

Rethinking Ecotravel

Ecotravel involves activities in the great outdoors — nature tourism, adventure travel, birding, camping, skiing, whale watching, and archeological digs that take place in marine, mountain, island, and desert ecosystems. Much of this travel is now called ecotourism, defined by The International Ecotourism Society (TIES) as "responsible travel to natural areas that conserves the environment and sustains the well-being of local people."[1] Although this definition sounds like a wise conservation choice for the environment and the local people, in practice the term is commonly used for tourism activities that do not fit the definition. In fact, the term is being used for almost any travel as long as something green is seen along the way.

Fortunately, some new guidelines and definitions that go further to protect local people and the environment are emerging. The WWF Artic Program assisted in the development of the Ten Principles for Arctic Tourism[2] that include suggestions such as promoting the recruitment, training, and employment in tourism of local people.

I use the term "ecotravel" to encompass all forms of ecotourism, sustainable tourism, conservation-focused tourism, and other types of nature travel that market the earth. The popular term, "ecotourism," is not limited to visits to natural areas. The number of tourists who travel solely to view natural surroundings or wildlife is actually quite modest. A majority of travelers also want an opportunity to experience a culture different from their own. Cultural activities and lifestyles are featured prominently in travel brochures. Ecotravel programs cover a wide variety of experiences — from spartan, hard-core, bury-your-own-poop backpacking in special conservation zones to the purely hedonistic, luxury vacations at typical resorts. They offer a participatory experience in the natural environment. At its best, ecotravel promotes environmental conservation, international understanding and cooperation, political and economic empowerment of local populations, and cultural preservation. When ecotravel fulfills its mission, it not only has a minimal impact, but the local environment and community actually benefit from the experience and even own or control it. At its worst, ecotravel is environmentally destructive, economically exploitative, culturally insensitive, "greenwashed" travel.

Most ecotravel is simply a way to get out of urban environments and back to nature, or to the nature that existed before human systems came to dominate it. But whatever the motive, the effects of global tourism on the environment are potentially terrifying. Huge amounts of fossil fuel are required for all forms of transportation. Tourists create a transient but permanent population increase in destination sites. The land required for expanding tourist sites around the world disturbs the ecological balance. Finally, tourism creates monumental waste and pollution. The result of all these secondary effects of tourism working in tandem is a rapidly shrinking land mass.

Ecotourism developed from different motives: conserving the environment, providing nature-based and adventure travel, and serving the growing tourist demand for more "authentic" experiences. While ecotourism has brought attention to the conservation of pristine areas, the reality is that tourism is not ecofriendly. An ecotourist, like any tourist, uses tremendous amounts of natural resources to jet halfway around the world to enjoy an outdoor experience. According to the World Watch Institute (WWI), "Airplanes are the most energy-intensive means of carrying people and cargo."[3] WWI reports that jet travel's impact on climate warming is a growing concern, as "commercial aircraft may be a major catalyst of the greenhouse effect due to the peculiarities of high-altitude flight."[4] Scientists calculate that each year airplanes produce nearly 4 million tons of nitrogen oxides, which react with sunlight to form ozone, a potent heat trapper; "nitrogen oxides from aircraft could be responsible for more than 30 percent of future global warming."[5] The World Wildlife Fund (WWF) noted in 2001 that air traffic is expected to increase 5 percent per year for a total increase of 75 percent by 2015. The combination of increased air travel and its high level of emissions is likely to "cause considerable environmental damage, and to have knock-out effects on the tourism industry itself."[6]

Not only do we need to be concerned about the environmental impact of tourism, we also need to think about how that environmental damage will impact the tourism industry. As a report from the WWF explains:

The tourism industry's heavy reliance on the local environment and climate to sell holidays means that it could face serious challenges as a result of climate change.... While the impacts of climate change on tourism will vary, it is already clear that small island states such as the Maldives in the Indian Ocean, an increasingly popular tourism destination, will be particularly vulnerable to sea-level rise.[7]

Indeed the impacts of climate change in tourism are so great that a recent WWF study, *Tourism and Climate Change*, recommends:

Action must be taken now by governments, individuals, and the tourism industry to reduce the threat of climate change. Governments worldwide should meet, and ideally go beyond, the commitments made through the Kyoto Protocol.

The tourism industry itself must take action to reduce its contribution to global greenhouse gas emissions. For example, in destinations, changes to energy supply should be introduced, creating a shift from fossil fuel to renewable sources of energy such as wind, biomass and solar power. This needs to be coupled with changes to planning procedures and laws, so that more opportunities for renewable energy sources can be developed. More stringent efficiency standards and a compulsory energy rating scheme could also be employed in buildings, such as hotels.[8]

In fact, what is now commonly called "ecotourism" is actually magnifying the negative impacts upon the earth, because it promotes development (destruction) of wilderness. For a tourist to have truly minimal impact, she would have to walk to the destination, use no natural resources, and bring her own food that she grew and harvested. She would also have to carry along her own low-impact accommodations (a tent) or stay in a place that is locally owned and uses alternative technologies and waste treatment. Of course she would also leave the destination in no worse and perhaps in even better condition than she found it and contribute funds to local environmental protection and community development. And most importantly, ecotourism would be the development choice of local people who would be fully in control.

Conservationists and government planners cite many reasons that ecotravel to protected areas can be advantageous. They believe ecotravel is a subjectively healthier kind of tourism that attracts desirable visitors. Given that ecotravelers are often more tolerant of rustic, basic facilities and infrastructure, tourism inflow can be increased without major expenditures. In some cases ecotourism can support the capital improvements over the long term, starting with just a trickle of undemanding tourists who prefer small-scale accommodations built by local people with native rather than costly and pretentious tourist facilities. Protection of certain natural areas for tourism encourages land use planning. In theory, rural communities will receive the economic benefits of ecotourism. Ideally, ecotourism's profits will help local people; they will in turn participate in integrated, regional planning. However, ecotourism may actually be worse for Indigenous Peoples and other rural communities because they have fewer facilities to support increased tourist populations and fewer policies and regulations to monitor its development than do other tourist destinations. Ole Kumuaro, a Maasi environmentalist working on tourism development issues in his community, writes:

> The trend toward the commercialization of tourism schemes disguised as sustainable, nature-based, environmentally friendly ecotourism ventures has become the subject of considerable public controversy and concern.... Kenya, Tanzania and South Africa reap significant economic benefits from these commercial ventures. But the negative psycho-social impact of this type of tourism, including physical displacement of persons and gross violation of fundamental rights, far outweigh[s] its intended medium-term economic benefits.[9]

The tourism industry regards ecotourism as an exciting product to market; environmental groups tend to see it more as a means of conservation and protection. A number of environmental groups and socially responsible organizations have joined the ecotourism industry, looking for ways to promote and finance conservation efforts, and developed the first models of ecotourism by using tourist fees to support conservation work. Initially, the targets of conservation were wildlife areas and national parks. International laws were implemented to protect endangered species, and large parcels of land were set aside as protected areas.

Local people opposed many of these conservation projects, which created conflicts in the nearby communities. Because of the fragility of the favored areas, the increased numbers of tourists soon began to take a toll on the environment. The original designers of ecotourism realized that ecotourists were loving nature to death and disrupting the lives of local people. So the question becomes, is ecotourism all that it's cracked up to be? Luis Vivanco, an anthropology professor at the University of Vermont, explores this very question:

> The big question for ecotourism, of course, is does it live up to its much-touted ability to save nature and redistribute money to local communities. This question is intimately wrapped up in the question of globalization and whether it's viewed as a positive or negative force in the world. Certainly, ecotourism is a vehicle for globalization: governments pursue tourism development on the advice of international aid and lending agencies, who want to see these countries make money to pay off their debts. But, as Joseph Stiglitz, the former chief economist of the World Bank, has argued in his recent book *Globalization and Its Discontents* (and of all people he should know), the economic schemes of the World Bank, IMF, and much of the aid industry have failed, for two reasons: first, they're more concerned with expanding free markets than improving the quality of life for people or protecting local environments, and second, the structural changes the IMF requires of countries (such as selling off state enterprises to private business and minimizing government involvement in the economy) have deepened poverty, not alleviated it. As anti-globalization protesters (and increasingly critics of ecotourism) have been arguing, the faith in free markets to solve the world's problems, which is the ideological cornerstone of both globalization and ecotourism, is a strategy that looks better to the few who benefit than the large majorities who suffer from its negative consequences.[10]

Despite such problems, many countries have sought new ways to address development issues by incorporating tourism. For example, countries or regions lacking in other natural resources have come to regard a favorable climate, beaches, and other tourist attractions as a different type of natural resource base for development. Because many of these countries had already established parks and protected areas, promoting tourism seemed an easy way for them to benefit. For example, in 1996 there were 30,361 parks covering more than 13 million square kilometers worldwide.[11] These parks were made for ecosystem protection and recreation, thus opening a space for tourism development within fragile ecosystems.

Ecotourism Saves the Planet?

Academic study programs with an environmental twist have boomed. These programs deliver thousands of new-breed ecostudents to tag turtles, bag leeches, and count plants in the wilds. No one knows how the environment will be affected by millions of people traveling around the world, using resources and invading fragile areas. Paul Erlich warns, "We are not able to support the present population on income from our natural capital: we're only doing it by exhausting our capital. That's a one-way street."[12]

Each community and culture has a different response to tourism. While some are working cooperatively with private enterprise, others feel that they are being invaded by tourists, just as they are by other colonists who take over their homelands. In Chiapas, Mexico, and Guatemala, organized resistance has emerged to massive tourism plans for the Mayan Biosphere; in Nagarhole, India, Indigenous People living in a national park were supported by an international campaign to resist tourism construction and their displacement from traditional lands by an "ecoresort." Most Indigenous lands have been turned into federal parks, refuges, cultural heritage sites, and monuments. These designations conflict with local use or multiple use traditions.

A traditional concept of conservation is that land should be preserved in its natural state. Such a mandate can infringe on traditional lifestyles by limiting subsistence activities. Comprehending the myriad of complex issues Indigenous Peoples face, often without the proper knowledge and tools to plan for their futures, is difficult. Many Indigenous communities hope that ecotourism will be a way to resist other destructive forms of development. They are alert to ecotourism strategies to protect their natural resources, environments, and cultures. But some have seen such projects backfire, creating conflicts and divisions within their communities. In March 2002, the International Forum on Indigenous Tourism (IFIT) was held in Oaxaca, Mexico, to examine issues that the mainstream ecotourism movement has marginalized. Emerging concerns included bioprospecting, protection of biological and cultural diversity, and even the right to say no to tourism development. No easy answers are available, but information must be shared with Indigenous communities confronting tourism development. Indigenous Peoples are organizing community, regional, and international networks to address these issues.

Ecotourism: Size and Space

Ecotravel is big business. On the one hand, the United Nations promotion of International Year of Ecotourism, the World Bank, international conservation and ecotourism organizations, the tourism industry, and many governments have made ecotourism or sustainable tourism a big business. Yet, according to Ron Mader, small, locally owned ecotourism projects are "a small niche" and have been grossly overpromoted — leading to "disappointments across the board." As a big business, ecotourism has greatly expanded jobs for tourism corporations, adventure travel companies, environmental organizations, and government officials. However, the scope of the ecotourism market is hard to gauge because the definition of ecotourism is not universally accepted. The incomplete record-keeping of most host countries further complicates the issue.

Ecotourism projects run the gamut from small-scale to monstrous. While many ecotour operators limit group size to ten or twelve people, ecoresorts are being designed to accommodate thousands of people at once. In terms of land area, some small ecotourism projects encompass just a few acres and others encompass hundreds or thousands of square miles. For example, Plan Puebla Panama (PPP) is a comprehensive plan to build major transportation for economic development as well as tourism use from the southeastern state of Mexico, Puebla, all the way to Panama, an area spanning eight countries. Action for Community and Ecology in the Regions of Central America (ACERCA), an environmental organization in Central America, explains the plan:

> [PPP] calls for vast displacement of native communities, rampant and uncontrolled ecological devastation, and massive industrial development [that] will irrevocably damage this region.... Plan Puebla Panama, the name given by [President] Fox to this disastrous scheme, has already seen tremendous alliances build to oppose it.... The geographical scope of the PPP includes... spectacular fresh water reserves, and the World Bank-created "Meso-American Biological Corridor," a much-coveted gold mine of biodiversity.[13]

Gregoria Flores, of the human rights group Organización Fraternal Negra Hondureña (OFRANEH), described Plan Puebla Panama as "one of the most hostile neocolonialist plans we are facing."[14]

Just how the income from ecotourism fees is distributed is difficult to determine. A major portion of the money generated on-site goes to maintaining the tourist attraction and hotels, staff, infrastructure, technical assistance, training, and other items contracted by the public sector. Once the private-sector costs are deducted, any remaining funds could be used to address issues such as encroachment around the ecotourism site. No examples are known of ecotourism projects that adequately pay for themselves; in other words, ecotourism is simply not sustainable.

New forms of ecotravel are supposed to save the planet and create economic advantages for local people. In reality few of ecotourism's benefits go to locals. "A study of twenty-three protected areas with projects designed to generate local economic development found that while many projects promoted ecotourism, few generated substantial benefits for either parks or local people."[15] More integrated approaches designed to generate local economic development have created relatively few jobs. Even at highly successful parks, such as KhaoYai National Park in Thailand, where tourists bring in about $5 million annually, the surrounding communities remain poor. Ecotourism revenues in Rwanda support the park system and the central government, but few economic alternatives exist for local populations.[16]

For any real benefits from ecotourism, local people must be involved in every stage, from the initial planning through the development, monitoring, enforcement, and ownership. In fact, during the IFIT in Mexico, Indigenous Peoples drafted a declaration on tourism which insists that "tourism projects must be undertaken only under the guidance and surveillance of an Indigenous Technical Team, and only after a full critical analysis of the long-term pros and cons of tourism development."[17] In Costa Rica, considered a model ecotourism destination, many biological reserves and stands of old-growth forest are owned by foreigners. One local community has formed an association to buy back these lands. "With the development of the ecotourism industry, local residents have garnered some benefits as employees of ecotourism entrepreneurs, but there seems to be no example of a local resident who is owner of a successful ecotourism establishment."[18] The locals hope some day to develop their own ecotourism operations.

Environmental Effects

The issues involved in ecotravel epitomize what is happening with tourism around the world. If ecotravel creates enormous environmental

Deborah McLaren, Nepal

More than sixty thousand annual trekkers along with the porters and pack animals they require have caused serious erosion in the Annapurna Circuit in Nepal; some ruts are several feet deep.

devastation when it is supposed to be "good" for the environment, what are the effects of conventional tourism on the environment? If ecotravel is the best-case scenario, what is the worst? Numerous examples of worst-case scenarios exist just in the United States. The beloved Grand Canyon is not designated as an ecotourism destination, but it is the forerunner of all such ecotravel programs and an excellent object of study regarding long-term impacts. Despite the number of tourists and the money spent to maintain it, the federal government can no longer manage it. Over 4.4 million people visit the park annually.[19] According to Julie Galton Gale of the Grand Canyon Trust:

> There are simply too many people, too many cars, too many air-planes. Despite current laws restricting flights, there were over 900,000 tour flights over the Grand Canyon in 1997. The Grand Canyon would be completely overrun if Park Service allowed tour operators free rein. Another problem is the incursion of roads and trails . . . in areas that were previously inaccessible. The impacts on

local communities is dramatic. This is a place that got "discovered" because of the increase in tourism development....There are no zoning laws; it's one hotel after fast food restaurant. The detrimental growth is directly a result of having been discovered as an "outdoor adventure" destination.[20]

The Grand Canyon Trust works with tourism-affected communities on the Colorado Plateau. They report an urgent need for education of local citizens, elected officials, and tourists and more integrated planning, dispute resolution, better forms of energy, and alternatives to harvesting old-growth timber. If we cannot stop the environmental destruction of the Grand Canyon, little hope remains for the national parks that Western conservationists are planning in other parts of the world.

"Greening" and "Sustaining" the Tourism Industry

Ecotourism is supposed to mean ecologically sound tourism, implying that one would take care of a place just as one would take care of one's own home. Yet how many ecotravelers are actively involved in environmental preservation in their own communities? Ron Mader, host of Planeta.com, also questions, "How many tourists develop an 'eco ethic' only when planning a trip?" All travelers should link their travels to their work and interests in their own communities. When we understand what is at stake, we can join with other people around the world and better confront the environmental challenges we face together.

Ecoterminology and philosophy continue to mutate. Just when we thought we might understand "ecotourism," environmentalists and futurists warn that we must develop "sustainable" patterns of tourism development. "Sustainable tourism development" has been defined as meeting the needs of present tourists and host regions while protecting and enhancing opportunities for the future. Sustainability is a concept that is not easy to translate into specific actions that individuals or governments can undertake. Critics suggest that sustainability is based on Western values and economic models developed on an anti-ecological basis, and early visions for sustainability fail to challenge some of the basic premises that have helped us into the environmental mess we now inhabit. Others warn that the term has become co-opted by private industry and is a "green" stamp of approval for business as usual — a trend that we will see more of in the future. One thing is certain: "sustainability" as a concept is used to promote the World Bank's reentrance into tourism and as a basis for many environmental organizations' work in the global South.

In addition, many ecotourism programs are designed using commercialized conservation methods. In other words, the value of natural resources and conservation efforts are measured purely in economic terms, according to present or future profitability, without taking into account the inherent ecological value of the environment. This formula simply sets aside land as "reserved" and does not address root causes of development expansion and colonization.

Truly sustainable tourism must be locally controlled, limited, and focused on local self-reliance without diminishing local resources for the local population. Sustainable tourism would include integrated planning that challenges the tourism industry at every level; would take up broad issues, from the reduction of energy-consumptive technologies to the society's religious practices; and would most likely be an impetus to halt further tourism development.

Strategies for Rethinking Ecotravel

Since all forms of tourism are unsustainable and Western development processes are threatening both biological and cultural diversity in every destination community around the world, true efforts toward ecotourism would move away from specific conservation and environmental protection strategies to integrate broad community and regional development priorities. Sustainable tourism would depend upon sustainable agriculture and sustainable forestry management. For example, in Bhutan, sustainable forestry focuses on using products from the forest floor, such as dried flowers, to make potpourri that is sold to tourists. Primary components would focus on education and promote critical thinking about development, growth-oriented economics, and other unsustainable practices; the strategies would design programs to counter the ideologies and effects of unsustainable, consumptive models of development. These projects would not only develop alternative tourism but would rethink these strategies as well.

In other places around the world, people are beginning to work actively against tourism development in their communities. Many resourceful activists are intent upon taking tourism a step further. Emerging from a number of concerns, the responsible tourism movement is designed primarily to make people-to-people connections so that citizens of the world can experience the realities of other societies and environments. This type of tourism is based on the principle that people matter and that humans are basically dependent upon — and responsible for — the earth's resources. Connecting with each other at a human level allows both the so-called hosts and guests to observe and learn from one another in more equitable, realistic terms. Most strategies for actively negating traditional, exploitative tourism practices are on a small scale. From tour operators to regional strategies developing from local communities, some of the best new ideas are emerging from this approach. Himalayan High Treks is an example of a small business that works to offset the effects of tourism. Owner Effie Fletcher told me:

> I'm concerned about locals' maintaining their traditional lifestyle. Development, unjust economics, and Westernization have made many so poor they must sell their animals, pack up, and move to a job in the city. They don't have the option to stay and have a pristine lifestyle: the land is gone, split up, and subdivided. Many tourists want to be "the first" and seek out pristine environments. I have strong opinions about that — there is no need to continue to simply exploit new territories when, as tourists, we have some responsibility for the problems we've helped to create. We [at Himalayan High Treks] go to impacted areas and work with locals to lessen those impacts. We use locally owned and produced items and services, eat local food, stay at local guest houses. It's much more expensive to do the research. It would be easier to fax and phone big hotels. But it's our responsibility and an investment in the future.

Where are the most successful ecotravel programs and policies formed? Invariably, they come from grassroots organizations that link with responsible tourism groups to develop educational programs. These ideas integrate real change and take the focus off of marketing "green" tourism or zoning off wilderness areas. Luciano Minerbi, a professor at the University of Hawaii at Manoa and a member of the Hawaii Ecumenical Coalition on Tourism, has worked with Native Hawaiians to develop ecocultural tourism. According to Minerbi, their goals include:

- allowing Indigenous Peoples back on their lands and promoting experimental homesteading arrangements, subsistence economies, and affordable and appropriate modern and Indigenous technologies;

- promoting research and development of eco-industry by involving local people with universities and industries;

- decentralizing environmental agencies so locals can develop and implement their own strategies;

- establishing partnerships among local communities, schools, landowners, and the industry to provide opportunities to merge traditional knowledge with modern science;

- halting monocrop agriculture, which displaces locals and leads to further development, deforestation, pollution, water diversion, soil erosion, and destruction of sacred sites;

- halting speculation of real estate development for resorts, golf courses, and the international market;

- allowing customary access to subsistence resources and religious sites and returning lands for community restoration;

- protecting and repossessing lands, particularly for community land trusts;

- undertaking cultural assessments to demarcate important areas, map resources, and suggest protection programs;

- regulating but legalizing small, locally owned accommodations for community-based service organizations so economic benefits of visitors remain within the community; and

- making Indigenous points of view known within the industry and to the public.[21]

Whom do local people consider good tourists? The villagers of Gundrung, Nepal, have on the wall of their community center a photograph of a smiling, bearded young man with a backpack. The villagers say he was the best ecotourist ever to visit their community: he brought much of his own food, stayed at a local's lodge, helped repair trails, and was concerned about the villagers' use of fuel wood — he never asked to take a hot shower. He even carried his own water jug to use in place of toilet paper. They say they wish all ecotourists could be as sensitive and helpful.

Some refute the growing crisis of the natural world and promote free trade and unsustainable, high technologies to "solve" environmental problems. Even McDonald's is funding ecotourism projects. McDonald's Indonesia Family Restaurants is a partner with environmental organizations to develop local enterprises in and around Gunung Halimun National Park, in West Java.[22] Perhaps the wave of the future is to have McDonald's restaurants at all ecotourism destinations around the world.

Virtually every place on earth has experienced significant human intrusion. Even the poles are littered with trash, toxic batteries, and plastics left by tour groups, a problem that the WWF International Arctic Programme is addressing. This program has developed the "Ten Principles for Arctic Tourism" and just recently held a conference on sustainable tourism in the Arctic.[23] Tourism is a population problem, for not only is the earth's population growing, but millions of people are not simply staying at home — they are consuming enormous amounts of natural resources to travel to other places. These populations are transient but often mean a permanent population increase in destination communities. Yet population experts do not take seriously the population problems associated with tourism.

What is the difference between conventional travel and ecotravel? The overwhelming answer seems to be "not much." Ecotravel may involve more of a focus on going out to see nature, but that doesn't necessarily mean protecting the earth. Rethinking tourism means finding activities that might never be considered ecotravel by the travel industry but can contribute to real environmental protection of the earth. For example, human rights groups, labor unions, and environmental groups are linking with workers in sweatshops along the border of Mexico to conduct "reality" tours about the increasingly dismal state of the border area and gain support for broad issues. Environmental organizations, universities, and other research expeditions and study programs recruit tourists to undertake valuable field studies and restoration projects. Hikers are turning into advocates to preserve wilderness areas.

Sustainable agriculture has disappeared in places where tourism was but the first wave of an international corporate incursion. Tourism has displaced small farms and in some cases promoted unsustainable agriculture. In places where sustainable agriculture still exists — for example, Costa Rica and Mexico — monoculture agricultural processes have turned coffee exporting into a commercialized tourist venture.

But new agricultural programs, eco-agro farms and villages, are concerned with self-sufficiency and local economies — promoting more control of investment, production, and sales; a healthier sense of community; and less reliance on the global economy. Eco-agro tourism is seen as a way to address problems in the agrarian sector. A recent study on this form of tourism in Poland reports: "One of the most interesting results concerns the fact that farmers and officials play into each other's hands. According to the officials the farmers should take the initiatives, according to the farmers the government and other institutions should provide financial and organizational support in order to make it possible to start agro-tourist activities."[24] Eco-agro tours offer tourists an opportunity to reconnect with the land — to learn about organic farming and less consumptive technologies — and become committed to preserving it. Yet they work to have highly diversified local economies and refrain from relying on the tourism sector. These programs may be the most integrated approach to protection of the natural world: true ecotravel.

A group of organic farmers has created a rapidly growing eco-agro tourism network of more than two hundred family farms worldwide. More than a hundred farms are part of the European Center for Eco-Agro Tourism (ECEAT), which promotes nature and lobbies politicians and the tourism sector to apply more integrated approaches in development policies and planning that relate to farming and agriculture. Members are involved in village restoration, conservation and waste management, and marketing organic foods. The farmers are organized in each country to support each other in a variety of ways, through linking, technical assistance, and policy. The eco-agro tourism initiative started by promoting organic farms, but the concept has widened to include programs with national parks, environmental NGOs, and sustainable villages and regions. Cooprena in Costa Rica is a cooperative consortium of small-scale, eco-agro tourism programs. Leila Solano, one of the program coordinators, told me, "This type of program spreads tourists through decentralized accommodations while supporting farmers and rural communities. . . . Eco-agro tourism is a step on the way toward a locally integrated plan that focuses on preserving the environment, agriculture, and rural economies." Indigenous Peoples are looking at broad, integrated sustainable development. After all, shouldn't sustainable tourism be interdependent upon sustainable agriculture, sustainable forestry, and sustainable fishing?

Rethinking tourism considers ecotravel and all other forms of alternative tourism as part of the massive global tourism industry. The effects of ecotravel are similar to conventional tourism and in many cases might even be worse, given that it has encouraged a boom of tourists and development in regions that are fragile and remote, some of the most important biologically and culturally diverse areas on the planet. As Zac Goldsmith states: "The addition of the word 'eco' to the word 'tourism' has so far remained cosmetic. Tourism today is incompatible with life tomorrow. If as an industry it is to be made consistent with ecological and human principles, then we must examine it thoroughly, both the pros and cons, and must be prepared to re-think what may well be a fundamentally flawed process."[25] Ultimately, all tourism greatly costs the earth.

Six

Ecotravel Issues
for a New Century

What are some of the issues now facing ecotravel and how are local communities responding to them? This chapter addresses the problems and some of the opportunities that offer hope for the future. It also brings together contributions from a number of writers.

Ecotourism Certification:
A Slippery Challenge

Certification involves setting criteria for measuring the quality and social, political, and environmental impacts of tourism businesses, carrying out audits, awarding eco-labels, and building consumer and industry demand for certification programs. A great deal of overlap and competition exists among the different certification programs, as do a lack of common standards and criteria, and much consumer confusion and ignorance. Dozens of efforts have been made to create ecotourism certification standards; all of them are voluntary, and many of them are attempts to put a green label on travel, although they actually do little to set standards for serious conservation efforts. Such attempts have included ecotourism principles and codes of conduct, "best practices," and awards. These self-regulatory guidelines have been criticized as simply a means to avoid real government directives or legislation.

The Green Globe initiative has been frank about avoiding governmental or international legislation and has come under fire time and time again by environmental organizations and others. The Certification for Sustainable Tourism Program (CST) in Costa Rica was designed to differentiate tourism-sector businesses on the degree to which they comply with a sustainable model of natural, cultural, and social resource management. CST is aimed at the hotel industry. The Nature and Ecotourism Accreditation Program (NEAP) was developed by industry for industry, addressing the need to identify genuine eco-tourism and nature tourism operators in Australia. NEAP aims to provide green standards to benefit operators, protected area managers, local communities, and travelers. The Blue Flag (run by the independent nonprofit organization Foundation for Environmental Education [FEE], in Denmark) is an exclusive eco-label awarded to more than twenty-eight hundred beaches and marinas in twenty-three countries across Europe and South Africa. The Blue Flag, a symbol of high environmental standards as well as good sanitary and safety facilities at the beach/marina, promotes environmental education and information for the public, decision makers, and tourism operators.

In November 2000, ecotourism "experts" from around the world gathered in upstate New York to discuss developing guidelines for ecotourism. As a result, the Rainforest Alliance, a U.S.-based organization, has the responsibility for coordinating efforts to develop the standards for ecotourism certification. The first step involves investigating the possibility of establishing an international accreditation body for sustainable tourism certification and providing a fully developed implementation plan. Rainforest Alliance also helped establish SmartVoyager to minimize the impact of tour boats in the Galapagos Islands by improving social and environmental conditions of boat operations.

Critics argue that while the need exists to develop standards for various players in the industry, standardizing communities and real people is extremely difficult where much ecotourism development takes place, not just hotels or other products. Further, critics note that these schemes are still insufficient as they usually only consider Indigenous Peoples as sideline players and fail to recognize treaty rights, land rights, sovereignty, their government-to-government status in many countries, or even their right to say no to tourism development.

In the following essays by Martha Honey (the director of the International Ecotourism Society in Washington, D.C.) and Ron Mader (host of Planeta.com, based in Mexico City), the reasoning behind certification efforts is laid out and critically examined.

Certification:
Why Ecotourism Needs Strong Ecolabels
Martha Honey

As the May 2002 World Ecotourism Summit in Quebec City demonstrated, a lot is put under the big "green" tent of ecotourism. Basically, ecotourism takes one of three forms. One is "greenwashing" or totally phony projects that don a "green" marketing mantle but are bold-faced imposters that include none of the tenants of ecotourism. A second, the largest swath, is ecotourism "lite" that includes businesses that claim to be green by making minor, largely cosmetic changes. One of the increasingly common practices of conventional or chain hotels is to market themselves as green because they offer guests the choice not to change their sheets and towels each day. A sensible step, but while it saves on the hotel's laundry bill, it does little to save the planet or fundamentally transform the way tourism operates. The third is genuine ecotourism, whose proprietors and proponents are trying to implement the multidimensional tenets of this revolutionary concept. Most basically, people and groups involved in genuine ecotourism are striving to do three basic things: (1) preserve and tangibly benefit the environment, (2) respect and tangibly benefit local communities, and (3) educate travelers to better understand the place and the peoples they are visiting.

For the traveling public, the challenge is sorting the wheat from the chaff — finding the environmentally and socially responsible companies and avoiding the greenwashing and lite variants. The concept of certification — eco-labeling — comes here. Certification is a procedure to assess, audit, and give written assurance that a facility, product, process, or service meets specific standards. To date, all tourism certification programs are voluntary (not government mandated), market-driven initiatives, which means companies choose to be certified and the consumer must choose whether or not to buy only labeled products.

As such, certification is a tool uniquely suited to our times. The prevailing notion for much of the twentieth century was that government intervention could and should solve social, economic, and environmental problems. However, over the last several decades, the role of the state has been rolled back, as corporations have moved outside national boundaries, developing new institutions of global corporate governance (World Trade Organization, North American Free Trade Alliance, Asia Pacific Economic Cooperation, etc.) and pushing a new ideology, dubbed the Washington Consensus, that trumpets free trade, privatization, deregulation, and economic globalization.

In response to the widening gap between rich and poor within and across countries, a dynamic global justice movement has taken to the streets in

Seattle, Washington, D.C., Prague, Davos, Quebec City, Genoa, Porto Ale-gre, Barcelona, and elsewhere. Youth, labor, environmentalists, human rights, social justice and peace activists, and other constituencies have joined forces to protest the World Trade Organization, World Bank, World Economic Forum, and other institutions dominated by the wealthiest countries and corpora-tions. Parallel with these protests, a variety of efforts — many spearheaded by NGOs — have sought to engage with industry and find tools for setting socially and environmentally responsible standards. Within the travel and tourism in-dustry, researchers have identified 104 certification and eco-labeling programs, about half of which are located in Europe.[1]

According to a recent analysis by Duke University researchers, "While cer-tification will never replace the state, it is quickly becoming a powerful tool for promoting worker [host country and local community] rights and protecting the environment in an era of free trade." Certification programs are all based on the assumption that a market — a public demand — exists for environmentally and socially responsible products. They assume that an informed public will reward socially and environmentally responsible businesses by purchasing its goods and services as well as punish (through boycotts, court cases, stockholder battles, and other methods) those businesses that are not. The Duke University researchers conclude that certification programs, as "voluntary governance mechanism," are "transforming traditional power relationships in the global arena."[2]

Certification can be thought of as a three-legged stool. One leg measures health and safety standards (many of which are legally required). The second measures quality and service, which has been the focus of traditional certifica-tion programs like AAA (Automobile Association of America). The third and newest leg measures "sustainability" which, properly done, includes standards for measuring both environmental and social impacts of, say, a hotel. Over the last decade — largely in the wake of the United Nations' seminal 1992 Earth Summit in Rio — there's been a proliferation of efforts to create eco-labels and to certify companies that meet certain criteria. Most are for particular countries or regions; only seven (Green Globe, ECOTEL) are global.

Unlike certification programs for other industries such as wood, coffee, and bananas, tourism is enormously complex, located in virtually every coun-try, with a wide variety of different types of business and a mix of services and products. This situation presents some real challenges for certification be-cause distinct certification must be developed for each business category. Like the traditional certifications programs tied to automobile travel, most "green" certification cover hotels and lodges. Increasingly, however, tourism certifica-tions are covering other areas: tour operators (CST in Costa Rica), naturalist guides (NEAP in Australia), beaches (Blue Flag in Europe, South Africa, and the Caribbean), parks (PAN Parks in Europe), and boats (*Smart Voyager* in the Galapagos), to name a few.

And, like ecotourism itself, wide variations exist in the types and rigor of these certification programs. Some — in fact, most — geared to the conventional tourism market, such as Green Globe, are based on setting up environmental management systems within businesses. These award eco-labels for establishing processes to, for instance, reduce electricity and water consumption. They don't set performance standards. Process-based certification programs therefore measure *intent* more than *outcome*. Many of these programs are run by industry associations or private, for-profit companies, and they tend to be very costly because they require outside consultants to implement. In addition, these programs focus only on environmental issues, not social or cultural areas, which are also vital to genuine ecotourism.

Stronger — and cheaper — certification programs are performance-based, which measure *achievement, not intent* — that is, they set clear environmental and social standards against which all businesses are measured. This may include, for instance, the requirement that more than 90 percent of a hotel's employees be hired locally, that at least 50 percent of electricity come from renewable energy sources, that all washing products be biodegradable, or that gardens be planted only with native species. All businesses within these types of certification programs can be compared against one another, which makes them much more meaningful for the consumer.[3]

Two of the best "green" certification programs are found in Costa Rica and Australia. Both incorporate some process criteria, but they are mainly based on set performance standards or benchmarks. For many in the United States, Costa Rica is the poster child for ecotourism. By the mid-1990s, the Costa Rican government, many in the tourism industry, academics, and environmentalists were becoming increasingly concerned that Costa Rica was losing its eco-image. They decided to create a strong certification system to help distinguish the genuine eco-lodges from the greenwashing and eco-lite variants. Today the Certification for Sustainable Tourism (CST) program has a tiered logo system, awarding between one and five "leaf" logos to lodges that score well on a checklist of 152 yes/no questions. Outside auditors inspect all hotels before certification. So far some 50 lodges have been certified, and many others are pending.[4] The other countries in Central America have agreed to adopt the CST, which is being considered as a model for elsewhere in Latin America.

In Australia, a strong nature tourism destination, the government has also helped underwrite the development of the NEAP program.[5] Run by a combination of "stakeholders" — academics, the Australian Ecotourism Association, industry associations — NEAP also uses a list of yes/no questions to rate hotels and provide three levels of logos: for nature tourism, ecotourism, and advanced ecotourism. NEAP's thick book of questions covers eight different categories, including "responsible marketing," "customer satisfaction," "working with local communities," "environmental sustainability," and "interpretation." Today, NEAP has certified about three hundred eco-lodges. NEAP is now being adopted as a model for elsewhere in Asia.

Over the last several years, efforts have been made to consolidate "green" certification programs. In 2000, the Institute for Policy Studies sponsored the first international workshop on ecotourism and sustainable tourism certification programs, which brought together some forty-five experts from twenty different countries. The resulting document, dubbed the Mohonk Agreement, laid out a common framework and set of criteria that should be part of all sustainable tourism and ecotourism programs.[6] In 2001 and 2002, a series of workshops held around the world as part of the United Nations' International Year of Ecotourism[7] helped stimulate further wide-ranging discussions of certification programs as well as a global accreditation system. The Rainforest Alliance has undertaken a study of how to create a global accreditation system for evaluating and certifying certification programs intended to cover businesses involved in either sustainable tourism or ecotourism.[8] As we move into the twenty-first century, setting standards via certification programs is increasingly viewed as vital in helping tourists distinguish authentic ecotourism from the lite and greenwashing variants. However, certification is not a panacea. Rather, certification should be viewed as only one of a combination of tools, both voluntary and regulatory, that are needed in order to promote both social equity and a sustainable environment.

Tourism Certification:
Taking Away Local Control
Ron Mader

Good intentions lie behind "ecotourism certification," but many of the programs betray one of the main components of ecotourism — local control and operation. The very notion of certification should be scrutinized as much as the operations themselves because if the programs are not implemented wisely, they could jeopardize the initiatives they intend to support.

Certification — formal documentation attesting compliance — requires infrastructure, coordination, and financial resources that are generally lacking in the developing world. One criticism of the certification process is that any "certifiers" of ecotourism lack certification themselves!

Ecotourism is a relatively new niche within the tourism industry, and it has multiple definitions. Its success or failure depends on the eye of the beholder. Conservationists measure the merits of a project by its contributions to local environmental protection. Travel agencies focus on the bottom line — are they making a sufficient profit? And travelers each come to an ecotourism destination with their own personal experiences and expectations.

Traditional tourism has a number of certification programs — from AAA ratings to associate programs for Bed and Breakfasts. They are as effective as they are strictly defined, enforced, and accepted by travelers. It's important to note the variety of interpretations for programs as simple as rating hotels on a scale from "one Star" to "five Stars."

Sadly, much of the discussion around certification is being conducted in private, closed-door meetings. That development agencies and foundations are pursuing dialogues about certification strategies without including local tour operators or community groups is a shame.

Any specific viewpoint has its pros and cons. For ecotourism to succeed, we must be aware of our own perspectives. If we insist on high environmental standards and minimal impacts, the costs skyrocket, placing the services and destinations into a "luxury" class of tourism — sometimes without the amenities to which people paying high-end prices are accustomed.

What is the best example of ecotourism: a rustic, community lodge or a foreign-owned, eco-friendly green hotel? Too often architects and consultants promote high technical standards and luxurious eco-lodges because they have a personal stake to certify those businesses that can pay them well.

At risk are rural and/or Indigenous guides who do not have the financial resources to take part in established guide training programs — not offered in the field, but usually in the capital city. People who might benefit from ecotourism — namely, farmers (campesinos) and residents of rural areas that lie next to or even coincide with protected areas — are never the focal point of evaluation or promotion, let alone certification.

While little or no consumer demand may exist for certified "eco" vacations, we should not accept the status quo. That said, the emphasis needs to be placed on evaluating the industry and offering training and promotion for local providers that strive toward sustainable tourism and ecotourism.

————— ◗◖ ◗◖ —————

The ecotourism certification push remains strong despite the lack of Indigenous Peoples and other locals. Their inclusion is important if these programs are truly motivated to bring them benefits. The challenge for NGOs and governments to include them continues.

Ecotourism's New International Players

New concepts in tourism that focus on sustainable development and ecotourism have opened the door for further expansion of the global industry. National government agencies, development agencies, private enterprise, and the World Bank are becoming infatuated with ecotourism programs. Northern environmental NGOs are providing abundant financing for ecotourism. New ideas for tourism have consistently proven problematic because they follow the traditional path of development and are often initiated in the global North. Attempts to link ecotourism to other sustainable development projects have been controversial, especially when tied to development strategies such as economic initiatives to market sustainable use products from the rain forests, collect medicinal plants, or cement other bioprospecting agreements with universities and pharmaceutical companies.

Tourism has long been of interest to U.S. government agencies. USAID recently renewed its interest in ecotourism. Its goal is to promote environmentally sound, long-term economic growth, often developing natural areas for their "sustainable yield." USAID has placed high priority on stimulating private investment, free markets, and free enterprise and regards "nature-based tourism as well suited for simultaneously meeting" these objectives.[9]

The Overseas Private Investment Corporation (OPIC) funds projects related to ecotourism and "has the potential to become a major source of financing for the ecotourism industry through its new 'Environmental Investment Fund'...which funds ecotourism projects such as guest lodges near natural attractions."[10] The eight-country Plan Puebla Panama anticipates funding from the World Bank, Inter-American Development Bank, and Central American Development Bank.

Multilateral financial institutions support ecotourism because it stimulates economic development. Yet many environmental groups, Indigenous Peoples, and other local people say the government and multilateral institutions neglect to include them in their programs. The

World Bank, for example, does not have a good history when it comes to tourism. In 1969 the World Bank created a tourism department that lent over $450 million directly to twenty-four tourism projects in eighteen countries throughout the developing world. The department was discontinued because of the "bad publicity associated with funding capital intensive projects, such as large hotels, which clashed with the Bank's evolving rural poor mandate."[11]

Currently the World Bank is only designing policy for tourism development; although its policies for working with Indigenous Peoples, protecting the environment, and encouraging participation of affected people should apply, they are often ignored. The Global Environment Facility (GEF), an arm of the World Bank, is currently undertaking ecotourism development under the term "biodiversity protection" in several countries. Environmentalists and Indigenous organizations have opposed some of the projects. However, the GEF bypasses these locals and links with more "cooperative" groups to continue the projects.

Many governments are becoming international players as they claim to be developing ecotourism projects, yet these programs are coming at a great expense to the environment. One of the worst acts of "eco-terrorism" yet, according to a watch group in Asia, is "unbelievable! In the name of ecotourism the Lao government has given the green light to the Malaysian Syuen Corporation to develop a mammoth resort [in a] national park . . . to pave the way for the US$211 million 'Phou Khao Khouay-Nam Ngum Ecotourism Resort,' including a mini-city of hotels, golf courses, casinos. . . . Local residents have to move out of the area."[12]

UN approval of the International Year of Ecotourism (IYE) in December 1998 under Resolution A/Res/53/200 made the United Nations a player in the ecotourism game, although many of the intergovernmental agencies had long ago introduced some concepts of "sustainable tourism" in their overall strategies. For example, UNESCO has a long history of integrating tourism in its strategies for World Heritage and Biosphere, and the Convention on Biological Diversity (CBD) is currently formulating "International Guidelines for Sustainable Tourism."

The World Tourism Organization (WTO/OMT) and United Nations Environmental Program (UNEP) were mandated as the co-leading UN organizations to develop and coordinate activities related to the IYE.

Analyzing the UN Tourism Lenses:
2002 — The International Year of Ecotourism (IYE):
An Indigenous Perspective
Crescencio Resendiz-Hernandez and Cynthia Harrison

The United Nations' sales pitch for the IYE was to encourage cooperation among governments, international and regional organizations, and non-government organizations (NGOs) to promote sustainable tourism development capable of protecting the environment. Four main objectives were developed under the framework of sustainable development of tourism. Only one made specific reference to Indigenous Peoples: "Empowerment and fully informed participation of local stakeholders, particularly local communities and indigenous peoples."[13] However, the events surrounding the IYE, including the preparatory meetings leading to the World Ecotourism Summit (the IYE main event) had very little input from Indigenous Peoples, whose land and culture are two of the main "targets" of ecotourism development. In fact, the year was largely conceived as a promotional opportunity for ecotourism development and industry, with almost no critical analysis of ecotourism and its long-term impacts on Indigenous Peoples, the environment, and local communities.

Another objective of the IYE was to "promote exchanges of successful experiences in the field of ecotourism."[14] For most NGOs and Indigenous organizations, this objective ignored the negative ecotourism projects that have had major impacts on Indigenous homelands. It did not question whether or not ecotourism is sustainable and sparked discussions about the fundamental promotion of a segment of the tourism industry that may not be sustainable. The objective also undermined the search for sustainability by only highlighting success and not delving into the factors that could define what is sustainable and for whom.

Because the appearance of the IYE objectives and the activities undertaken was merely to promote rather than critically analyze ecotourism, Indigenous Peoples and numerous NGOs around the world called for reassessing of the IYE. A major event organized as a response to the IYE was the International Forum on Indigenous Tourism held in Oaxaca, Mexico, in March 2002. Indigenous Peoples from thirteen countries and twenty-one states in Mexico took part in this Forum, where they learned from one another and forged an Indigenous tourism network. One of the outcomes of the Forum was the *Declaration of the International Forum on Indigenous Tourism* (Oaxaca Declaration), a document that was presented at the World Ecotourism Summit (WES) in May 2002. The Oaxaca Declaration was critical of the IYE and the events leading up to the WES, highlighting how tourism and ecotourism guidelines were developed behind closed doors with very little Indigenous participation, and pointing out the danger that the IYE could be used to legitimate the invasion and displacement of Indigenous homelands and communities. The Oaxaca Declaration also underscored the need to respect and implement internationally recognized rights, and stressed the need for active Indigenous participation in policy development and in receiving equitable share of the derived benefits.

The Oaxaca Declaration[15] acknowledged Indigenous Peoples as internationally recognized holders of collective and human rights with the rights and responsibilities to our territories and the processes of tourism planning, implementation, and evaluation. A second point indicated that tourism is beneficial for Indigenous communities only when it is based on and enhances self-determination. A third point stated that Indigenous Peoples must be the natural resource and wildlife managers of their environments. A final recommendation stated that Indigenous Peoples must establish and strengthen strategies of coordination and information sharing both regionally and internationally — that is, an Indigenous Tourism Network — in order to assert participation in initiatives like the IYE. The participants of the Forum sent a strong message to urge the development and implementation of guidelines and regulations for ecotourism development and visitation based on principles of respect for local cultures and the integrity of ecosystems, and that they would consider illegitimate any drafting process that does not include the active and full participation of Indigenous Peoples.

Indigenous Peoples throughout the world are clearly struggling with common tourism issues, and the IYE together with all the activities organized around it could have served as a springboard for the implementation and respect of internationally recognized Indigenous rights. However, the present situation regarding the IYE does not look very promising for Indigenous Peoples as it mirrors the UN's Decade of Indigenous Peoples, which produced few results.

Creating spaces for the gathering of Indigenous Peoples to discuss important tourism issues like the Forum are very much needed and must be promoted in order to facilitate the articulation of relevant concerns, needs, and priorities that could be put forward directly to the policy makers or those able to influence policies. Furthermore, tourism is one of many arenas in which Indigenous Peoples are organizing themselves around the expression of their political concerns in international public arenas, including issues like biodiversity conservation and human rights.

Ecotourism Examples: Myths and Realities

From overpopulation that threatens both wildlife and people in the Galapagos, to "green" corporations, to land development paving the way for ecotravel, the problems are growing rapidly. Lands have been cleared and locals displaced for a huge dam project to provide eco-travelers with electricity in Malaysia. Elsewhere around the world, developers are building major airports to bring in more ecotravelers and the imports they require to set up golf courses, ecoresorts, eco-condominiums, ecolodges, ecomarine parks, and ecoranches. In July 2002, farmers in Mexico staged a four-day standoff, even taking hostages, in an effort to stop the government from seizing their lands at obscenely low prices to build yet another airport. There is a limit to how far tourism can go toward rescuing an economy, however.

>«(◊)»

Leaving Out People:
Ecotourism in the Solomon Islands
Charles R. de Burlo

In the 1990s, the Solomon Islands government, the Tourism Council of the South Pacific, and foreign conservation groups were promoting an ecotourism plan as a development and conservation alternative to logging. The plan included a resort at Lauvi Lagoon, on the Weather Coast of Guadalcanal, and a rain-forest hiking trail crossing the island north to south, linking villages along the route. Throughout the planning process, local people of the southern Weather Coast repeatedly issued formal objections to the Guadalcanal provincial government and over the national radio concerning tourism development on their lands. In response, local political elites and tourism ministry officials have pressed for the project to proceed, in spite of local resistance and cyclone damage to the area. Villagers and landowners resisted on the grounds that the ecotourist project would deny them customary rights to their trees and lands, as well as lagoon fishing resources. International conservation groups' resource evaluation studies for the project omitted both local peoples' knowledge and use of the area's natural resources, and the real health, agricultural, and education needs perceived by local people of this rugged region of Guadalcanal. In fact, villages along the walking trail would have been hard pressed to produce food or materials for tourist guesthouses. Instead of desiring tourists, local people of southeast Guadalcanal want better health care, safe drinking water supplies, and educational facilities. Researcher Brenda Rudkin states, "Despite the rhetoric of tourism organizations, conservation groups, consultants, and aid donors, the concept of ecotourism in the South Pacific has been promoted within a particularly narrow band of conservation and business thought which has often failed to appreciate the role of social and political values within sustainable tourism development and the maintenance of biodiversity."[16] In the South Pacific, the "environment" is preeminently a cultural domain and resource.

Selling Out in Costa Rica

In Costa Rica the ecodevelopment Papagayo Project has been a center of controversy. The massive project includes the construction of 1,144 homes, 6,270 condo-hotel units, 6,584 hotel rooms, a shopping center, and a golf course along the shores of Bahia Culebra.

> The enormous scope of this project is entirely inconsistent with the concept of sustainable and socially responsible ecotourism.... The use of the title "Ecodesarrollo Papagayo" [Ecodevelopment Papagayo] is a sad attempt to disguise this huge construction project under the all-too abused umbrella of ecotourism. The project has nothing to do with ecology, much less with responsible development for Costa Rica. Papagayo is nothing more than a high-profit real estate scheme designed to make a bundle of money for a few Costa Rican investors and their foreign corporate allies.[17]

Costa Rica has lost sight of small, locally owned accommodations and conservation and is moving toward privatization and the development of megaresorts. Costa Rica guidebooks are full of advertisements inviting tourists to pick out the piece of virgin forest or beach they would like to purchase, many promising "American construction company on-site." Tours have turned into real estate outings for foreigners. Since Costa Rica is considered the ecotourism model of the world, we should take note of how this "perfect" example of ecotravel exploits nature, conservation ideas, and locals by selling lands, constructing megaresorts, and otherwise paving paradise. Costa Rica has become the ultimate ecotourism lie.

The Galapagos Islands:
Tourism in (the Lack of) a Social Setting

Norbert Hohl and Deborah McLaren

The Galapagos Islands, long considered a model for tourism management worldwide, today faces new perils induced by tourism and the booming immigration of job-seeking Ecuadorians from the mainland. The troubles are twofold. On the one hand, the unpredictable and often negative spin-off effects of an evermore intertwined and growing tourism branch are increasing. On the other hand, conflicts over natural resources are becoming more violent and local ownership issues are surging, despite the lack of a long history of human settlement on the islands.

Galapagos' "Development"

Large-scale tourism to the Galapagos started in the late 1960s, when the islands were still virtually uninhabited. Until then, fewer than a thousand adventurous settlers had learned to successfully cope with the islands' rugged and unpredictable environment. Then as now, human settlement was restricted to four islands.

In 1959 the Galapagos National Park was created, covering some 97 percent of the islands' surface and leaving 3 percent of the land to be developed and used by humans. Together with the Charles Darwin Foundation, the park's research counterpart, management concepts were conceived of and implemented to allow for ecologically sustainable and economically beneficiary tourism activity. The exclusive, high-range products soon benefited a group of powerful Ecuadorians living on the mainland. Part of the benefits was reinvested into conservation efforts, leaving all partners content. With virtually no local population, almost no conflicts took place.

The number of cruise ships operated on the Galapagos soon surged from one in 1972 to eighty-four in 1997.[18] Annual tourist arrivals during the same period rose from a mere five thousand to more than sixty thousand. The tremendous rise in tourism activity created the need for local infrastructure and personnel, fueling the influx of settlers on the four populated islands. Today, despite the existence of the Special Law of Galapagos, which attempts, among other things, to restrict immigration, nearly twenty thousand registered inhabitants live on the islands, not counting a large number of illegal residents. At least two out of three inhabitants are directly or indirectly dependent on tourism.[19] On some islands, around 90 percent of the population work in tourism.

To be sure, the relatively large number of tourist arrivals doesn't pose the only risk to the islands, given that tourism is highly regulated. The tourism-induced side effects, combined with globalization phenomena and a weak institutional sector, represent significant threats to the extremely fragile Galapagos ecosystem.

Galapagos' Disputed Resources

The Galapagos hold two main resources that have become the focus of volatile disputes between local and other interest groups. These resources pertain to two ecosystems — namely, the marine reserve with its wealth of sea life, incidentally a bonanza fishing site due to its protected status, and the volcanic island land reserve, justifiably famous for its natural-historic beauty and singularity. The fact that no human group has an ancestral right to control these resources makes them prey to various economic interests that are not fundamentally embedded in sustainable land-use concepts, nor are decisions based on traditionally sustainable patterns of resource use.

Commercial fishing companies from the mainland and from abroad compete for marine resources. Only local small-scale fishermen are allowed to fish within the Galapagos Marine Reserve, which includes waters within a forty-mile offshore boundary. All other fishing parties are restricted to fish outside the reserve. Park authorities are faced with the daunting task of controlling the marine reserve. Many legal infractions, mostly relating to illegal fishing, were reported during the recent past, and even though the park and navy have captured several ships laden with illegal catches, many of them were released again without having been fined because of political intervention. Local fishermen are often engaged in illegal fishing within the reserve, be it for shark fins, sea cucumbers, or lobster, where black market prices earn local fishermen more money in two months than would an entire year's pay working in the tourism industry.

The tourism industry "is a very complex sector, composed of a number of powerful mainland-based companies, some with foreign capital, and small and medium-sized local operators."[20] The high-priced, elitist product earns the country valuable foreign exchange. However, aside from positive local employment effects, locals receive no benefits from such "external" tourism practices. Even worse, the few local operators that do exist must compete for their share of the medium-priced segment with nonlocals who entered the market by taking over the businesses of failures that were sold to mainlanders.

Add to this situation the following ingredient: The only group that actively and financially advocates preservation of both the marine and tourism resource is the conservationists, a group supported by international and national stake-holders. However, past policy shows that this activity was done mostly without the involvement of the local population.

> From the early 1970s to the 1990s, a number of powerful interests were focused on defending their various positions without making sufficient effort to understand the needs, interests, and concerns of the weaker stakeholders, represented, among others, by the local community of small-scale fishers.[21]

The Unsocial Side of Tourism

Recently, tourism has caused more pressure on the Galapagos ecosystem. In January 2001, a fueling tanker called *Jessica* sank off San Cristóbal Island at "wreckage bay" in an attempt to express fill the eco-certified tourism boat *Galapagos Explorer II*. The boat was the only one on the island that used the heavy bunker fuel, which is known to be more harmful to the ecosystem than the lighter diesel. A certification program for tour boats had been introduced a year earlier, generously leaving out fuel specification and refueling procedures from certification. A team of scientists has now confirmed long-term damage to the ecosystem due to the spill.[22] Another permanent threat to the islands' ecosystems is invasive species, a threat that becomes more likely with every tourist setting foot on the island. A control and quarantine system is in place, but because of funding restrictions is still not very effective.

The still dormant, but largest, threat to the islands' ecosystems stems from the local population. Drug abuse among youths, illegal drug dealing, prosti-tution, and an alarmingly increasing HIV rate are symptoms of an underlying malady especially in scattered towns. For decades, neither politicians nor park managers concentrated their efforts on locals; now the malaise of low-quality education, poor health services, a low level of social cohesion and cultural identity, and a low level of ecological awareness is making itself felt all too much.

The social disorientation experienced by so many on the islands is presently accompanied by an overwhelming price inflation. Compared to the mainland, normal prices on the Galapagos Islands are at least twofold in comparison, and often much higher still. Employees in tourism who earn minimum wage, and in some cases even less, are impoverishing at an accelerated rate. This situation encourages a sufficiently large group of individuals to become involved in illegal activities to earn a living and support their family. A parallel development is that children, often inspired by the behavior of a wealthy leisure class, are increasingly tempted to engage in fast-money-earning activities.

Conclusion

The Galapagos Islands' twenty thousand tourism-pulled inhabitants are a fact today, and their collaboration in conservation efforts is crucial for the survival of the islands' ecosystems. Tourism on the Galapagos is a fragile vehicle for conservation. The extreme dependency by the islands' populations on the volatile tourism sector creates incentives to partake in ecologically destructive but short-term high-profit activities like cucumber, lobster, and shark fin fishing. The negative social impacts of tourism together with uncontrolled drug dealing, a poor education system, the lack of a common social identity, and low environmental awareness have all contributed over the past decades to create a time bomb for a generation without roots.

The legacy of former conservation policy, which did not take into account the local human factor, will arguably be the most difficult to overcome. In the 1990s, park management policy was officially changed to become a participatory stakeholder policy. However, several decades of distrust and ambiguity by the locals combined with successful illegal and opportunistic behavior, often supported by powerful political interest groups that undermine national park management, make it difficult for the conservation sector to regain cooperation by locals. To highlight this dilemma, one need think only of the recurring protests and acts of violence by local fishermen over the past years that have repeatedly culminated in kidnapping tortoises and threatening to kill them, damaging property of the national park and the Charles Darwin Station, and assaulting tourist buses to get what they want, such as increased fishing quotas.

Christophe Grenier spent a year and a half researching tourism impacts and conservation in the Galapagos. He conducted a survey of almost two thousand tourists and locals, and summarizes the development as follows: "The ecological damage is being done at a terrific speed: more people, tourists, boats, cars, concrete, introduced plants and animals, and the boom for sharks for Asian markets." The Ecuadorian government is incapable of stopping this disastrous evolution:

> The government, the Darwin Foundation, and some international experts developed tourism policy for the Galapagos and want to limit migration by reducing the monetary flow poured by tourism into the local economy. This policy is actually "selective tourism" although it claims to be ecotourism. The goal is to transform the islands into an expensive tour destination — higher airline prices, higher national park taxes, higher yacht tariffs — so it will discourage the "cheap" tourists, who contribute directly to the locals. The result is both tourists and prices have increased

while limits are not enforced. The Galapagos National Park Service allows cruise boats while it's officially forbidden. Migration continues and the lack of local jobs in the tourist economy has resulted in people taking jobs in illegal fisheries, which have boomed. The ecological degradation is very rapid while the locals oppose any type of conservation. The locals believe the Foundation naturalists don't care about human beings living in the archipelago, partly because they use the islands' nature to make money. Thirty to forty percent of the Darwin Foundation budget comes from tourist donations. What I have learned about conservation is that there is no way to protect natural areas without putting their inhabitants at the core of conservation policy.[23]

Craig MacFarland, former director of the Charles Darwin Research Station and president of the Charles Darwin Foundation, comes to the following conclusion:

Overall, the Galapagos Islands are a good model for nature tourism to this type of large dispersed protected area, with many positive lessons for design, planning, and implementation. . . . However, it cannot be taken as a good model for local ecotourism which intensely involves local communities as the primary service providers and beneficiaries, and which attempts to provide for minimizing impacts to their cultural and social life.[24]

Mass "Ecotourism," Thai-Style
Anita Pleumarom

As with tourism in general, "ecotourism" schemes in Thailand often proceed without proper involvement of local communities in decision making. No adequate discussion takes place on who owns the land and natural resources, how land should be used, and where and how tourist facilities should be built. The result is aggravated ecological problems and conflict between the government, private industry, and ordinary citizens.

A glaring example was the strong opposition by local residents and environmentalists against landscape changes in Phi Phi Islands National Park in Krabi province for the filming of 20th Century Fox's movie The Beach, starring Leonardo DiCaprio, in 1999. The reason given by the government to allow the controversial film project to go ahead was to promote the country's tourism industry and income for local communities. But critics insisted such actions make a mockery of conservation efforts and the legal system, showing that the commercialization of natural and cultural heritage for tourism purposes can override any other issue in Thailand.

Such concerns persist as many natural and rural areas have been newly earmarked for ambitious tourism projects. Recently, the plan to develop a huge golf resort at the junction of the Thai, Laotian, and Cambodian border provoked another protest. Local conservation groups argued the project in the so-called "Emerald Triangle" area should be rejected as the Thai land is located in a 1A watershed area, which is part of Ubon Ratchathani's Phu Chong Na Yoi National Park. Yet, government officials maintained the project was "needed at any price" because it would bring in a large amount of tourism revenue. In response to environmental opposition, a senior forestry official said the golf resort could be defined as an "ecotourism" project and as such would co-exist well with the surrounding protected forest as golfers could watch wildlife while playing on the fairways.

A similar conflict is evolving around the government's plan to turn the Chang Islands in Trat province, which are currently 86.5 percent national park protected from development by law, into a luxurious retreat for high-spending "ecotourists." Local residents say they have not been properly informed about the project, and worries are increasing about rampant land speculation and the mushrooming of five-star hotel projects on the main island, Koh Chang. Apart from massive infrastructure works such as roads, boat piers, and a freshwater pipeline system to all fifty islands in the park area, the project also provides for an "entertainment zone" that will include a golf course to be developed by private concessionaires.[25]

Indigenous Ecotourism in Mexico: An Opportunity under Construction
David Barkin

The National Indigenous Congress, a coalition of most of the Indigenous communities in Mexico, reports about 15 million Indigenous People in Mexico. Dispersed throughout the country, they speak more than sixty different languages, reflecting the large number of distinct ethnic groups that have survived.[26] Many Mexicans are reclaiming their ties to the past, in the wake of the Zapatista uprising in 1994. Although embroiled in a life-and-death struggle,

Deborah McLaren, northern Thailand

With no recycling or waste management, plastic trash (brought in by tourists) accumulates behind trekker huts in Thailand. Local people must burn the plastic, causing hazardous toxic chemicals to be released.

Indigenous organizations are finding that they may have a brighter future if they insist on placing first their cultural heritage and the center of their struggle to forge viable alternatives for themselves and their regions, rather than denying its importance.[27] Explaining this diversity and activism is part of the secret to understanding the extraordinary opportunities that Indigenous People have and the challenges they face when attempting to participate in tourist activities.

Mexico's Indigenous Peoples are active participants in the country's integration into the world economy. Whether they like it or not, their fortunes are intimately tied into the global economy, be it the result of centuries of systematic discrimination against their communities and inhumane treatment of their peoples, the expropriation of their lands, or myriad forms of outright racism. The world economy has also been cruel, paying low prices for their products and unthinkably low wages for their labor. Many have been forced from the most fertile of their lands into the inhospitable "regions of refuge" that today are considered "their" territories; others are reluctant migrants, forming numerous communities of poorly paid workers in Mexico's urban centers and its agricultural emporia or settling in growing communities in urban centers in the United States, most notably in Southern California. Some remain in their regions of origin, tenaciously conserving their customs and their lands — living in and among the monuments constructed by their forefathers and the cemeteries that continue as important links to a complex historical memory. Nowhere has this been more forcefully illustrated than in the southern state of Chiapas, where the region's predominantly Indigenous population has not only actively organized to defend the small band that rose up in battle, but also to join their clarion cry for a measure of self-government and the basic guarantees enshrined in the Mexican Constitution, as a result of the peasant victories in the 1910 Revolution. While conditions are particularly hostile in Chiapas, all of Mexico's Native populations suffer from the results of discrimination and neglect.

Although they are definitely traditional, these societies are anything but stagnant. They are constantly adapting to changing conditions as their members attempt to survive. One of the most important innovations in Indigenous communities in recent years is the realization that their customs and traditions, as well as their accumulated wisdom, are not just important for their identity and their survival. Nor are they simply objects to be described by anthropologists or captured by photographers, as has been their fate in the past. Recognition is growing that significant groups in the "outside" world also treasure this heritage and are willing to collaborate to defend these societies while also enjoying the pleasure of participating in the activities that are intrinsic to Native societies. As in many other parts of the world, Native peoples in Mexico are rediscovering their own identities and beginning to organize; as part of this movement, they are beginning to regulate the way in which outsiders are permitted to visit their communities and territories, and, in some instances, they are learning to charge for the privilege.[28] Although visitors have always imposed themselves on these communities, assuming the right to intrude, especially during the most sacred (and colorful) of ceremonial occasions, without giving prior notice or seeking permission, they have generally been tolerated or welcomed, with few concessions to accommodate them, save by the merchants who along with federal or state tourism authorities viewed their custom with delight.

This situation is changing as local peoples become aware of the possibilities and dangers of such visits continuing without regulation. Today, throughout Mexico, Indigenous communities are actively involved in the tourist trade, many without any planning or preparation. Shops typically have local products on display, together with the normal inventory of consumer items, but in many regions where artisan production is important, specialized shops and even museum-like displays are common; an outstanding example is the community museum program established jointly by twenty villages in Oaxaca and the local museum of artistic copper pieces in Michoacán. These efforts are often complemented by regional or statewide fairs where local artisans compete for recognition and prizes and merchants gather to negotiate for local and international markets; the federal government's promotional organization (Fondo Nacional de Artesanías, FONART) also provides limited credit and outlets for quality producers.

Local artisan production continues to grow, although market relations are frequently exploitative and often reproduce themselves within the communities themselves as intermediaries cut margins on the assumption that the local contractors will simply take advantage of community members by insisting on greater productivity or imposing lower wages as well as onerous and dangerous working conditions. These goods are marketed as "hand-made" by local artisans, and often resold on cosmopolitan markets at substantial mark-ups; occasionally, a local tradition or skilled individual is "discovered" and its practitioners learn how to charge correctly for the products, but this is the rare exception, save those that are distributed through FONART or by a few non-government organizations (NGOs) seeking to expand channels for "fair trade" products.

A few communities and local organizations have gone beyond the traditional forms of interaction with outsiders. Instead of passively waiting for the tourists to arrive, they are developing new mechanisms to attract visitors, interested in learning more about local cultures and the environments in which they live. Some non-government organizations and an occasional government promotional scheme are also involved in helping to establish and even promote this approach, as it has become a new fashion within the development community. From the analysis in other parts of this book, such projects are evidently much more difficult to organize and make profitable than it might seem.

Visitor interest and local communities willing to participate in such an enterprise are readily available in Mexico. Even without any concerted effort, the single most important category of tourist destinations is archeological sites operated by the National Institute of Anthropology and History, surpassing beach tourism in numbers by a considerable margin, including both local and international visitors. Furthermore, commercial tour operators have been selling packages for visitors to observe traditional ceremonies honoring the Day of the Dead and the Virgin of Guadalupe for quite some time, to mention just two dates that are celebrated nationally, but with specific local variations among rural and Indigenous communities. Unfortunately, most of the visitors to religious and other ceremonial occasions in Indigenous communities offer little benefit and often cause damage as they are unaware of the appropriate forms of behavior and the possibility of harm, as they grope for better vantage points from which to observe the events and are frequently unaware of the significance of the ceremonies they are witnessing.

Indigenous/Ecotourism Experiences

In spite of the many problems, however, numerous communities are searching for ways to take advantage of this new interest and the opportunities tourism creates. At the same time, numerous civil society groups and some government programs are offering assistance and sometimes even financing to help make these programs operational. The rest of this short article offers some reflections based on various experiences in Mexico, going from the relatively successful to the extreme abuse of the concept, a result that often leads to actual harm to the Indigenous communities and the ecosystems in which they live.

Urban Communities

Perhaps the most successful example of collaboration between people who have developed technical expertise and established solid networks with international groups seeking to promote responsible ecotourism in community-operated programs is Balam Consultants[29] operating out of Mexico City. Their experts are working with numerous communities and regional groups throughout the country to help develop or perfect local efforts to provide visitor experiences well-suited to the needs and abilities of the communities and their physical surroundings. A relatively modest effort involved building hiking trails of varying degrees of difficulty in an area surrounding Mexico City designated as a "lung" or green area; managed by local peasants of Indigenous extraction, the project involved using state-of-the art concepts in trail design, certified by international evaluators, to create an accessible offering that would allow people with different abilities to enjoy some greater contact with their natural surroundings. The effort is expected to generate sufficient income to enable the communities to also dedicate greater effort to care for the region and plant crops and trees most appropriate for the area and to supply local needs. City government is supporting this project as one strategy for strengthening their environmental protection programs, reducing the use of the lands for destructive grazing and ending the threat of land invasions by people from other parts of the metropolitan area. A more ambitious program supported by Balam involves building a private park on communal lands in Mexico City to provide a variety of recreational activities well-attuned to the customs of a large segment of the region's people, but explicitly designed to help them to learn more about how rural people can undertake environmental management that is both beneficial for the area and reverse the economic decline afflicting most rural people in Mexico. This private park offers sports and other recreational facilities, and a fishery open to the public now produces trout to supply a community restaurant that caters to the visitors.

Forest Environments

Another well-known project developed from a widespread movement for communities to retake control of forest lands that had been poorly managed by logging companies through concessions granted by the federal government. After developing a new forest management program, one of the members, a university-trained biologist, organized a group within his Indigenous community in the mountains of Oaxaca to offer a variety of trips to outsiders interested in enjoying the splendor of the regional pine forests and in learning about the local efforts to stem the tide of migration and improve living conditions; the new model for ecosystem management is also contributing to increase water supplies in the valley surrounding the city of Oaxaca. The community is beginning to produce artisan products, made from wood gleaned from the ongoing efforts to manage the forests. Another nearby community has "rehabilitated" a pre-Columbian religious monument that was "lost" in the shrubbery and expanded the local city hall to accommodate a small collection of pieces of historical and archeological interest; advisors helped a local restaurant improve the quality of its offerings and "reinvented" what must have been a system of transporting underground spring water for domestic use while building a small bottling plant, selling the water to local visitors and in the capital. Both of these villages received modest amounts of outside financing from international sources interested in promoting productive activities that also contribute to environment protection. Even with the small numbers of visitors that these projects have attracted in their first years, a marked change has occurred in the attitude of many other communities in this region, which boasts a millennial tradition of collective self-government and ecosystem management.

The Indigenous Past

But not all projects are successes, nor do all tourist visits to Indigenous areas leave benefits for the natives. Although most archeological sites in Mexico are managed by the federal government and are surrounded by Indigenous communities, local populations are virtually excluded from participating, except by hawking their wares — cheap souvenirs or artisan goods, reproductions of archeological pieces, soft drinks, candy and other "junk" food; local commerce is tightly controlled by wealthier merchants who regulate the market stalls at these tourist meccas, relegating the natives to the fringes or to outright begging.

Government Sponsorship

In recent years, new government programs have helped establish "ecotourist" programs managed by Indigenous communities in attractive but isolated regions. Unfortunately, their top-down design — subject to centralized control and unrealistic business plans — condemned them to fail, even when implemented by honest, well-meaning officials in an office devoted to creating small business opportunities. A particularly egregious example of a poorly executed government program (by another government program) is the Special Reserve created to protect the Monarch butterfly — one of the densest sites of tourist visits in west-central Mexico. Although more than four hundred thousand people flock to the area to see the millions of lepidopters during their four-month visit to escape the harsh North American winter, and in spite of relatively generous financing and the active participation of international NGOs seeking to promote community-based conservation based on ecotourism, only one of the dozens of Indigenous communities in the region has really benefited from this bonanza. In essence, the errors are the same as those committed by the government program cited above, with the difference that in this case a great deal of money is spent by tourists and most of the benefits are captured by tour operators and well-connected vendors of tourist services, groups that have effectively blocked all efforts to allow the local people to implement their own models of tourist development, tied directly to a concept the local people sometimes call "productive conservation." Tragically, the "free-market" model of tourism that now prevails is leading to a progressive degradation of the ecosystem and a lost opportunity to integrate conservation efforts and tourism into a creative program for sustainable regional resource management. Compounding the damage, this growth may actually endanger its continued success, as tourists become disenchanted by the effects of the disorganization and opportunism, although other communities in nearby areas less tightly controlled by vested interests are creating a variety of alternative visitor models, but without creating the external benefits of "productive conservation" offered by the alliance of peasant communities within the area of influence of the reserve.[30]

The example of the Monarch butterfly is also illustrative of another poorly understood but potentially important contribution of effective programs promoting Indigenous tourism. Contrary to most stereotypes, more than 90 percent of visitors are Mexican, since the region is readily accessible to more than 30 million people in just a few hours from the two major metropolitan areas. Although disdained by tourism agencies in many poorer countries, in most parts of the world tourism is predominantly from within the

same country, or from neighboring countries.[31] As a result, a serious examination of the role of tourism in promoting sustainable regional development
must consider the impact of and potential for native visitors.

Local Tourists as Patrons

Considering the potential of in-country tourism in many parts of the world,
some analysts are reevaluating tourism as a force for stimulating environmentally friendly programs that contribute to improving local welfare. Rather
than focus exclusively on international travel and facilities, community tourist
projects aiming to promote local development might find that small groups
of local visitors can be more readily attracted and better served than larger
international groups. This reasoning lies behind a local development alternative incorporating tourism as a part of a broader strategy for rehabilitating a
degraded ecosystem on the Pacific coast of Mexico.[32] Focusing on a strategy
of rebuilding biodiversity in an endangered dry tropical forest, the Centro de
Soporte Ecológico is collaborating with local community leaders to develop
a variety of productive activities that are generating employment and income;
because of the beauty of the area, and the continued growth of beach tourism,
ecotourism is an especially promising complementary activity for diversification
and growth.

Internal Cooperation and Discord

Unfortunately, here again the great potential of local tourism as an area for
future growth reveals a common problem that communities must face when
attempting to develop their own offerings. After working diligently with local
and interested community members to develop management and design skills
and identify appropriate sites at which to erect bungalows along a mountain
creek, project organizers were forced to call a halt to the project because a few
unscrupulous individuals set up competing business nearby without abiding by
the guidelines required for a high-quality project. Such problems are common
where decisions requiring voluntary compliance are attempting to introduce
innovative projects; this example underscores the importance of collective responsibility and implementation that many Indigenous communities incorporate
as fundamental principles in their organization. The breakdown in this authority in the coastal project in Mexico further highlights the complexity of the
process of implanting successful tourist projects, even when cohesive groups,
like those in many Indigenous peoples' communities, provide the driving force
behind the effort.[33]

New Avenues for Cooperation

Indigenous and ecotourism projects can offer important benefits for all concerned. They can also make potentially significant contributions to a national
environmental protection program. One especially innovative proposal is offered by the Zoques who live in Mexico's largest remaining tropical rain forest
(a community of about twenty-five thousand people who inhabit six hundred
thousand hectares in south-central Oaxaca). After successfully thwarting repeated attempts to implant development programs to take advantage of the
region's abundant water resources and forest reserves, the Mexican scientific
community proposed creating a professionally managed UNESCO "Biosphere
Reserve" to protect the area from continued degradation. In response, the
Indigenous community proposed taking charge of managing the project, developing a suitable program to assure their own sustenance and assuming
responsibility for their professional training to enable them to collaborate with
outsiders who might want to conduct research and assist in developing conservation programs. Although the scientific community supported the proposal,
opposition arose from numerous regional forces, each promoting its own program for livestock development, export agriculture, or logging, as well as from
national politicians concerned that such a proposal might confer too much political independence from regional *caciques*. State government programs were
implemented to attempt to defuse this Indigenous strategy and to divide the
community against itself.

In view of the impasse, important parts of the Zoque community, with political support from national environmental groups and financial assistance from
the British government,[34] began to implement their project for a peasant-
administered conservation program, including guided visits for the scientific
community and the interested public. Exceptional students from local schools
were offered fellowships to study biology at the national university and forest
and water resource management at regional technical schools. The communities have initiated research programs in collaboration with professionals and
students from local and international scientific organizations, while they continue to improve their capability to protect the forests from fire and invasion
by ranchers. Selective planting of nurseries for endangered species of trees has
been started. A small ecotourism program has been implemented to provide an
additional source of income and to generate a broader base of understanding
of the concept of locally administered conservation by interested outsiders.

Now that the southern part of Mexico has taken on greater importance
with the announcement of an ambitious regional development program, Plan
Puebla Panama, Indigenous communities are intensifying their efforts to build

alliances with other communities that are also developing their own proposals for "productive conservation," as it is being titled. Las Chimalapas offers a promising example of an innovative project to promote the "sustainable management of regional resources," allowing local peoples to improve their living standards while raising levels of environmental protection and contributing to a better understanding of our planet.

Although opposition to these "independent" initiatives continues in Oaxaca and other parts of the country, and intensifies at times when political conditions are propitious, environment authorities grudgingly recognize that the communities offer a viable and economically attractive model for participatory conservation. In fact, the model of local participation in ecosystem management has become a fundamental principle in the design of conservation programs in the country's protected area program, although the government is still struggling with mechanisms to make it workable, given the complex array of local interests in each area.

Forging Alternatives to Globalization

Indigenous communities and many of their peasant neighbors are actively searching for alternatives to globalization. They have become painfully aware of the process of productive polarization and homogenization that spills over into every aspect of their social existence. Throughout the Third World, we have witnessed an impoverishment of excluded peoples and an intensification of environmental problems, resulting from the lack of mechanisms for adequate ecosystem management. Their search for alternative strategies for sustainable regional resource management offers a means to confront the destructiveness of the present forms of international integration with activities that generate opportunities and promote social cohesion, while also producing goods that are both useful and marketable.

The theory behind this approach has emerged from a search for alternatives to globalization. The approach combines an important reflection on the meaning of sustainability with innovative projects to assure a greater measure of self-sufficiency while insisting on the development of new products and new markets that will free small-scale producers from the tyranny of monopolistic markets; tourism is ideally suited to be part of a diversified strategy that will contribute to these objectives.[35] Although many groups are working on this problem around the world, some are promoting small businesses without delving into their social and environmental impacts. A serious examination of the role of Indigenous and rural peoples, like the material in this book, confirms the need to broaden our analysis.[36]

The prevailing pattern of concentrated development does not contribute to a durable model. Large segments of people in many countries are searching for their own mechanisms to construct ramparts against the advance of globalization. Local initiatives to promote sustainable regional resource management offer a promising approach that requires greater attention. Indigenous and rural communities can actively participate in this process, but only if they are allowed to seize the initiative and overcome the patterns of political, economic, and cultural discrimination so common in today's world.

Seven

Rethinking Tourism

"Welcome to Paradise...before it's gone" is macabre. Do we really want to destroy paradise before it's gone? Current high-consumption forms of tourism are *not* sustainable. Realistic information must be made easily available. As we travel, we need to ask ourselves, "Why am I traveling? How can I help change the destructive aspects of the travel industry?"

I asked these questions of several responsible tourism advocates. Virginia Hadsell, founder of the Center for Responsible Tourism, told me that despite the efforts of the worldwide responsible tourism movement that began to emerge in the 1970s, the negative impact of irresponsible tourism has increased. She sees some hopeful signs, however, as the issue of irresponsible tourism is being placed on the agenda in many parts of the world. Increasingly, from many quarters, the rights of Indigenous Peoples, concern for the deteriorating environment, the homogenization of cultures, and the rights of women and children are being addressed — and often connected with the tourism industry.

Over the past few decades, the world has truly shrunk, in a large part because of tourism. As citizens of the global North, we can fly to Rio de Janeiro tomorrow and float down the Amazon the day after. Our ability to see the world close up has made us more concerned about international problems. News about environmental threats to the rain forests, the plight of the people who live there, human rights abuses around the world, and the increasing poverty and economic gaps between citizens reach us speedily each day. Issues like the uncontrolled power of corporations and the destruction of the planet have become central in many of our lives. Yet in some ways the rapid rate at which information is being thrown at us makes it almost too much to comprehend. We feel overwhelmed, sometimes jaded, by the surplus of information. We see the problems but remain unsure how to effect change.

Numerous "alternative" types of tourism are evolving, and the real danger is that travelers will simply consume these new products, places, and peoples without recognizing the urgent need for a critical reevaluation of global tourism and their participation in it. To rethink tourism is to challenge the travel industry at every level, including the booming new forms of travel, which, even if well intended, have many of the same detrimental effects as conventional tourism. Olivier Pouillon, a tourism activist who works in Indonesia, warns, "Stop looking for alternatives or technical solutions to tourism. When you scream ecotourism, agritourism, and alternative tourism, it makes people forget to look at what is wrong with tourism." Tourism scholar and activist Shelley Attix asks:

> Why are we "activists" afraid of the "t" word? Tourism industry people aren't. If we are concerned about what tourism is doing and come from different backgrounds — business, Indigenous sovereignty, environmental — then we should talk instead of waiting until there is a crisis. It is very difficult, except in strategic boycott situations, to shut down tourism. We have to keep alliances strong and prepare for transitional efforts. We need to train young people to be managers and handle policy decisions during these transitions from mass tourism. We have to make plans in terms of finances and management skills to take over the helm and make big changes. We're making the "t" word so bad that no one wants to talk about it, and that's counterproductive.

The remedy is within tourism itself. To counter tourism's economic, social, and environmental devastation, we must learn to recognize corporate tourism's messages and methods. Tourism has provided us with fantasies. At the same time, it provides potentially free public relations that may help to encourage rethinking of the industry and create alternatives. Tourism provides people-to-people contacts and an opportunity to utilize the ability to communicate with one another, to meet, and to organize. On a global level, this can help foster an appreciation for rich human, cultural, and ecological diversity and can cultivate a mutual trust and respect for one another and for the dignity of the natural world.

You and I are tourists, even if we are traveling to learn about or change the world. Unless we are willing to stay at home and reject the transportation systems, communication lines, technologies, and the tremendous amount of resources that we consume each time we travel, we need to understand not only our participation in the promotion of the global tourism industry but also its importance and potential as a tool for change. Tourism can raise awareness of and action for the global nature of problems like poverty, pollution, and cultural erosion. Close human relationships and activities liberated from preoccupations with profits and bottom lines are crucial to this awareness. The past three decades have witnessed a return to social responsibility and social idealism. This value shift is reflected to a small degree in the tourism industry (in the tourism-for-peace movement, for example) in the consciousness of the cross-cultural impact a travel experience has for both a visitor and the communities visited. The trend in travel is for more tourists and locals in alliance with schools, NGOs, religious groups, the media, cities, and governments to work to stop the paving of paradise.

So where do we start? With ourselves. We can read, learn, make personal changes, be more involved in our own communities, pressure governments and corporations, denounce exploitation, change policies, and investigate the global forces transforming our lives. We can discuss, educate, and organize. I believe that most tourists understand the many things that are wrong with tourism. What we need is a clear outline for change.

The first requirement is for more tourism research and analysis, which can occur as activism goes forward. Travelers from the global North can link with people in other places to make progress on issues that concern us all. By building on experiences and developing relationships and networks, we can challenge international trade and tourism policies, misinformation produced by the travel industry, and exploitative practices. We can make sure that monies from tourism go to the local economy.

Many developing countries are on the brink of abandoning traditional organic practices and moving toward more capital-intensive methods of development. The responsible tourism movement can draw attention to development policies that are undemocratic and promote reliance on the global economy as opposed to local resources. In many places around the world, people are building sustainable communities that focus on the well-being of the community, rely more on renewable energy, discourage consumption, and create less pollution.

The Need for Education

While a fair amount of critical analysis of tourism has come from the academic community, most tourism education focuses on hospitality management, training, and operations. Critical studies in economics, political control, culture, the North-South dichotomy, and the way tourists view themselves have contributed important insights.

According to Luis Vivanco,

> Many tourism programs are designed to reproduce the industry, validate its basic capitalist paradigms, and create the next generation of managers. Will they allow for more critical, deconstructive work to happen under their umbrella? My guess is that if it's allowed, truly critical social scientific and political perspectives will be marginalized by the business and technique-focused emphasis of the industry.

Real changes in tourism will not be created until people from diverse communities, backgrounds, and disciplines take a more integrated approach. Anthropologists, political scientists, and sociologists must connect with tourism management and training programs to share information, challenge unsustainable practices and unfair labor, and develop critical analysis.

A few programs exist that are not completely industry-focused. Texas A&M is an example of an interdisciplinary approach to tourism in the United States. The University of Waitago in New Zealand has a very unique program in tourism that is completely interdisciplinary and based in geography, and which offers some critical analysis. At the same time it hopes to serve the Maori, the Indigenous Peoples of New Zealand.

Women of all colors are urgently needed to look at gender issues in tourism and change policies that exploit, discriminate, and cause violence to women. Support for tourism gender studies at universities and colleges will support education for women to work in tourism in areas other than as prostitutes, waitresses, maids, bar attendants, and housekeepers.

Indigenous students of tourism need tremendous support. While understanding Western systems is necessary in order to tackle the issues of tourism, it is important to remember that Western education has produced the systems that are threatening the planet. Educational programs must introduce and integrate lessons from Indigenous eco-logical values and traditional and subsistence economics. I encourage students reading this book to research tourism, to undertake an analysis of advertising strategies or investigate the corporate responsibility of a tourism company. When educational programs encourage critical thinking and opportunities for people from diverse perspectives, they can create the tools, information, and education for those who are affected to change tourism. The global tourism industry must be persuaded to set aside some of its trillions of dollars in profits to advance the education of young people around the world to rethink tourism.

Tourists as Activists

The Center for Responsible Tourism suggests tourists ask themselves: Is this trip necessary? "Tourism has become a supermarket of illusions, exotic lands promising to satisfy secret desires. Ask yourself, why am I buying this trip? What do I leave behind? How many trips does it take to renew my soul and body? What do I do with my experiences when I return home?"[1] As tourists questioning tourism, the role we play, and the impact of our very presence in destination communities, we can start by considering the amount of natural resources it takes to transport us to our destination, to get us around while we are there (whether the oil used by airplanes and cars or the energy for the lights and air conditioning in the hotel room), where our waste is going, whether the locals have adequate water resources, how much land has been "reconstructed" for the place we stay, and whether residents have been moved to make room for us. Who owns the hotels, and where do our dollars go? We tourists can make some powerful political choices by voting with our feet and our pocketbooks.

As tourists, we must make educated economic choices and support small-scale, locally owned and operated businesses. Get involved in your own community so that when you travel you will have a reason to be involved in other communities and will *stay involved*; acknowledge the modern realities of Indigenous and rural communities and learn to respect, not romanticize, other cultures. Support responsible tourism organizations. Subscribe to their magazines and newsletters. Volunteer. Study. Learn about local currency programs and how you can start one in your community. Pressure large tourism companies to do more than greenwash. Organize a "reality tour" of your own community to examine environmental, economic, or social justice issues. Invite teachers, students, local community members, your family, city officials, religious leaders, local businesses (including those in tourism) and others to participate. Make activism a goal of the tour. Contribute funds to support more integrated, diverse critical tourism studies.

Travelers can act responsibly by seeking out accurate information about the places they intend to visit. In the United States and elsewhere, many Indigenous organizations will provide a list of recommended readings by authors they believe accurately describe their culture and history. Environmental and social justice groups that work with Native and Indigenous Peoples will have information about important current issues. Indigenous Peoples face any number of issues, ranging from health care and uranium mining cleanup to sovereignty rights and free trade agreements. In the United States, travelers can support the protection of sacred religious sites. Many such places have been turned into tourist destinations, rock climbing walls, and even resorts. Sacred Sites International Foundation advocates for "the preservation of natural and built sacred places. We believe that protecting sacred sites is key to preserving traditional cultures and time-honored values of respecting the earth."[2]

While social activists are developing new tourism strategies, concerned tourists are changing their focus from relaxation to activism. Global Exchange, a San Francisco organization, has been a leader in people-to-people tourism. Their reality tours explore grassroots movements, offering travelers an opportunity to meet people behind the scenes, from Zapatistas in Chiapas and young people in Cuba to women organizers in South Africa and Vietnamese facing injustices created by capitalism. Tourists are now monitoring elections in Mexico, speaking out on behalf of Indigenous Peoples being forced from their lands by oil companies, and trying to uphold human rights in Bosnia. They are sharing information about fair trade, organic farming or permaculture, and less-consumptive technologies.

Deborah Tull joined a reality tour organized by Bard College:

I spent nine months traveling, meeting local people and helping out. I still have questions about what we did — did it really make a difference? Some places I could see that, yes, it did. However, in other places I felt we were contributing to problems. Yet, overall, we traveled in a different way — meeting and learning from local people involved in important issues. It certainly changed my perceptions about tourism. It actually changed my life. I will never see tourism in the same light, I will never travel in a conventional way. I've talked to a lot of friends, family, and my teachers about it and believe I have been influential.

Travel Industry Changes

Some segments of the travel industry are more aware of environmental and human rights issues and are actively involved in reform. A growing number of small tour operators are rethinking their industry. Although many alternative ideas claim to benefit local people, we must not lose sight of the fact that tour operators are in the business to make money, and the tourist is the paying consumer they cater to. Tourism researcher Barbara Johnson warns against some tourism ideas that are emerging:

> Alternative tourism represents an industry whose ventures capitalize on the increasing global concern with disappearing cultures, lifestyles and ecosystems.... [However], the vision of responsible tourism includes more than this potentially exploitative relationship. Responsible tourism encompasses those ventures that are consciously designed to enhance the socio-environmental milieu of the host while educating and entertaining the guest. These ventures sell the "exotic" to gain money, labor, and/or foreign presence — all in an effort to restore the degraded environment while attacking the roots of social inequity.[3]

Many ecotourism projects are extremely misleading and exploitative. Some may be well intentioned but are misguided attempts to sell nature and culture. One example of a tour company that not only follows responsible tourism guidelines but also monitors the global travel industry is The Travel Specialists (TTS). A member of Co-Op America, a fair-trade organization, TTS serves as a link between concerned travelers, tour operators, tour programs, and local community projects. It evaluates other travel programs, promotes responsible tourism, and monitors the impact of tourism on local communities and the environment. TTS established the Eagle Eye Institute, a program to get urban youth out of the cities and into nature for hands-on learning experiences. The group also publishes a newsletter that includes travel opportunities, suggested readings on responsible tourism, and updates about the travel industry.

The Alaska Wilderness Recreation & Tourism Association (AWRTA) is a statewide model of how local business and industry, conservation, and communities — including Native communities — come together to improve the tourism industry. AWRTA, a nonprofit trade organization, promotes the recognition and protection of Alaska's recreation and tourism resources and the businesses that rely on them. AWRTA's mission is to support the stewardship of the wild in Alaska and the development of healthy, diverse travel businesses and communities by linking business, community, and conservation interests. AWRTA promotes the recognition and protection of Alaska's recreation and tourism resources including scenic qualities, wildlife, fisheries, wilderness, wildlands, and rivers. AWRTA also developed an innovative funding mechanism for environmental and conservation groups. The *Dollars a Day for Conservation* program, aimed at tour operators arranging travel to Alaska, can help clients and the habitat and wildlife they enjoy by putting their money toward conservation efforts. The voluntary program asks tour operators to simply introduce the concept to their clients and "passing through" their donations. AWRTA consists of members from Native communities and therefore offers travelers to Alaska more realistic expectations and connections to Native cultures.

More Natural Experiences

The real argument for environmental protection through any form of tourism requires a departure from the global marketplace economy that exploits the natural world. Accomplishing this departure is almost impossible within the context of the global tourism industry, which gobbles up resources. We must expect to pay for the environments we visit. In the global North, we pay taxes to keep up our sewer systems, water, and even national parks. In many other countries, no such public support exists. If you plan to travel, factor the cost of the environment and public services into your trip. Better yet, set aside funds especially for this purpose and donate them to an environmental organization or community development project. But understand as well that Western solutions to saving the planet are not always compatible with those of the people who live in wilderness areas. For example, conservation — a Western concept — is an idea that land should be preserved in its natural state. Under conservation statutes, new parks, wildlife refuges, wilderness areas, and monuments have become protected lands. The designation of wilderness lands may actually impinge on Indigenous ways of life because limitations are placed on traditional and subsistence activities. Instead of developing new sites and new destinations, we should consider the pressing issues related to tourism that are already on our doorstep, investigate the "corridors" and peripheral areas of protected lands.

Local Action

Local people in destination communities are speaking out and taking action against exploitative tourism. Some paint murals on walls near tourist resorts to graphically illustrate their antitourism sentiments. Others have developed educational programs for residents and designed regional tourism strategies to protect their natural resources and limit the numbers of tourists and developers who enter their lands. Still others are setting up their own travel companies that promote responsible tourism through people-to-people links, some of which focus on human rights; they are developing tour programs that recruit scientists and volunteers to work directly with them to preserve their environments. Native people are taking over operations of parks — their ancestral homelands — and training others to do the same. While they share the use of these areas with tourists, their own communities are the first priority. They are establishing local currencies that keep dollars within the communities. Some are working with universities and local governments to come up with new policies on land planning and use in their regions. Some programs are even assessing the reasons that record numbers of stressed tourists are escaping from urban environments. Many programs examine the impacts of tourism upon their environments, teach tourists about the impact of their mere presence, and invite them to take action to help offset the damage. Projects have even been created for individuals or organizations in the United States and Europe to help purchase land in the global South to set aside as protected areas for wildlife and for local people.

Indigenous Peoples are resisting tourism with increasing strength. The Masai in Africa, the Mayans in Chiapas, the Quechuas in the Amazon, many Native people in the United States, and many others are resisting irrational development of their lands in the name of ecotourism. These groups have organized opposition both from within their own countries and in the international community, and their voices are being heard. Responsible tourism groups, environmentalists, and others have responded by providing support and publicizing injustices. Concerned citizens rallied in 1996 to oppose the construction of a sprawling resort in the heart of India's Nagarhole National Park, one of the world's biological "hot spots" and home to Indigenous Peoples. The opponents denounced the development, organized locally with tribal people, and called upon responsible tourism organizations around the world to help publicize their plight. In 1997 the Indian courts ruled against the resort, at least for the time being. Unfortunately the hotel continues to press for development, and the community members live in a precarious situation.

Rural communities are organizing to address conflicts caused by tourism. Chris Beck, a member of AWRTA, explains one such project in Alaska.

The Talkeetna Community
Chris Beck

Since 1998, visits to the small, end-of-the-road town of Talkeetna increased dramatically. Talkeetna traditionally has been a destination for modest numbers of climbers, anglers, and independent sightseers. These travelers come for spectacular views of the Alaska Range, proximity to Denali National Park and Preserve, and the town's historic and colorful character. In recent years, the opening of two new hotels led to a rapid increase in package tourist visits. Annual visitation is up at least threefold, from about 30,000 to 120,000 annual visitors.

Many townspeople are feeling overwhelmed by the sudden rush of tourism. In a town of fewer than seven hundred residents, as many as a thousand visitors per day has led to congestion, parking problems, and new commercial development. Perhaps most important, many people have the sense that they're losing the things they most like about their town—a sense of contact with history, the natural world, and their neighbors.

To respond to these changes, the town is currently in the middle of an ambitious tourism planning project. One goal of the project is to address the immediate side effects of rapid tourism growth—for example, finding ways to reduce congestion by parking motorcoaches and RVs on the edge of town, rather than having them drive through the middle of the community. Another goal of the project is to establish, for the first time, land use controls so future development is compatible with the town's funky/rustic/historic character. Finally, the project is working to build better lines of communication and improved decision-making capacity, both within the community and between the community and "outside" interests such as major cruise lines.

While not yet complete, the project has already helped find common ground among the often divergent views in the community, and give residents hope that they can both accommodate growth and hold onto the qualities that make Talkeetna a unique community.

Creating links within communities is essential. Foreign-owned or foreign-operated tourism companies could help support local agriculture and more sustainable practices by buying local goods and services such as food and transportation. They could recognize the harm in building cluster sites and make sure broad planning in the area included agricultural lands and other lands used by locals.

The Media

Most travel advertising of destination communities is created in the global North or by private industry and government tourist offices in the global South. This medium dominates the planet and promises paradise while other sectors of the media discuss how backward, poor, and degraded these same locations are. Any argument to rethink tourism must see through this corporate vision and its methods of propaganda. While responsible tourism organizations and tourism scholars have provided the best critiques of global tourism, the mainstream media are taking notice, especially with the growing concern about threats to national parks and protected areas. More travel writers, newspapers, and magazines are responding to the alerts about negative tourism activities and providing more realistic accounts of the life of locals, the dismal conditions that tourism has helped create, and the antitourism campaigns launched by grassroots groups everywhere.

Clay Hubbs, an educator, started the alternative travel magazine *Transitions Abroad* in the mid-1970s to provide information on economical, purposeful international travel opportunities — travel that involves learning by living, studying, working, or vacationing alongside the people of the host country. Hubbs describes his magazine's mission:

A lot of tourists have a consumer attitude — what can I get, instead of what can I learn. We have to put aside our own cultural biases and learn as much as possible from the people we visit. I find that if you stay long enough, learn the language, you get a sense of who locals are as "people." Through the magazine we are providing people-to-people links and small-scale programs, and with the numbers of people traveling "independently" mushrooming, it is obvious that people benefit and the travel industry does not.

Indigenous brochures describe cultural taboos and warn tourists from certain areas. Internet services speak to broad issues that affect both travelers and people in local destinations. Ron Mader, who coordinates the Internet service Planeta.com, told me, "It seemed to me that there were all of these groups not talking to each other about 'ecotourism.' I set up Planeta to run both positive and critical articles on ecotourism in the Americas and to hear from many people throughout the hemisphere. Many have been excluded from the governmental arena or the larger circles of powerhouse NGOs."

New and interesting media tools for tourists abound. One is *On This Spot: An Unconventional Map and Guide to Lhasa,* published by the International Campaign for Tibet. It provides uncensored stories behind Lhasa's tourist sites and commemorates dozens of places and events that the Chinese government is trying to hide from tourists and the international community. The map explains the contemporary political situation and gives the exact locations where Tibetan prisoners of conscience are held today. Linking travelers with Tibetan support organizations around the world, this map is a great example of a rethinking-tourism tool.

The Green Tourism Association, based in Toronto, is the first such organization to offer a written green tourist guide for a particular city and a companion green map to show people all the best ways to experience a rich and sustainable urban existence. *The OTHER Guide to Toronto: Opening the Door to Green Tourism* and the accompanying *The OTHER Map of Toronto* provide resources that link tourism to the environment and celebrate the green city.

What can you do to encourage the media and marketers to present a more realistic image of tourism and its effects? Don't buy travel magazines that are simply advertisements for corporations and reject the "awards" they give themselves. Support the alternative press that does not depend upon corporate funds and offers critical analysis of travel. Educate your local news media. As a tourist, researcher, or activist, you can write about your tourism experiences. Always make sure to include resource information to link people, and illustrate how the issues you learned about on your travels are related to you and your community. For example, a traveler to the Amazon wrote about irresponsible, exploitative oil and gas development and linked her story to increased consumer demand for petroleum in the United States.

Human Rights

On several occasions the United States has sought to use tourism as a political weapon. As Linda Richter, a tourism scholar who has researched politics and tourism in Asia, wrote: "The United States demonstrated opposition to the regimes of the People's Republic of China and Cuba by forbidding travel to those countries for many years. Now it is symptomatic of the desired change in political relationships that the United States has lifted the travel ban on the People's Republic of China (and) allowed some travel to Cuba."[4] By opening the doors of free trade, countries are "rewarded" with an expanding force of superconsumers, the tourists. They are also "rewarded" with expanding infrastructures, technologies, imports and exports, Western homogenization, and all the other tools of capitalism, consumerism, and globalization.

Despite the "rewards," some countries continue to oppress people. Individual tourists, as opposed to tour groups, have played a role in documenting some of the abuses simply by being part of the community. According to tourism analyst Ronald Schwartz, following demonstrations in Tibet in 1987, tourists who witnessed the events "became the principal source of information to journalists denied access to Tibet and gathered material on arrests, torture, and imprisonment for human rights organizations. A loosely knit network that arose in the first few days following the demonstrations continued to function for more than two years, recruiting new volunteers [tourists] to take the place of those who left."[5] They also provided medical treatment to wounded Tibetans who were afraid to go to government hospitals. Yet Schwartz emphasizes that this special group of independent travelers might have been concerned about human rights in Tibet in the first place. Such "engaged" tourists have not simply stepped out of their own societies, leaving behind obligations and seeking relaxation and luxury: "The ease with which travelers from different nationalities, a group of strangers, were able to create a clandestine organization and pool their skills . . . is remarkable. But their ready agreement on goals and tactics suggests a common culture of shared perceptions and values."[6] Engaged tourists share skills and values that belong to a larger social world.

Monitoring Corporations

Some corporations are taking steps to become more responsible, but only after facing tremendous pressure from the public. The public is needed to monitor and challenge corporations at every level. Community resistance to tourism corporations has been mostly unsuccessful. Nevertheless, resistance is increasing, and workers in the tourism industry are also organizing to resist. Any argument to rethink tourism calls for investigation of the power of international tourism corporations in order to move large corporations out of the local planning process and reduce their local political influence and control. In the United States, disclosure laws mean that information about global tourism corporations is fairly easy to obtain. The U.S. Securities and Exchange Commission requires corporations to file quarterly and annual reports. Any environmental liabilities — significant remediation or cleanup — must be reported. Investigating overseas corporations is much more difficult. The best way is to locate and work with a grassroots group in the destination country. Friends of the Earth publishes the booklet *How to Research Corporations*. Other groups like the Multinational Monitor and Transnational Resource Action Center (TRAC) can also assist in investigating corporate actions and responsibility, and may help publish your own investigative work.

Travelers can learn more about corporate responsibility, oppressive governments, and actions against human rights abusers from the numerous publications that monitor human rights, corporations, the environment, and government actions. *Boycotts in Action* (BAN) provides information about boycotts of corporations, countries, and organizations, including tourism and travel-related corporations. A dedicated hiker told me, "People underestimate the power they wield. I became an environmental activist to save the places I love. It makes me angry to see politicians 'selling' wilderness areas, designing bills with loopholes allowing for construction of roads, power lines, and pipelines. I write about my experiences to encourage others to get involved. There is no doubt it is effective. Public pressure is the only way to make sure politicians don't sell out to private interests."

Tourism Revisited

In rethinking tourism, we must analyze the role we tourists play in promoting current destructive practices. With pressure, the industry can be reshaped so that profits from tourism are distributed more equitably. We must reduce consumption and respect natural limits rather than merely think "green." Technology is not neutral but interacts with society and nature. An essential step is replacing environmentally and socially obsolete high technology with more appropriate, less-consuming, and traditional technologies.

This task is enormous. The developed world is in a state of denial about such severe problems and voluntary change is unlikely. The developed world will have to be forced to change by community groups in the global South and by cross-border organizations everywhere. A more generous spirit and greater volunteerism with respect to tourism issues goes hand in hand with a condemnation of the elitist, materialistic view that tourists are entitled to purchase other environments and cultures. Travelers must be willing to be on equal footing with locals, to try to understand cultures widely disparate from their own, and to contribute to the community (perhaps through manual labor or professional expertise).

People in the North who reject the advance of commercialized global culture and those from the South who are victimized by it vociferously oppose the continued devastation of the environment and Indigenous populations. We need to take a hard look at the travel industry, at the self-exploitation of communities, and the roles we play as individuals. This inner journey of reevaluation won't be easy, but it is essential.

Some say we are too late. At a conference to rethink current economic directions, a former executive of one of the largest travel companies in the world was asked if he could see an alternative future.

Deborah McLaren, Ladakh, India

In an alternative tourism program, American and Ladakhi youth participate in a cultural exchange to examine development processes and common issues that affect them all.

He replied, "There is no way to stop economic globalization because tourism and travel have already created globalization." Yet because of global grassroots movements for change, developing a deeper understanding of the course we're on and the role of global tourism may be possible. Alternative strategies and movements are available, as are alternatives to tourism.

Tourism has become politicized within global institutions, nations, communities, industry, the environment, and within almost all of us, whether we are tourists or persons affected by tourism in our own community. The field begs for more research, monitoring, linking, policymaking, and change. Meanwhile, despite the slowdown caused by the September 11, 2001, terrorist attacks, global tourism is growing at a phenomenal rate — particularly in areas deemed "safe," such as the Arctic. An urgent need exists to rethink tourism and ecotravel and to stop paving paradise.

Almost twenty years has passed since my trip to Jamaica. My continual journey through "tourism" over those years has been one of learning — sometimes frustrating, always challenging, often delightful, and in many ways transformative. When I think back to the day when I rode horseback among the shantytowns and hills near Montego Bay with Joseph, one thing seems clear to me: in many ways we were both searching for dignity and an opportunity for self-realization. Throughout the world, among different cultures and classes, people are looking for self-determination. The world we are now born into and the society we know measures humans in terms of their economic worth. Human potential is enormous and largely unrealized. Western-style capitalism and consumerism have undermined the possibility for people to make their own choices about their lives and to have opportunities for their futures. Tourism continues to play a tremendous role in spreading the corporate empire. However, this industry is different from many others. One of its primary functions is to develop human relationships, which I see as a chance to rethink and change our future. *That* would be paradise.

Notes

Chapter 1: An Overview of Tourism

1. "Tourism Works for America" (Washington, D.C.: U.S. Dept. of Commerce, 2001).

2. "The Globalization of Tourism," *UNESCO Courier*, July/August 1999, www.unesco.org/courier/1999_08/uk/dossier/txt13.htm.

3. This figure is compiled from the World Tourism Organization and The World Travel & Tourism Council. It is commonly used in tourism studies.

4. François Vellas and Lionel Bechard, *International Tourism: An Economic Perspective* (New York: St. Martin's Press, 1995). These figures are compiled from various data in the book.

5. Ibid., 268.

6. IFC/World Bank, *IFC Tourism Sector Review* (Washington, D.C.: International Finance Corporation and the World Bank, 1995), 1.

7. Maggie Black, *In the Twilight Zone: Child Workers in the Hotel, Tourism and Catering Industry* (Geneva: International Labor Organization, 1995), 9.

8. Martin Khor, "Global Economy and the Third World," in *The Case against the Global Economy*, ed. Jerry Mander and Edward Goldsmith (San Francisco: Sierra Club Books, 1996), 47–48.

9. Quoted from "The Trouble with Trade," in *ISEC/Ladakh Project Newsletter* 12 (Bristol, U.K., and Berkeley, Calif.): 1, 6.

10. IFC/World Bank, *IFC Tourism Sector Review*, 4.

11. David Korten, *When Corporations Rule the World* (West Hartford, Conn.: Kumarian Press, 1996), 54.

12. Alexander Goldsmith, "Seeds of Exploitation: Free Trade Zones in the Global Economy," in *The Case against the Global Economy*, 267.

13. United Nations Economic and Social Council, "*Resolution 1998/40 — Declaring the Year 2002 as the International Year of Ecotourism*," 46th plenary meeting, July 30, 1998.

14. *Declaration of the International Forum on Indigenous Tourism*, International Forum on Indigenous Tourism, Oaxaca, Mexico, March 2002 (copies available from Indigenous Tourism Rights International, St. Paul, Minn.).

15. USTTA, *World Tourism at the Millennium: An Agenda for Industry, Government and Education* (Washington, D.C.: U.S. Department of Commerce, U.S. Travel and Tourism Administration, 1993), 36.

16. Ibid., 34.

17. Bernice Powell, telephone interview with the author, February 1997.

18. Helena Norberg-Hodge, *Ancient Futures: Learning from Ladakh* (San Francisco: Sierra Club Books, 1991), 3.

155

19. Richard Barnet and John Cavanagh, "Homogenization of Global Culture," in *The Case against the Global Economy*, 73.

20. Paul Gonsalves, speech at the UNESCO-sponsored conference "Sustainable Tourism Development in World Heritage Sites — Planning for Hue, Vietnam," May 1996. Available from the Ecumenical Coalition on Third World Tourism (ECTWT) or EQUATIONS (see p. 167 below).

21. Jules Siegel, "Holding On to the Dream in Cancún," *London Observer/Guardian Foreign News Service*, January 17, 2000, *www.mexconnect.com/mex_/travel/jsiegel/jscancundream.html*.

Chapter 2: The Promises of Tourism

1. Marshall McLuhan, *Understanding Media: The Extensions of Man* (New York: McGraw-Hill, 1964), from the CD-ROM series by Paul Benedetti and Nancy DeHart, *On McLuhan: Forward through the Rearview Mirror* (Cambridge, Mass.: MIT Press, 1996).

2. Pratap Rughani, "From This Month's Editor," *New Internationalist* 245 (1993): 1.

3. For back issues on tourism, contact *Cultural Survival Quarterly*, 46 Brattle Street, Cambridge, MA 02138.

4. See Shelley Attix, *U.S. Based New Age Spiritual Tour Operators* (Albuquerque: University of New Mexico, 1996). Attix, a Ph.D. candidate, undertook the survey, which includes new-age tour operators in the United States offering shamanistic experiences, spiritual experiences, vision quests, and trips to sacred sites. Attix claims that while the tour operators can offer a basic spiritual or cultural orientation, "they can never claim to offer an authentic spiritual 'experience'; it would be false advertising." Attix points to a "considerable lack of awareness among the tour groups surveyed as to the protocols followed by local Indigenous Peoples when visiting their traditional sacred sites. Many of the companies have no local contacts in the communities they visit, or relationships with Indigenous elders" and therefore do not understand the protocols or preparations, what Attix refers to as "basic spiritual manners" required to visit important cultural and religious sites. "Many of these places are used daily by local people and are not simply historical sites with no contemporary value; they are not places that should be available for the wealthy consumer who can afford to displace locals for a chance to take photos." Yet thousands of individuals seeking spiritual journeys are not only nudging the locals out but are perpetuating cultural taboos in the process.

5. Deborah McLaren, "Earthwise Travel: Socially and Ecologically Responsible Tourism — A Global Analysis," M.A. thesis, Institute for Social Ecology, Goddard College, 1991.

6. Katrina Brandon, *Ecotourism and Conservation: A Review of Key Issues* (Washington, D.C.: World Bank, 1996), 11.

7. Polly Pattullo, *Last Resorts: The Cost of Tourism in the Caribbean* (London: Cassell, 1996), 39.

8. M. Cleverdon and C. Edwards, "Tourism Strategies for Transnationals in Belize," in *Annals of Tourism Research* (Elmsford, N.Y.: Pergamon Press, 1982), 528–29.

9. Elizabeth Boo, *Ecotourism: The Potentials and Pitfalls* (Washington, D.C.: World Wildlife Fund, 1989), 12.

10. David Helvarg, "Perception Is Reality: Greenwashing Puts the Best Public Face on Corporate Irresponsibility," in *E: The Environmental Magazine* (November/December 1996): 40.

11. Susan Newell, "Holiday Inn: China's Profiteering Partner," *Tibet News* (London) (Spring 1996): 20.

12. Ibid.

13. Free Tibet Campaign, "Holiday Inn Pulls Out of Tibet," Press Release August 1, 1997.

14. Charles Kernaghan, *Setting the Record Straight/The Real Disney in Burma, Haiti, Indonesia, China* (Disney Memo: Separating Fact from Fiction), National Labor Committee, New York, January 17, 1997, 9–10. The memo cited a December 17, 1996, *NBC Dateline* report, "Toy Story," by Stone Phillips. Transcripts are available from Burrell's Transcripts, PO Box 7, Livingston, NJ 07039-0007.

15. USAID, *Ecotourism: A Viable Alternative for Sustainable Management of Natural Resources in Africa*, report prepared by International Resources Group for the U.S. Agency for International Development, Bureau of Africa, 1992, 34.

16. Linda K. Richter, *The Politics of Tourism in Asia* (Honolulu: University of Hawaii Press, 1989), 4–5.

17. Geoffrey Wall, "Planning the Rate of Social Change: Bali, Indonesia," paper presented at the Tourism and Socio-Cultural Change Conference, Trinidad and Tobago, 1990, 56.

18. Jerry Mander, *In the Absence of the Sacred: The Failure of Technology and the Survival of Indian Nations* (San Francisco: Sierra Club Books, 1991), 158.

19. Jamaica Kincaid, *A Small Place* (New York: Penguin Books, 1988), 10.

20. Hawaii Ecumenical Coalition on Tourism, *Responsible Tourism: A Hawaiian Point of View* (Kapa'a: Hawaii Ecumenical Coalition on Tourism, 1996).

21. Rughani, "From This Month's Editor," 1.

Chapter 3: Guests and Hosts

1. Helena Norberg-Hodge, "The Pressure to Modernize," in Edward Goldsmith, Martin Khor, Helena Norberg-Hodge, and Vandana Shiva, *The Future of Progress: Reflections on Environment and Development* (Berkeley: International Society for Ecology and Culture, 1992), 81–101.

2. David T. Schaller, "Indigenous Ecotourism: Rio Blanco, Ecuador," M.A. paper, University of Minnesota, 1996.

3. James T. Yenckel in the *Washington Post*, January 28, 1996, E11.

4. bell hooks, "Eating the Other," in *Black Looks: Race and Representation* (Boston: South End Press, 1992), 25.

5. Ibid.

6. Ibid., 28.

7. Nancy Keates, "Tourists Take 'Human Safaris' in Pacific," *Wall Street Journal*, December 20, 1996, B-12.

8. Ibid.

9. John Lennon and Malcolm Foley, *Dark Tourism — The Attraction of Death and Disaster* (London and New York: Continuum International), 2000.

10. Haunani Kay Trask, *From a Native Daughter* (Monroe, Maine: Common Courage Press, 1990), 11.

11. Ibid.

12. These figures are from the 1996 *Visitation* statistics available from the Rapid City Convention and Visitors Bureau, Rapid City, S.D., 29.

13. Dean MacCannell, *The Tourist: A New Theory of the Leisure Class* (New York: Shocken Books, 1989), 6.

14. Trask, *Native Daughter*, 11–12.

15. Quoted from the standard information letter sent in response to tourists' inquiries from the Hopi Tribal Office, Kykotsmovi, Ariz., 1996.

16. World Travel and Tourism Council, *www.WTTC.org*.

17. *www.salmonarmedc.com*.

18. "Travelers Should Boycott Burma," May 9, 2001, *TIMEasia.com*.

19. *2000: Burma and Lonely Planet*, from the Tourism Concern (London) website *www.tourismconcern.org.uk/campaigns/campaigns_burma.htm*, July 2002.

20. *Trekking Wrongs, Porters Rights*, Tourism Concern's porter page online at *www.tourismconcern.org.uk/pdfs/porters.pdf*.

21. Daniel Hiernaux Nicholas and Manual Rodriguez Woog, *Tourism and Absorption of the Labor Force in Mexico* (Washington, D.C.: Commission for the Study of International Migration and Cooperative Economic Development, 1990), 16.

22. Christopher de Bellaigue, "Packaged Confusion," *India Today* (New Delhi), February 28, 1995, 187.

23. Nina Rao, interview via email, July 2002.

24. de Bellaigue, "Packaged Confusion," 189.

25. Ibid.

26. Ibid.

27. Rebecca Cunningham, "Peru: Tourists Flock to Cuzco," *Responsible Traveling* 14, no. 1: 3.

28. Jim Molnar, "In an Era of Mass Travel, Tourism Becomes the New Colonial Power," *Seattle Times*, September 10, 1989, J-12.

Chapter 4: Tourism Development in the Local Community

1. "Ethnic Villages Overrun and Commercialized," *New Frontiers* 8, no. 3 (May–June 2002), edited from an article by Agence-France Presse (AFP) correspondent Michael Mathes (*The Nation* 23, no. 5 [2002]).

2. Helena Norberg-Hodge, *Ancient Futures: Learning from Ladakh* (San Francisco: Sierra Club Books, 1991), 94–95. The pressure to modernize, argues Norberg-Hodge, stems from the psychological pressure that consumerism and conventional development have focused on unprepared cultures. The luxurious images of consumerism are enforced through media and tourism and create artificial "needs" previously unknown in self-sufficient traditional cultures. These "needs" contribute to insecurity and loss of self-esteem and create an artificial scarcity that puts people who were traditionally close-knit in competition with

each other and pressures them to conform to Western models they cannot emulate. Norberg-Hodge presents this concept more fully in the essay "The Pressure to Modernize," in Edward Goldsmith, Martin Khor, Helena Norberg-Hodge, and Vandana Shiva, *The Future of Progress: Reflections on Environment and Development* (Berkeley, Calif.: International Society for Ecology and Culture, 1992), 81–100.

3. Quoted from "The Facts," a compilation of tourist arrivals from the World Tourism Organization, *New Internationalist* 245 (1993): 19.

4. Ibid.

5. Ibid., 13.

6. M. Kelly, "West Beach Is Only the Beginning for Wai'Anae," *Contours* (Bangkok) 3, no. 7 (1997): 17.

7. Ibid.

8. Jean Keefe, "Whose Home Is It Anyway?" *In Focus* (Spring 1995): 5.

9. Chee Yoke Ling, "A Rough Deal: Golf Displaces People," *In Focus* (Spring 1995): 12.

10. Ibid., 13.

11. Ibid.

12. *Cruise Industry Information* from the website of American Association of Port Authorities, Alexandria, VA. *www.aapa-ports.org*, July 2002.

13. Quoted from *Responsible Cruising: Background Information.* Brochure available from the Center for Seafarers' Rights, New York, and the Center for Responsible Tourism, San Anselmo, Calif.

14. Ibid.

15. Valene L. Smith, ed., *Hosts and Guests: The Anthropology of Tourism,* 2d ed. (Philadelphia: University of Pennsylvania Press, 1989), 8.

16. Norberg-Hodge, *Ancient Futures,* 109.

17. Norberg-Hodge, "The Pressure to Modernize," 81.

18. Wiert Wiertsema, "Paths to Sustainability," in *The Future of Progress,* 167.

19. Matthew Rothschild, "Multinational Corporations: Affecting Lives on a Global Scale," in *Native Resource Control and the Multinational Corporate Challenge: Aboriginal Rights in International Perspective* (Cambridge, Mass.: Cultural Survival, Anthropology Resource Center, 1982), 8.

20. Linda K. Richter, "Indonesian Tourism: The Good, the Bad and the Ugly," *Contours* (ECTWT: Bangkok) 14, no. 1 (1993): 29–30.

21. "Target Industries: Tourism" (Anchorage: Anchorage Economic and Development Corp., July 2002), *www.aedcweb.com/content/subpages/target_tourism.*

22. Vine Deloria Jr. and Clifford M. Lytle, *American Indians, American Justice* (Austin: University of Texas Press, 1983), 7.

23. Kaleo Patterson, "Aloha! Welcome to Paradise," *New Internationalist* 245 (1993): 15.

24. Yareth Rosen, "Last Frontier Image Pulls Growing Crowd of Tourists to Alaska," *Christian Science Monitor,* August 19, 1991, 9.

25. Contributed by Chris Beck; see contributors section.

26. Abrium G. Escárzaga, Monica E. Parise, and Jacquelin M. Roberts, "Provisional Data Report on Malaria Surveillance and Use of Antimalarial Chemoprophylaxis August–December 2000" (Atlanta: Centers for Disease Control and

Prevention, 2001), at *www.cdc.gov/ncidod/dpd/parasites/malaria/chemoprophylaxis/index.htm.*

27. Ritchie Witzig, "New and Old Disease Threats in the Peruvian Amazon: The Case of the Urarina," *Abya Yala News: Journal of the South and Meso American Indian Rights Center* (Summer 1996): 6–7.

28. Ibid., 7, 9.

29. Ibid., 7.

30. Ibid.

31. Ibid., 46.

32. Quoted from "Boy Prostitution in Sri Lanka," *Prostitution Tourism Development Documentation* (report includes news clips and other information and is available from ECTWT, Bangkok, n.d.), 31.

33. Sue Wheat, "Tourism: An Unwanted Guest?" *Tibet News* (London) 20 (1996): 5.

34. D. H. Donnelly, *Where Have All the Children Gone?* reported in an alert from Broken Bud, Berkeley, Calif., 1996, 1.

35. Kund Daeng, "Alternative Tourism," *Alternative Tour Thailand* 2 (1990): 3.

36. Chatrudee Theparat, "Resort Islands Growing Thirsty," *Bangkok Post* (Bangkok), May 10, 2002.

37. David Dudenhoefer, "Ecotourism Boom Forces Nation to Seek New Alternatives," 1991–1992 *Guide to Costa Rica* (San José: Tico Times, 1991), 9.

38. James Stark, "Hawaii: Tourism Action Network," *Contours* (ECTWT: Bangkok) 4, no. 4: 20.

Chapter 5: Rethinking Ecotravel

1. See the International Ecotourism Society at *www.ecotourism.org.*

2. Ten Principles for Arctic Tourism, WWF International Arctic Programme, Oslo, Norway, 2001.

3. Hal Kane, "Air Travel Growth Resumes," *Vital Signs 1993: The Trends That Are Shaping Our Future* (New York: W. W. Norton and World Watch Institute, 1993), 90.

4. Ibid., 36.

5. Ibid.

6. World Wildlife Fund International, "Tourism and Climate Change," June 2001, online at *www.wwf.org.uk/filelibrary/pdf/tourism_and_climate_change.pdf.*

7. Ibid., 2.

8. Ibid., 2–3.

9. Ole Kamuaro, "Ecotourism: Suicide or Development," United Nations Non-Governmental Liaison Service, *Voices from Africa* website, no. 6: Sustainable Development Part 2, Geneva, 2002. *www.unsystem.org/ngls/documents/publications.en/voices.africa/number6/vfa6.12.htm.*

10. Luis Vivanco in an interview with Cynthia Harrison, Tourism Rights, July 9, 2002.

11. Paul Eagles, "International Trends in Park Tourism," prepared for *Europarc 2001*, September 17, 2001, 6.

12. Jim Motavalli, "Conversations: Paul and Anne Erlich," in *E: The Environmental Magazine* (November–December 1996): 10.

13. ACERCA, "New Corporate Development from Southeastern Mexico to Panama: Plan Puebla Panama," Briefing paper, Winter 2001: 1–3.

14. Gregoria Flores, interview with Cynthia Harrison, Tourism Rights, July 2002.

15. M. Wells and K. Brandon, *People and Parks: Linking Protected Area Management with Local Communities* (Washington, D.C.: World Bank, 1992), cited in Katrina Brandon, *Ecotourism and Conservation: A Review of Key Issues* (Washington, D.C.: World Bank, 1996), 11.

16. Brandon, *Ecotourism*, 11.

17. International Forum on Indigenous Tourism, *Declaration of the International Forum on Indigenous Tourism*, Oaxaca, Mexico, March 2002, 4 (copies available from Indigenous Tourism Rights International, St. Paul, Minn.).

18. John Vandermeer and Ivette Perfecto, *Breakfast of Biodiversity: The Truth About Rain Forest Destruction* (Oakland, Calif.: Food First and Institute for Food and Development Policy, 1995), 110.

19. Statistic obtained from Maureen Oltrogge, public affairs officer at the Grand Canyon National Park; interview with Cynthia Harrison, Tourism Rights, July 2002.

20. Julie Galton Gale, interview with the author, January 1997. Statistic of nine hundred thousand commercial aircraft is an update obtained from Maureen Oltrogge.

21. Luciano Minerbi, "A Framework for Alternative and Responsible Tourism: Eco-cultural Tourism," paper presented at the Hawaii State Conference on Ecotourism, Honolulu, September 26, 1994.

22. Biodiversity Conservation Network, "Ecotourism in the Rain Forest of Western Java," in *Biodiversity Conservation Network* (BCN) *1996 Annual Report* (Washington, D.C.: Biodiversity Conservation Network and World Wildlife Fund, 1997), 18. BCN is a consortium of the World Wildlife Fund, the Nature Conservancy, and World Resources Institute and is funded by USAID and the United States–Asia Environmental Partnership.

23. WWF International Arctic Programme, *www.ngo.grida.no/wwfap.*

24. Marcel Jansen, Jan W. Te Kloeze, and Han van der Voet, *Wakacje Na Wsi: Agritourism in Southwest Poland* (Wageningen, Netherlands: Center for Recreation and Tourism Studies, Agricultural University, 1996).

25. Zac Goldsmith, "Eco-tourism: Old Wine — New Bottle?" paper presented at the Oko Himal Sustainable Tourism Conference, Kathmandu, Nepal, December 1996. Available from International Society for Ecology and Culture, Bristol, United Kingdom.

Chapter 6: Ecotravel Issues for a New Century

1. Panel presentation by Eugenio Yunis, Head, Sustainable Development of Tourism, World Tourism Organization, IATOS World Conference, Chicago, February 21, 2002; World Tourism Organization, *Voluntary Initiatives for Sustainable Tourism* (Madrid: World Tourism Organization, 2002).

2. Gary Gereffi, Ronie Garcia-Johnson, and Erika Sasser, "The NGO-Industrial Complex," *Foreign Affairs* (July–August 2001): 64–65.

3. Martha Honey and Abigail Rome, *Protecting Paradise: Certification Programs for Sustainable Tourism and Ecotourism* (Washington, D.C.: Institute for Policy Studies, October 2001).

4. See the website *www.sustainable-tourism.co.cr.*

5. See the website *www.ecotourism.org.au/About_NEAP.htm.*

6. Abigail Rome and Martha Honey, "Summary Minutes: Ecotourism and Sustainable Tourism Certification Workshop," November 17–19, 2000, Mohonk Mountain House, New Paltz, New York (Washington, D.C.: Institute for Policy Studies, December 29, 2000); Honey and Rome, *Protecting Paradise.* Available on website *www.ips-dc.org.*

7. See the websites at *www.world-tourism.org/sustainable/IYE-Main-Menu.htm* and *www.uneptie.org/pc/tourism/ecotourism/iye.htm.*

8. See the website *www.rainforest-alliance.org/programs/sv/stsc.html.*

9. USAID, *Ecotourism: A Viable Alternative for Sustainable Management of Natural Resources in Africa* (Washington, D.C.: International Resources Group and the U.S. Agency for International Development, Bureau for Africa, 1992), 40.

10. Ibid., 44.

11. Ibid.

12. Quoted from *New Frontiers* (Bangkok, March 1997): 1.

13. From a CD-ROM "A Portfolio of Statements and Presentations," United Nations, *The International Year of Ecotourism (IYE): United Nations Mandates and Objectives*, official document of the UN World Ecotourism Summit (Quebec, Canada, May 2002).

14. Ibid.

15. IFIT, *Declaration of the International Forum on Indigenous Tourism*, 3–4.

16. Brenda Rudkin and C. Michael Hall, "Unable to See the Forest for the Trees: Ecotourism Development in the Solomon Islands," in Richard Butler and Thomas Hinch, eds., *Tourism and Indigenous Peoples* (London: International Thomson Business Press, 1996), 203–26.

17. Jeffrey S. Marshall, "Papagayo Project Is Not Ecotourism," *Contours* (Bangkok) 7, no. 8: 25.

18. WWF-Fundación Natura, "Tourist Use of the Galapagos National Park and the Carrying Capacity of Tourist Sites," *Galapagos Report*, 1997–98.

19. Paola Oviedo, "The Galapagos Islands: Conflict Management in Conservation and Sustainable Resource Management," in *Cultivating Peace: Conflict and Collaboration in Natural Resource Management*, ed. Daniel Buckles (Ottawa: IDRC; Washington, D.C.: World Bank, 1999).

20. Ibid., chap. 8.

21. Ibid.

22. Martin Wikelski et al., "Marine Iguanas Die from Trace Oil Pollution," *Nature* 417 (2002): 607–8.

23. Letter to Deborah McLaren from Christophe Grenier, February 12, 1996, and subsequent discussions.

24. Craig MacFarland: *An Analysis of Nature Tourism in the Galápagos Islands*, 1998. *www.darwinfoundation.org/articles/br15049801.html.*

25. "Golf Courses Threaten Food Security," *Nation*, November 14, 1996. As in the case of Costa Rica, many new ecoprojects now include golf courses, though

few environmentalists would promote golf courses as a sustainable tourism option, because they put pollution, herbicides, pesticides, and contaminated water into the natural environment; take up huge amounts of land that is often needed for agriculture; and displace farmers and traditional communities. But in the 1990s hundreds of golf courses were built throughout Asia and the Pacific. At the United Nations–sponsored World Food Summit in 1996, it was pointed out that golf had in effect taken food out of people's mouths. "If tens of thousands of hectares wasted on golf course construction had been planted in grain, it would have supported hundreds of thousands of people. . . . Building golf courses has led to the destruction of forests and farmland and also drained much-needed water from agricultural use in the area. . . . [One expert said,] 'Tourist earnings may be important but golf courses are catering to an upper elite and contribute little to the welfare of the 1.2 billion people in the world believed to be surviving on less than US$1 a day.'"

26. This number of Indigenous People is in sharp contrast to the 8 million reported at the end of the 1980s by Guillermo Bonfil Batalla (1989) or the 6 million reported in the national census of the year 2000. Bonfil argued that Mexico would not be able to overcome many of the principal obstacles to development until it comes to terms with its Indigenous past rather than trying to eradicate remaining vestiges.

27. The support of the Zapatista struggle by Mexico's Indigenous groups is crucial to understanding the increasing success of local communities in designing and implementing their own alternatives to global integration, firmly anchored in their demand for greater local autonomy — a capacity for self-management and a recognition of their unique identities. For a lengthy discussion of some of these issues, see N. Harvey, *The Chiapas Rebellion: The Struggle for Land and Democracy* (Durham, N.C.: Duke University Press, 1998), and W. Assies, G. van der Haar, and A. Hoekema, eds., *The Challenge of Diversity: Indigenous Peoples and Reform of the State in Latin America* (Amsterdam: Thelathesis, 1999).

28. Of course, as in other places, some groups are staunchly resisting this tendency, attempting to sharply restrict access to their territories and their communities to outside visitors.

29. Balam s.c. Asesoría y Capacitación, Ciudad de Mexico, Mexico. *www.planeta.com/ecotravel/mexico/balam/balam.html*. Email at *febobalam@laneta.apc.org* or at *jbalam1@prodigy.net.mx*, A Mexico-based consultancy focusing on community-based rural tourism development.

30. For a detailed analysis of the Monarch butterfly, see David Barkin's article, "The Economic Impact of Ecotourism: Conflicts and Solutions in Highland Mexico," in: P. Godde, M. F. Price, and F. M. Zimmerman, eds., *Tourism and Development in Mountain Regions* (London: Cab International, 1999), 157–72.

31. This phenomenon is examined at length in a collection of essays by K. Ghimire, ed., *The Native Tourist: Mass Tourism within Developing Countries* (London: Earthscan and UNRISD, 2001).

32. Cf. D. Barkin and C. Paillés, "NGO-Community Collaboration for Ecotourism: A Strategy for Sustainable Regional Development," *Current Issues in Tourism* 6, no. 3 (2002).

33. The extensive literature on the regulation of access to and use of common property raises many of these same issues in great detail. Local management, far

from being the "tragedy" envisaged by some, has proved to be quite effective in assuring satisfactory results when the rules are clear and widely accepted. In the case of the tourist development mentioned in the text, the group formulating the project was unable to obtain unqualified support from the larger community of which it is a part, in part because of opposition from local leaders who tried to take advantage of the situation for their own benefit. For an authoritative review of this very important issue for Indigenous resource management, including references to many case studies, see E. Ostrom, T. Dietz, N. Dolsak, P. Stern, S. Stonich, and E. Weber, *The Tragedy of the Commons* (Washington, D.C.: National Research Council, National Academy Press, 2002).

34. In 2000, this assistance was withdrawn at the insistence of the Mexican government, which decreed that the local NGO was not fulfilling its functions and was preventing the creation of the biosphere reserve. Following the Zapatista uprising, political conflicts intensified in this region. Cf. D. Barkin and M. A. Garcia, "La estructura social de la deforestación en México," In: *Los Incendio Forestales en México*, México: Consejo Nacional Forestal (1998): 41–55. An English version is available: *www.bionet-uc.org/uc-na_barkin.pdf*, and S. Salas Morales, L. Schibli, and E. Torres Bahena, *Chimalapas: La última oportunidad* (México: World Wildlife Fund and Secretary of the Environment and Natural Resources, 2001).

35. D. Barkin, *Wealth, Poverty and Sustainable Development* (Mexico: Editorial Jus, 1998).

36. See, for example, J. Mander and E. Goldsmith, eds., *The Case against the Global Economy and a Turn toward the Local* (San Francisco: Sierra Club Books, 2001).

Chapter 7: Rethinking Tourism

1. Quoted from "Third World Travel — Buy Critically," brochure adapted from a TEN publication and distributed by the Center for Responsible Tourism, Berkeley, Calif.

2. Quoted from website, Sacred Sites International Foundation, 1442A Walnut St. #330, Berkeley, CA 94709, 510-525-1304, *sacredsites@aol.com*, *www.sitesaver.org*.

3. Barbara Johnston, "Save Our Beach Dem and Our Land Too? The Problems of Tourism in 'America's Paradise,'" *Cultural Survival Quarterly* 14, no. 2 (1990): 31.

4. Linda K. Richter, *The Politics of Tourism in Asia* (Honolulu: University of Hawaii Press, 1989), 6.

5. Ronald David Schwartz, "Travelers Under Fire: Tourists in the Tibetan Uprising," *Annals of Tourism Research* (New York: Pergamon Press, 1991), 588.

6. Ibid., 589.

Resources

This chapter is divided into sections that list organizations directly or indirectly involved in rethinking tourism; the final few sections consist of a more or less traditional bibliography. Please note that many small, non-profit groups cannot respond to blanket requests for information, and they greatly appreciate contributions to cover the costs of processing requests. In addition, readers are encouraged to share information with the organizations. The author and publisher do not endorse the organizations listed throughout this directory. Readers are encouraged to investigate resources. Updates should be sent to the author, care of Indigenous Tourism Rights International, 366 Prior Avenue North, Suite 205, Saint Paul, MN 55104. Resources are listed under the following categories:

- Responsible Tourism Organizations
- Ecotourism Organizations
- General Environmental, Development, and Indigenous Resources
- Responsible Tour Operators and Programs
- Social and Environmental Justice Programs (Tours, Delegations, Volunteer Programs)
- Human Rights and Social Justice Organizations (information only)
- Short-Term Travel Study Programs
- Tourism-Specific College and University Programs
- U.S. Government Contacts
- International Organization Contacts
- Magazines, Newsletters, Journals, Surveys, and Travel Guides
- Audiovisuals
- Books
- Guides for Students
- Helpful Websites

Responsible Tourism Organizations

Action for Conservation through Tourism (ACT), CREATE Center, Smeaton Road, Bristol, BS1 6XN, UK; 0117-927-3049, Fax: 0117-930-0076, *act@gn.apc.org*. Supports local communities, NGOs, governments and tour operators in developing and marketing sustainable tourism projects.

African Indigenous Women Organization (AIWO), PO Box 74908, Nairobi, V6K 1X4, Kenya; 254-2-723-958, Fax: 254-2-729-607, *iin@swiftkenya.com*. African Indigenous women working on issues affecting their community, including tourism issues.

Alaska Wilderness Recreation and Tourism Association (AWRTA), 2207 Spenard Road, Suite 201, Anchorage, AK 99503, USA; 907-258-3171, Fax: 907-258-3851, *www.awrta.org*, *info@awrta.org*. Statewide association promotes the protection of Alaska's wild places, responsible tourism, and community tourism planning.

Arbeitskreis Tourismus und Entwicklung, Missionsstrasse 21, CH-4003, Basel, Switzerland; 41-61-2614-742, Fax: 41-61-261-4721, *www.akte.ch*, *info@akte.ch*. A Swiss NGO working on fair trade and responsible tourism.

Asian Women's Association, Sakuragaoka, Shibuyaku, Tokyo 155, Japan; 81-3-346-9752. Affiliated with the Japanese Men's Group Against Prostitution in Asia; anti-prostitution organization; promotes responsible tourism.

Asia-Pacific Peoples' Environment Network (APPEN), 27 Lorong Maktab, 10250 Penang, Malaysia; 60-422-76930, Fax: 60-4227-5705. A regional anti-golf-course and environmental network.

Asia Tourism Action Network (ANTENNA), 15 Soi Soonvijai 8, New Petch-buri Road, Bangkok, 10310, Thailand. Promotes locally controlled tourism; publishes a newsletter.

Bina Swadaya, Wisma Jana Karya, Jl Gunung Saharj 111/7, Jakarta Pusat 10610 (PO Box 1465, Jakarta 10014), Indonesia; 62-21-420-4402 or 62-21-425-5354, Fax: 62-21-420-8412, *bst@cbn.net.id*. Indonesian community-development NGO. Organize responsible tours.

Center for the Advancement of Responsible Travel (CART), 70 Dry Hill Park Road, Tonbridge, Kent TN10 3BX, UK. Center of information on responsible tourism in Europe.

Center for Responsible Tourism, 1765-D Le Roy Avenue, Berkeley, CA 94709, USA; *CRTourism@aol.com*. Works to end tourism that traffics in women, especially tourism that involves child prostitution and pornography.

Center for Seafarers' Rights, Seamen's Church Institute, 241 Water St., New York, NY 10038, USA; 212-349-9090, *www.seamenschurch.org*, *csr@seamenschurch.org*. Documentation about workers on cruise ships; publications.

Coalition on Child Prostitution and Tourism, Christian Aid, 35 Lower Marsh, Waterloo, London SE1 7RT, UK; 44-020-7620-4444, Fax: 44-020-7620-0719, *www.christian-aid.org.uk/news/stories/011210s2.htm*, *info@christian-aid.org*. Responsible tourism group; anti-prostitution tourism advocacy network.

Coalition Against Trafficking in Women — Asia Pacific (CATWAP), Suite 406 Victoria Condominium, 41 Annapolis Street, Greenhills, San Juan, Metro Manila 1500, Philippines; 632-722-0859, Fax: 632-722-0755, *www.catw-ap.org*, *catw-ap@catw-ap.org*. Network of feminist groups, organizations, and individuals fighting the sexual exploitation of women globally.

Coalition of Organizations for Solidarity Tourism, Postal Box 1172, Attn: PH c/o Philcom, 8755 Paseo de Roxas, Makati 1200, Philippines. Alternative tourism in the Philippines.

Ecumenical Coalition on Third World Tourism (ECTWT), CCA Center, 96, 2nd District, Pak Tin Village, Mei Tin Road, Shatin, N.T. Hong Kong SAR; 852-(0)2602-3669, Fax: 852-(0)2602-3649, *www.pacific.net.hk/~contours*, *contours@pacific.net.hk*. Organizes conferences; publishes *Contours* magazine, other resources.

End Child Prostitution in Asian Tourism (ECPAT), ECPAT-Canada, 11 Madison Avenue, Toronto, Canada M5R 2S2; 416-323-9726, *www.ecpact.org*, *ecpat@globalpassage.com*. ECPAT-USA, 475 Riverside Drive, Room 621, New York, NY 10115; 212-870-2427, Fax: 212-870-2055. An international campaign to end child prostitution and trafficking; educates tourists, the tourism industry, and governments about prostitution tourism. They have offices around the world.

EQUATIONS: Equitable Tourism Options, No. 198, II Cross, Church Road (Behind old KEB Office), New Thippasandra, Bangalore 560 075, India; 9180-528-2313, Fax: 9180-528-2313, *www.equitabletourism.org*, ADMIN@equitabletourism.org. Responsible tourism advocacy; helps travelers locate environmentally and culturally sensitive projects in India.

European Center for Ecological Agriculture and Tourism-Poland (ECEAT-Poland), 34-146 Stryszow 156, woj. Malopolskie, Poland; Tel/Fax: 48-33-8797114, *www.sfo.pl/eceat*, *eceat@sfo.pl*. Works with small farmers to use ecological tourism to organic farms as a tool to help the farmers through the transition from conventional agriculture to ecological agriculture.

Euroter, 82, rue François Rolland, F 94130 Nogent-sur-Marne, France; 331-4514-6421, Fax: 331-439-49144. Publishes principles for developing green tourism in European villages.

Fair Trade in Tourism Campaign, Tourism Concern, Stapleton House, 277–81 Holloway Road, London N7 8HN, UK; 44-0-20-7753 3330, Fax: 44-0-20-7753 3331, *www.tourismconcern.org.uk/fair_trade/fair_trade.htm*, *info@tourismconcern.org.uk*. Highlights industry initiatives that promote good management and trade practice in other to achieve sustainable tourism.

Friends of the Earth (Amigos de la Terra), Tourism Campaign, c/o PO Box 19199, 1000 GD Amsterdam, The Netherlands; 31-20-6221369, Fax: 31-20-6392181, *foei@foei.org*. Research and networking on tourism industry activities and impacts.

Friends of Malaekahana, PO Box 305, Laie, HI 96762, USA; 808-293-1736, Fax: 808-293-2066, *www.alternative-hawaii.com/fom*, *fom@hawaii.rr.com*. Native Hawaiian civic group operates state park; provides training to other Native groups to manage parks.

Friends of PRONATURA, 240 East Limberlost Drive, Tucson, AZ 85705, USA; 602-887-1188, *closfree@aol.com*. Network of ecological groups working in Mexico.

Gambia Tourism Concern, Adama Bah: Bakadaji Hotel, PO Box 2066, Serrekunda, The Gambia; 220-462-057, Fax: 220-462-307, *concern@qanet.gm*. Campaigns to bring more of the benefits of tourism in the Gambia to local people; promotes fair trade.

Global Anti-Golf Movement and Global Network for Anti-Golf Course Action (GNAGA), 1047 Naka Kamogawa, Chiba, Japan 296-01; 81-47097-1001, Fax: 81-47097-1215. GAG'M, 27 Lorong Maktab, 10250 Penang, Malaysia; 604-227-6930, Fax: 604-227-5705, *utenti.lycos.it/dossierisarenas/golf.htm, aatzor@tin.it*. Anti-golf initiative, work with grassroots and Indigenous groups throughout Asia and the Pacific displaced by golf development.

Global Exchange, 2017 Mission Street #303, San Francisco, CA 94110, USA; 415-255-7296, Fax: 415-255-7698, *www.globalexchange.org, info@globalexchange.org*. Reality tours focus on public education about globalization issues and visit countries like South Africa, Haiti, Cuba, Mexico; publications.

GoNOMAD Network, PO Box 4, South Deerfield, MA 01373, USA; 413-374-3866, Fax: 413-665-7907, *www.gonomad.com, editor@gonomad.com*. A community of independent and alternative travelers dedicated to sustainable and responsible travel.

Green Globe Asia Pacific, GPO Box 371, Canberra ACT 260. Australia; +61 2 6257 9102; Fax: +61 2 6257 9103; *customer.services@ggasiapacific.com.au; www.ggasiapacific.com.au*. Green Globe provides a benchmarking and certification service in support of environmentally sustainable management for the Travel and Tourism industry. The GREEN GLOBE brand logo symbolizes better business and better sustainable environments to consumers, companies, and communities.

Green Globe 21 Americas, Caribbean Alliance for Sustainable Tourism, 1000 Ponce de Leon 5th Floor, San Juan, Puerto Rico 00907, 787-725-913; Fax: 787-725-910; *herawford@caribbean hotels.org; www.cha-cast.com/ggamericas.html*.

Green Tourism Association, 590 Jarvis Street, 4th Floor, Toronto, Ontario, M4Y 2J4 Canada; 416-392-1288, Fax: 416-392-0071, *www.greentourism.ca, greento@city.toronto.on.ca*. An NGO committed to developing and cultivating an urban green tourism industry in Toronto.

El Grupo Ecologist del Mayab (GEMA), Av. Uxmal 24 Sm. 2A, Cancún Q. Roo, Mexico; 98-84-69-44, Fax: 99-84-9857, *retcarib@cancun.com.mx*. Local group working to protect X'cacel, the most important sea turtle nesting beach in Mexico's Atlantic.

Hawaiian Ecumenical Coalition on Tourism (HECOT), 766 North King Street, Honolulu, HI 96817, USA; 808-256-7218, Fax: 808-843-0711. Research, activism, advocacy, publications.

Hopi Tribe, Office of Public Relations, PO Box 123, Kykotsmovi, AZ 86039, USA. Cultural Preservation Office: 928-734-3000, Fax: 928-734-2435, *www.itcaonline.com/Tribes/hopi.htm*. Information about tourism policy and visitor guidelines.

Indigenous Tourism Rights International, 366 North Prior Avenue, Suite 203, Saint Paul, MN 55104, USA; 651-644-9984, Fax: 651-644-2720, *www.rethinkingtourism.org, info@rethinkingtourism.org*. An educational and networking group for Indigenous Peoples, focusing on tourism-related issues like biodiversity protection.

Indonesian Resources and Information Program (IRIP), PO Box 190, Northcote 3070, Australia; 03-481-1581, *www.insideindonesia.org*. Fosters active links with Indonesians working for change; publications.

Initiatives for International Dialogue (IID), 27d Rosario Townhouse, Galaxy Street, GSIS Heights, Matine, Davao City, Philippines; 6382-299-2574, Fax: 6382-299-2052, *www.skyinet.net/~iiddvo, iid@skyinet.net*. Philippine NGO that campaigns for responsible tourism.

International Institute for Peace Through Tourism, Fox Hill 13, Cottage Club Road, Stowe, VT 05672, USA; 802-253-8671, Fax: 802-253-2645, *www.iipt.org, iipt@together.net*. Facilitates tourism initiatives that contribute to international peace and cooperation.

International Porter Protection Group (IPPG), PO Box 53, Repton, NSW, 2454, Australia; 612-66534241, Fax 612-66534130, *www.ippg.net, info@ippg.net*. A campaign to improve conditions and safety for trekking porters in the Himalayas.

Kenya Tourism Concern, PO Box 22449, Nairobi, Kenya; 254-2-535-850, Fax: 254-2-557-092. A Kenyan campaign for more sustainable tourism.

Los Angeles Alliance for a New Economy (LAANE), 548 S. Spring Street, Suite 630, Los Angeles, CA 90013, USA; 213-486-9880, Fax: 213-486-9886, *www.laane.org, info@laane.org*. Works to improve the working conditions and income of low-wage workers focusing on several industries including the tourism industry.

Namibia Community-Based Tourism Association (NACOBTA), Theo Ngaujake/Maxi Louis, PO Box 86099, 18 Lilliencron Street, Windhoek, Namibia; 264-61-250-558, Fax: 264-61-22-647, *www.nacobta.com.na, nacobta@iafrica .com.na*. An association of community tourism projects in Namibia.

Ökologischer Tourismus in Europa e.V., Am Michaelshof 8–10, 53177 Bonn; 0228-359008, Fax: 0228-359096, *www.oete.de, OeTE-Bonn@t-online.de*. Responsible tourism group.

Partners in Responsible Tourism, PO Box 237, San Francisco, CA 94104, USA; 415-675-0420, *www2.pirt.org/pirt, info@pirt.org*. Primarily a network of representatives of tourism companies concerned about the impact of tourism on local environments and cultures; promotes cultural and environmental ethics and practices.

respect (Austrian Center for Tourism and Development), A-1150 Vienna, Diefenbachgasse 36/4, Austria; 43-1-895 62 45, Fax: +43-1-8129789, *www.respect.at, office@respect.at*. Organization standing up for responsible and sustainable tourism in developing countries.

Responsible Tourism Network (RTN), PO Box 34, Rundle Mall SA 5000, Australia; 08-8232-2727 or 61-8-8232-2727, Fax: 08-8232-2808 or 61-8-8232-2808, *www.caa.org.au/travel/rtn, info@tours.caa.org.au*. Responsible tourism in Pacific region; works with travel industry and tourism activists; publishes responsible travel guide.

Sahabat Alam Malaysia (Friends of the Earth Malaysia), 1 No. 27, Lorong Maktab, 10250 Penang, Malaysia; 604-227-6930, Fax: 604-227-5705, *www.surforever.com/sam, smidris@tm.net.my*. Works on tourism issues.

Save Goa Campaign, Attn: Frederick Noronha: near Lourdes Convent, Saligao 403511, Goa, India. A local organization campaigning against the harmful effects of tourism in Goa.

Stichting Retour (Retour Foundation) Dutch, PO Box 1570, 6501 BN Nijmegen, The Netherlands; Tel/Fax: 31-24-360-6224, *www.do.nl/retour, retour@do.nl.* A tourism consultancy whose income is reinvested into campaigns/projects supporting communities affected by tourism.

Studienkreis fur Tourismus und Entwicklung (German), Kapellenweg 3, D-82541 Ammerland, Germany; 49-8177-1783, Fax: 49-8177-1349, *www.studienkreis.org, studienkreistourismus@compuserve.com.* Organizes the ToDo! Awards.

Third World Network, 228 Macalister Road, 10400, Penang, Malaysia; 604-226-6728, 604-226-6159, Fax: 604-226-4505, *www.twnside.org.sg, twn@igc.apc.org.* Produces a magazine and other information about development issues in the global South, including tourism.

Third World Tourism European Ecumenical Network (TEN), Missionsstrasse 21 4003 Basel, Germany; 41-061-261 47 42, Fax: 41-061-261 47 2120, *www.akte.ch, info@akte.ch.* Responsible tourism.

Tourism Concern, Stapleton House, 277–81 Holloway Road, London N7 8HN, UK; 44-0-20-7753 3330, Fax: 44-0-20-7753 3331, *www.tourismconcern.org.uk, info@tourismconcern.org.uk.* Advocates, investigates, educates; publishes quarterly magazine. Videos, documentation, teaching resources.

Tourism with Insight (Arbeitsgemeinschaft Tourismus mit Einsicht), Hadorter Strasse, 9B, 8130 Starnberg, Germany; *trraper@ksc.net.th.* Responsible tourism study group.

Tourism Investigation and Monitoring Team (t.i.m.-team), PO Box 51, Chorakhe-bua, Bangkok 10230, Thailand; Fax: 66-2-519-2821, *www.twnside.org.sg/ tour.htm, timteam02@yahoo.com.* Investigates tourism development in the Mekong subregion; publications.

Tourism Watch, Church Development Service, Ulrich-von-Hassell-Str. 76, 53123 Bonn, Germany; 49-0-228/81010, *www.tourism-watch.de, tourism-watch@ due.org.* Coordinates a European network of responsible travel organizations.

Transverses, 7 rue Heyrault, F-92100 Boulogne, France; Tel/Fax: 331-49-10-9084, *www.chez.com/transverses, transver@club-internet.fr.* Promotes responsible tourism and has a resource center on tourism and the Third World.

Trekking Wrongs: Porters Rights Campaign, Tourism Concern, Stapleton House, 277-281 Holloway Road, London N7 8HN, UK; 44-0-20-7753 3330, Fax: 44-0-20-7753 3331, *www.tourismconcern.org.uk/campaigns/campaigns_porters .htm, lara@tourismconcern.org.uk.* A campaign aims to put a stop to the abuse of porters' human rights.

Uganda Community Tourism Association (UCOTA), PO Box 24503, Kam-pala, Uganda; 256-41-344986, *www.visituganda.com/community/ucota.htm, uta@infocom.co.ug.* An association representing community tourism projects in Uganda.

Wisnu Foundation, Jl. Muding Indah 1/1, Kerobokan, Denpasar 8117, Bali, In-donesia; Tel/Fax: 62-0361-424-758, bali*www.com/wisnuenviroworks/home.htm,* *greenbali@denpasar.wasantara.net.id.* Concerned with environmental problems caused by tourism; works with small-scale, locally based enterprises; conducts environmental audits of resorts and hotels.

Ecotourism Organizations

Asociación Ecuatoriana de Ecoturismo (ASEC), Victor Hugo E10-11 e Isla Pinson, Sector Jipijapa, Quito, Ecuador; 593-2-466295, Fax: 593-2-245055, *www.ecoturismo-ecuador.com/Asec.html* or *ute.edu.ec/~mjativa/ce/aseceng.html, asec@accessinter.net.* Promotes ecotourism that is well managed for the operators as well as the tourists.

Asociación Méxicana de Turismo de Aventura y Ecoturismo (Mexican Association of Adventure Travel and Ecotourism — AMTAVE), Camaron 32, sm 27, Cancún Q. Roo, CP. 77509, Mexico; 52-998-884-3667, *www.amtave.com, info@amtave.com.* A group of about eighty-plus travel providers who work in the fields of ecotourism and adventure tourism and promote sustainable tourism.

Balam s.c. Asesoría y Capacitación, Ciudad de Mexico, Mexico. *febobalam@laneta .apc.org* or *jbalam1@prodigy.net.mx, www.planeta.com/ecotravel/mexico/balam/ balam.html.* A Mexico-based consultancy focusing on community-based, rural tourism development.

Belize Ecotourism Association, Tropical Wings Nature Center, San Jose Succotz, Cayo District, Belize; *www.belizeecotourism.org.* Membership ecotourism groups.

Certification for Sustainable Tourism (CST), PO Box 777-1000, San José, Costa Rica; 506-223-1733 ext 247, Fax: 506-258-2912, *www.turismo-sostenible.co.cr/EN/home.shtml, info@turismo-sostenible.co.cr.* A product of the Costa Rican Tourism Institute (ICT), CST was designed to differentiate tourism sector businesses based on the degree to which they comply with a sustainable model of natural, cultural, and social resource management.

COOPRENA (National Eco-Agricultural Cooperative Network of Costa Rica), Aptdo. 6939-1000 San José, Costa Rica; 506-225-1942, Fax: 506-225-1942, *www.agroecoturismo.net/english/index/htm, cooprena@sol.racsa.co.cr.* Consortium of cooperatives developing eco-agro tourism to relocalize and diversify tourism, conserve resources, and support small farms.

Ecotourism Australia (EA), GPO Box 268, Brisbane Qld 4001, Australia; 07-3229-5550, Fax: 07-3229-5255, *www.ecotourism.org.au, mail@ecotourism.org.au.* Promotes ecotourism in a responsible manner. Developed the International Ecotourism Standard, which is based on the Australian Nature and Ecotourism Accreditation Program (NEAP), Agenda 21, and guiding principles for sound ecotourism certification.

Ecoventure, Ronald Ziegler, Washington State Univ. Libraries, Pullman, WA 99164-5610, USA; Fax: 509-335-6721, *www.wsulibs.wsu.edu/ecoventure/!ecovent.htm, ziegler@wsu.edu.* Ecoventure has a database, BaseCamp, to provide travelers with information on ecotourism.

Estonian Ecotourism Association, PO Box 84, EE-3600 Pärnu, Estonia; 372-44-79739, Fax: 372-44-43779, *www.ee/ecotourism/intro.html, ecotourism@www.ee*. A network of small tour operators living in or nearby protected areas in rural settings; reference manual.

European Center for Eco-Agro Tourism, PO Box 10899, Amsterdam 1001 EW, Netherlands; 020-668-1030, 020-463-0594, *www.eceat.nl, eceat@antenna.nl*. Over two hundred small farms are members of the network; feasibility studies, guides to farms; assists other countries to develop networks.

Foundation for Environmental Education (FEE), Scandiagade 13, 2450 Copenhagen SV, Denmark; 45-33790079, Fax: 45-33790179, *www.blueflag.org, bf.int@friluftsraadet.dk*. International organization promoting education on sustainable development and the environment. Has an ecolabel called Blue Flag, which symbolizes high environmental standards and good sanitary and safety facilities.

Fundación Golondrinas Cloudforest Conservation Project, Calle Isabel La Católica 1559 (n24-679), Quito, Ecuador; 011-593-2-226-602; *www.ecuadorexplorer.com/golondrinas, manteca@uio.satnet.net*. A conservation organization conserving twenty-five thousand hectares of cloud forests on the northwest slopes of the Andes. They have volunteer and educational programs, including a four-day trek through the Cerro Golondrinas area.

The Green Tourism Association Resource Center 590 Jarvis Street — 4th Floor, Toronto, Ontario, M4Y 2J4, Canada; 416-392-1288, Fax: 416-392-0071, *www.greentourism.ca, greento@city.toronto.on.ca*. The Green Tourism Association Resource Center also includes information on: ecotourism, responsible tourism/sustainable tourism development, sustainable transportation and green accommodation initiatives.

Hawaii Ecotourism Association, PO Box 61435, Honolulu, HI 96822, USA; 808-956-2866 or (toll-free) 877-300-7058, *www.planet-hawaii.com/hea*. Promotes responsible tourism, resource network for Hawaii and the Pacific.

Indonesian Ecotourism Network (INDECON), Jalan H. Samali No. 51, Pejaten Barat, Pasar Minggu, Jakarta 12510, Indonesia; Tel/Fax: 62-21-799-3955, *indecon@indosat.net.id* or *indecon@cbn.net.id*. Developing an ecotourism database, information center, newsletter, manuals, guidebooks; conducts workshops, seminars.

The International Ecotourism Society (TIES), 733 15th St. NW, Suite 1000, Washington, DC 20005-2115 USA, 202-347-9203, Fax: 202-287-7915, *www.ecotourism.org, ecomail@ecotourism.org*. Dedicated to making tourism a viable tool for conservation and sustainable development; publications and videos; educational programs.

Kiskeya, PO Box 109-Z, Zona Colonial, Santo Domingo, Rep. Dominicana; 809-537-89 77, *kiskeya-alternative.org/cangonet, kad@kiskeya-alternative.org*. Enterprising organization focusing on ecotourism as well as Indigenous dance. Works mostly in the Caribbean.

Kodukant Ecotourism Initiative, SAARISOO, EE 3482 Joesuu, Parnumaa, Estonia; 011-372-446-6405. A network of small tour operators living in or near protected areas.

Las Cañadas: Bosque de Niebla, A.P. 24, 94100 Huatusco, Veracruz, Mexico; Tel/Fax: 011-2-734-1577. Contact: Ricardo Romero, *www.bosquedeniebla.com.mx*, *bosquedeniebla@infosel.net.mx*. Ecolodge, cloud forest treks, agro-ecology workshops, environmental education, research, bird watching, and Temazcal (sweat lodge).

Maya Ik', Turismo Ecológico y Cultural del Pueblo Maya, San Cristóbal de las Casas, Chiapas, Mexico; 967-86998, *mayaik@sancristobal.podernet.com.mx*. An alternative ecotour group organized by Indigenous Peoples in Chiapas.

Oceanic Society Expeditions, Fort Mason Center, Building E, San Francisco, CA 94123, USA; 415-441-1106, Fax: 415-474-3395, *www.oceanic-society.org*. Promotes environmental stewardship, education, and research through ecotourism.

Samoan Ecotourism Network (SEN), PO Box 4606, Matautu-utu, Western Samoa; 685-26-940, Fax: 685-25-993, *public-www.pi.se/~orbit/eco-sen.html*, *ecotour@pactok.peg*. Concerned about deforestation of primary rain forests; organizes ecotours.

Sikkim Biodiversity and Ecotourism, Opp. Krishi Bhawan, PO Tadong, Sikkim 737102, India; 011-91-3592-31046, Fax: 011-91-3592-31090, *sce@gokulnet .com*. Developing regional ecotourism program with local communities in the Himalayas.

SmartVoyager Certification and Sustainable Tourism Stewardship Council (STSC) of the Rainforest Alliance, 665 Broadway, Suite 500, New York, NY 10012, USA; 212-677-1900 or 888-693-2784, *www.rainforest-alliance.org/programs/sv/index .html, canopy@ra.org*. Ecotourism certification programs.

Talamanca Association of Ecotourism and Conservation (ATEC), Puerto Viejo de Talamanca, Limón, Costa Rica; Tel/Fax: 506-750-0398; *greencoast.com/atec .htm, atecmail@sol.racsa.co.cr*. Community group that promotes small, locally owned, socially responsible tourism businesses in Talamanca (Atlantic coast area). Local people are Bribri and Cabecar Indians and West Indian (Afro-Caribbean) immigrants.

Toledo Ecotourism Association (TEA), 65 Front Street — Box 75, Punta Gorda Town, Belize; Tel/Fax: 011-501-07-22-119, *belizehome.com/home/ads_web1 .shtml, ttea@btl.net*. Network of Indigenous farm cooperatives; requesting paying volunteers to help with their programs.

UCOTA (Uganda Community Tourism Association). Elissa Williams: PO Box 26318, Kampala, Uganda; 256-41-269-982, *prof@swiftuganda.com* or *ucota@swiftuganda.com*. An association representing community tourism projects in Uganda.

General Environmental, Development, and Indigenous Resources

Aboriginal Tourism Team Canada (ATTC), 275 Slater Street, Suite 820, Ottawa, Ontario, K2L 2E9, Canada; 613-235-2067 or 800-724-7872, Fax: 613-235-0396, *www.attc.ca, admino@attc.ca*. The national tourism association that influences and develops tourism policies and programs to benefit Aboriginal people in Canada.

Action for Community and Ecology in the Regions of Central America (ACERCA), PO Box 57, Burlington, VT 05402, USA; 802-863-0571, Fax: 802-864-8203, *www.acerca.org, acerca@sover.net*. Protects the ecological and cultural integrity of the Central American Region. Information on Plan Puebla Panama.

Alliance of Tribal Tourism Advocates, PO Box 673, Chamberlain, SD 57325, USA; 605-245-2327, Fax: 605-245-2266, *www.atta.indian.com*. Focusing on enhancing tourism development prospects for tribes to provide employment and economic benefits for Indian people on the reservations and in off-reservation Indian communities.

Amanaka'a, PO Box 509, New York, NY 10276, USA; 212-479-7360, *www.amanakaa .org, amanakaa@amanakaa.org*. Organizes an annual "Amazon Week" to discuss and learn about issues affecting Indigenous Peoples in the Amazon, including tourism issues.

Amazon Alliance, 1367 Connecticut Avenue NW, Suite 400, Washington, DC 20036, USA; 202-785-3334, Fax: 202-785-3335, *www.amazonalliance.org, amazon@amazonalliance.org*. Coalition of Amazonian and U.S. groups; publishes newsletter.

Bank Information Center (BIC), 733 15th Street NW, Suite 1126, Washington, DC 20005, USA; 202-737-7752, Fax: 202-737-1155, *www.bicusa.org, info@bicusa.org*. Provides information and strategic support to NGOs and social movements throughout the world on the projects, policies, and practices of the World Bank and other Multilateral Development Banks. Has information about Plan Puebla Panama.

Biodiversity Support Program (BSP), 1250 24th Street NW, Washington, DC 20037, USA; 202-861-8348, Fax: 202-861-8324, *www.bsponline.org*. Consortium of environmental organizations funded by USAID; funds ecotourism projects.

Bluewater Network, 300 Broadway, Suite 28, San Francisco, CA 94133, USA; 415-788-3666, Fax: 415-788-7324, *www.bluewaternetwork.org, bluewater@ earthisland.org*. A national environmental organization aggressively confronting the root causes of climate change and fighting environmental damage from the shipping, oil, and motorized recreation industries.

Cambodian Center for Protection of Children's Rights (CCPCR), #08, St. 311, Boeung Kork 2, Khan Toul Kork, PO Box 2487, Phnom Penh 3, Cambodia; Tel/Fax: 855-23-363-316, *ccpcr@forum.org.kh*. Organization working protecting children.

Chilean Ecological Action Network (RENACE), Seminario 774, Nunoa, Castilla 16784 Correo 9, Santiago, Chile; 56-2-223-4483, Fax: 56-2-223-8909, *chilesus@RDC.CL*. Coalition of more than one hundred Chilean environmental, Indigenous, and social action organizations.

Coalition for Environmentally Responsible Economies (CERES), 11 Arlington Street, 6th Floor, Boston, MA 02116, USA; 617-247-0700, Fax: 617-267-5400, *www.ceres.org, info@ceres.org*. Coalition of environmental, investor, and advocacy groups working for a sustainable future. One project is the Green Hotel Initiative (GHI), whose objective is to increase and demonstrate market demand for environmentally responsible hotel services.

Conservation Foundation, 1 Kensington Gore, London, SW7 2AR, England, UK; 440-207-591-3111, Fax: 440-207-591-3110, *www.conservationfoundation.co.uk*, *conservf@gn.apc.org*. UK-based environmental organization.

Conservation International, 1919 M Street NW, Suite 600, Washington, DC 20036, USA; 202-912-1000 ext. 421, Fax: 202-912-1044, *www.ecotour.org*. An environmental organization that promotes conservation through community development, including ecotourism projects.

Co-op America, 1612 K Street NW, Suite 600, Washington, DC 20006, USA; 800-58-GREEN, Fax: 202-331-8166, *www.coopamerica.org*, *info@coopamerica.org*. Membership group of businesses and cooperatives dedicated to creating a just and sustainable society by harnessing economic power for positive change. Publishes boycott information, alternative travel links, and magazine.

Corpwatch, PO Box 29344, San Francisco, CA 94129, USA; 415-561-6568, Fax: 415-561-6493, *www.corpwatch.org*, *corpwatch@igc.org*. Works to build global links for social justice, ecological sustainability, and democratic control over corporations. Hosts Corporate Watch, an online resource on transnational corporations.

Cousteau Society, Project Ocean Search, 870 Greenbrier Circle, Suite 402, Chesapeake, VA 23320, USA; 800-441-4395, *www.cousteausociety.org/indexmain.html*, *cousteau@cousteausociety.org*. Marine guidelines and information about threats to the world's oceans.

Earth Island Institute, 300 Broadway, Suite 28, San Francisco, CA 94133, USA; 415-788-3666, Fax: 415-788-7324, *www.earthisland.org*. A network of environmentalists working on various campaigns.

Global Ecovillage Network (GEN), Ecovillage Network of the Americas, 64001 County Road DD, Moffat, CO 81143 USA; Tel/Fax: 719-256-4221, *www.gaia.org*, *ena@ecovillage.org*. Global network of communities working towards sustainability. Allows visitation to Ecovillages, communities living sustainably.

Global March Against Child Labour, International Secretariat, L-6 Kalkaji, New Delhi 110 019, India; 91-11-622-4899, Fax: 91-11-623-8919, *www.globalmarch.org*, *childhood@globalmarch.org*. Organization dedicated to setting children free from servitude including child tourism labor and sexual tourism labor.

Global Response — Environmental Action & Education Network, PO Box 7490, Boulder, CO 80306, USA; 303-444-0306, *www.globalresponse.org*, *action@globalresponse.org*. Environmental action and education network.

Global Witness Limited, PO Box 6042, London, N19 5WP, UK; 44-0-20-7272-6731, Fax: 44-0-20-7272-9425, *www.globalwitness.org*, *mail@globalwitness.org*. A non-governmental investigative organization working to expose the link between natural resource exploitation and human rights abuses. Operates in areas where environmentally destructive trade is funding conflict or human rights violations.

Grand Canyon Trust, 2601 N. Fort Valley Road, Flagstaff, AZ 86001, USA; 928-774-7488, Fax: 928-774-7570, *www.grandcanyontrust.org*, *info@grandcanyontrust.org*. Protects and restores the canyon country of the Colorado Plateau. Works on tourism issues facing the area.

GreenNet, 33 Islington High Street, London N1 9LH, UK; 44-20-7713-1941, Fax: 44-20-7837-5551, *www.gn.apc.org, info@gn.apc.org.* Uses the Internet to support the community working for peace, the environment, civil rights, and social justice.

Greenpeace International, 702 H Street NW, Washington, DC 20001, USA; 800-326-0959, *www.greenpeaceusa.org, supporter.services@ams.greenpeace.org.*

Greenpeace International, Keizersgracht 176,1016 DW Amsterdam, The Netherlands; 31-20-523-6222, Fax: 31-20-523-6200, *www.greenpea.org.* Information about ecotourism and alternative technologies.

Honor the Earth, 2801 21st Avenue South, Minneapolis, MN 55407, USA; 612-278-7165, Fax: 612-278-7162, *www.honorearth.com, contact@honorearth.org.* Provides funding and public support for Native environmental initiatives.

Indigenous Affairs, International Work Group, IWGIA, Classensgade 11 E, DK 2100 Copenhagen, Denmark; 45-35-27-05-00, Fax: 45-35-27-05-07, *www.iwgia.org, iwgia@iwgia.org.* An independent international organization to support Indigenous People; magazines and publications available in English and Spanish.

Indigenous Environmental Network, PO Box 485, Bemidji, MN 56601, USA; 218-751-4967, Fax: 218-751-0561, *www.ienearth.org, ien@igc.org.* Alliance of grassroots Indigenous Peoples whose mission is to protect the earth from contamination and exploitation by strengthening, maintaining, and respecting the traditional teachings and natural laws.

Indigenous Peoples of East Africa Foundation, PO Box 59516, Nairobi, Kenya; 254-2-723-002. Information center for Indigenous organizations in East Africa.

Indigenous Peoples Intellectual Property Rights Center, IPBN-IPR Center, Mataatua Declaration Directorate, PO Box 13-177, Johnsonville, Wellington, Aotearoa, New Zealand; Tel/Fax: 64-4-479-7781, *www.undp.org/csopp/CSO/NewFiles/ ipindex.html, aroham@nzonline.ac.nz.* Research, advocacy in support of intellectual property rights (biodiversity, Indigenous knowledge).

Indigenous and Tribal Peoples Center (ITP), PO Box 319-6100, San José, Costa Rica; 506-205-1620 or 506-205-9085, Fax: 506-249-4187 or 506-249-3500, *www.itpcentre.org, ipinfo@ecouncil.ac.cr.* Promotes sustainability while fostering a better understanding of traditional values and knowledge.

Indigenous Women's Environmental Network, 1575 17th Street, West Prince Albert, Saskatchewan S6V 3Z5, Canada; *www.indians.org/library/iwen.html.* An ad hoc group of Aboriginal women in Saskatchewan who are concerned about environmental issues and the impact that megaprojects have on Indigenous People.

International Arctic Program of WWF, Kristian Augustgate 7 A, PO Box 6784, St. Olavs plass, N-0130 Oslo, Norway; 47-22-03-65-17, Fax: 47-22-20-06-66, *www.ngo.grida.no/wwfap, arctic@wwf.no.* Focuses on improving and protecting the natural environment of the Arctic. A network of eight organizations working in collaboration on sustainable tourism in the region.

International Society for Ecology and Culture/Ladakh Project (ISEC), UK: Foxhole Dartington, Devon TQ9 6EB, UK; 01803-868650, Fax: 01803-868651, *www.isec.org.uk, info@isec.org.uk;* US: PO Box 9475, Berkeley CA 94709,

510-548-4915, *isecca@igc.org*. Educational campaigns on globalization issues, including tourism study groups; educational materials.

Katmandu Environmental Education Project (KEEP), PO Box 9178, Jay-atha Road, Thamel, Katmandu, Nepal; 977-1-239567, Fax: 977-1-256615, *www.keepnepal.org*, *keep@info.com.np*. Provides advice and information on low-impact trekking in Nepal. Has an information center in Kathmandu.

Maasai Environment Resource Coalition (MERC), International Program Office, 2020 Pennsylvania Avenue NW, Suite 136, Washington, DC 20006, USA; 202-785-8787, Fax: 202-785-1557, *www.maasaierc.org*, *mercmaasai@aol.com*. Represents a broad spectrum of Maasai grassroots groups working to reclaim land rights and culture, with its traditional respect for Maasailand and its wildlife.

Mexican Action Network on Free Trade (RMALC), Calle Godard No. 20, Col. Guadalupe Victoria, D.F. 07790, Mexico; Tel/Fax: 525-335-1177, *rmalc@laneta.apc.org*. Information about grassroots groups and NGOs in Mexico; some monitor tourism development.

Multinationals Resource Center, PO Box 19405, Washington, DC 20036, USA; 202-387-8030, Fax: 202-234-5176, *resourcesfirst.org*, *mrc@essential.org*. Provides workers, environmental activists, consumer groups, and local journalists in less-industrialized countries with crucial information for their research and campaigns; specializes in information about U.S.-based multinational companies but can help answer a variety of environmental, consumer, and labor-related questions.

National Audubon Society, 700 Broadway, New York, NY 10003, USA; 212-979-3000, Fax: 212-979-3188, *www.audubon.org*, *audobon@neodata.com*. Works to conserve and restore the natural environment. Publishes travel ethics.

Native Lands Institute, 211 12th Street NW, Albuquerque NM 87102, USA; 505-842-6123, Fax: 505-842-6124. Advocacy for the land, water, cultural, and religious rights of Native Americans.

Native Tourism, Western American Indian Chamber, 1900 Wazee, Suite 100, Denver, CO 80002, USA; *www.nativetourism.org*, *bsherman@indiancountry.org*. Supports the growth of the economic vitality of sustainable Native American tourism.

The Nature Conservancy, 4245 North Fairfax Drive, Suite 100, Arlington, VA 22203, USA; 800-628-6860, *www.nature.org/ecotourism*, *comment@tnc.org*. Works to bring sustainable protection to natural areas. Ecotourism projects and other environmental protection programs throughout the world.

Northern Ontario Native Tourism Association (NONTA), Site 7, Comp. 154, R.R.#4, Thunder Bay, Ontario, P7C 4Z2, Canada; 807-623-0497, Fax: 807-623-0498, *www.nonta.net*, *nonta@norlink.net*. A member organization that facilitates Native involvement in the tourism industry.

Nuestra Tierra, Miembro de Youth Action for Peace (YAP), Apdo. Postal No. 2-119, C.P. 48350, Puerto Vallarta, Jalisco, Mexico; *www.nuestratierra.20m.com*, *ntmex-yap@pvnet.com.mx*. A youth environmental organization seeking to protect biodiversity and minimize tourism impacts in the Puerto Vallarta, Mexico, area.

Oceans Blue Foundation, 405-134 Abbott Street, Vancouver, BC V6B 2K4, Canada; 604-684-2583, Fax: 604-684-6942, *www.oceansblue.org*, *sails@oceansblue.org*. Canadian environmental charity that helps conserve coastal environments through environmentally responsible tourism.

Pacific Peoples Foundation, 1921 Fernwood Road, Victoria, BC V85 2Y6, Canada; 604-381-4131, *www.sppf.org*, *sppf@sppf.org*. Information about organizations, issues in South Pacific; magazine.

RARE Center for Tropical Conservation, 1840 Wilson Boulevard, Suite 402, Arlington, VA 22201, USA; 703-522-5070, Fax: 703-522-5027, *www.rarecenter.org*, *rare@rarecenter.org*. Assists communities in designing conservation programs, including ecotourism.

Sea Turtle Restoration Project, PO Box 400, Forest Knolls, CA 94933, USA; 415-488-0370, *www.seaturtles.org*. Fights to protect endangered sea turtles in ways that make cultural and economic sense to the local communities. Links ecotourists with community-based conservation programs.

Sierra Club, 85 Second Street, 2nd Floor, San Francisco, CA 94105, USA; 415-977-5500, Fax: 415-977-5799, *www.sierraclub.org*, *information@sierraclub.org*. Dedicated to protection of the wilderness; education, advocacy, and publications. Sponsors environmental outings.

SOMO Center for Research on Multinational Corporations, Keizersgracht 132, 1015 CW Amsterdam, Netherlands; 020-6391291, Fax: 020-6391321, *somo@xs4all.nl*. Investigates multinational corporations.

South and Meso American Indian Rights Center (SAIIC), PO Box 7829, Oakland, CA 94604, USA; 510-534-4882, Fax: 510-834-4264, *saiic.nativeweb.org*, *indian@igc.org*. Resource center on Central and South American Indigenous organizations; publishes magazine that covers development issues, including tourism.

Survival International, 6 Charterhouse Buildings, London EC1M 7ET, UK; 44-0-20-7687-8700, Fax: 44-0-20-7687-8701, *www.survival-international.org*, *info@survival-international.org*. Advocacy, information, education about survival for tribal peoples; concerned about tourism impacts.

Sustainable Energy Institute (SEI), PO Box 4347, Arcata, CA 95518, USA; 707-826-7775, Fax: 603-825-2696, *www.culturechange.org*, *info@culturechange.org*. Highways watchdog group; promotes restructuring of the American way of life away from growth, toward ecodemocracy. Publishes magazine titled *Culture Change*.

Sustrans, 35 King Street, Bristol BS1 4DZ, England; 0117-926-8893, Fax: 0117-929-4173, Sustrans Information Line: 0117-929-0888, *www.sustrans.org.uk*, *info@sustrans.org.uk*. Works for sustainable transport in the United Kingdom, and is developing a national cycle network.

Trees for the Future, 9000 16th Street, PO Box 7027, Silver Spring, MD 20907, USA; 800-643-0001, Fax: 301-565-5012, *www.treesftf.org*, *info@treesftf.org*. Organization committed to planting trees. Two of their programs are titled "Trees for Travel" and the "Global Cooling Program."

Trust for Public Lands, 116 New Montgomery Street, 4th Floor, San Francisco, CA 94105, USA; 415-495-4014, Fax: 415-495-4103, *www.tpl.org*, *info@tpl.org*.

Works nationwide to conserve land for people; opposes irrational development of wild spaces.

World Rainforest Movement Maldonado 1858 — 11200 Montevideo, Uruguay; 598-2-413-989, Fax: 598-2-418-0762, *www.wrm.org.uy, wrm@wrm.org.uy*. The World Rainforest Movement is an international network of citizens' groups of North and South involved in efforts to defend the world's rain forests.

World Resources Institute, 10 G Street NE, Suite 800, Washington, DC 20002, USA; 202-729-7600, Fax: 202-729-7610, *www.wri.org, front@wri.org*. Policy research center assists governments, international organizations, and private businesses to address sustainable development, biodiversity protection, analysis of ecotourism programs.

World Wildlife Fund — UK, Panda House, Weyside Park, Godalming, Surrey GU7 1XR, UK; 01483-426444, Fax: 01483-426409; *www.wwf-uk.org/core/index.asp, info@wwf.org.uk*. Has a tourism program that promotes long-term preservation of the natural environment through sustainable tourism.

World Wildlife Fund — US, 1250 24th Street NW, Washington, DC 20037, USA; 202-293-4800, Fax: 202-775-8287, *www.worldwildlife.org*. Collaborates with environmental efforts in developing countries to design ecotourism projects and protected areas; offers travel programs to members.

Responsible Tour Operators and Programs

Above the Clouds, PO Box 388, Hinesburg, VT 05461, USA; 802-482-4848, Fax: 802-482-5011, *www.aboveclouds.com/ethic.htm, info@aboveclouds.com*. Provides worldwide adventure travel.

Bicicletas Pedro Martinez, J. P. Garcia 509-A, 68000 Oaxaca, Mexico; 951-514-3144, *www.bicicletaspedromartinez.com, oaxmb@prodigy.net.mx*. Offers bike tours lasting from three hours to four days in Oaxaca.

Las Cañadas: Bosque de Niebla, A.P. 24 94100 Huatusco, Veracruz; Tel/Fax: 273-734-1577; *www.bosquedeniebla.com.mx, bosquedeniebla@infosel.net.mx*. Ecolodge, cloud forest treks, interpretative paths, organic farming area, agro-ecology workshops, community action, environmental education, research, bird watching.

Earthwyz Journeys, PO Box 16177, Portland OR 97292, USA; *www.teleport.com/ earthwyz*. Promotes responsible travel worldwide.

Eco Paraíso, Celestun, Yucatan; 991-621-00, *www.ecoparaiso.com, info@ecoparaiso .com*. Eco-friendly hotel on the Gulf of Mexico.

Eco-Travel Services, 5699 Miles Avenue, Oakland, CA 94618, USA; 510-655-4054, *ecotravel@wonderlink.com*. Nationwide individual and corporate travel arrangements, uses smaller operators; supports local economies and environmentally conscious operations instead of quick profits; publishes newsletter.

Ecoturismo Yucatan, Calle 3 #235 (between 32-A and 34), 97219 Merida, Yucatan; 999-25-21-87; *www.ecoyuc.com, alfonso@ecoyuc.com*. Tours of the world of the Maya including archeology, culture, birdwatching, kayak and bicycle tours.

Freedom ONE, Inc. 3 Cushing Road, Newmarket, NH 03857, USA; Tel/Fax: 603-659-8120, *www.freedomone.com*, *hspande@freedomone.com*. Works cooperatively with Qimuk, an Inuit Tourism Organization, offering cultural/adventure tours to Nunavut, Canada.

Green Hotels Association, PO Box 420212, Houston, TX 77242, USA; 713-789-8889, Fax: 713-789-9786, *www.greenhotels.com*, *info@greenhotels.com*. List of hotels around the world that are becoming green.

Green Tracks, 10 Town Plaza, Suite 231, Durango, CO 81301, USA; 800-966-6539, Fax: 970-884-6107, *greentracks.com*, *info@greentracks.org*. Adventure travel in the rainforest.

Himalayan High Treks, 241 Delores Street, San Francisco, CA 94103-2211, USA; 800-455-8735, Fax: 415-861-2391, *www.himalayanhightreks.com*, *effie@himalayanhightreks.com*. A small trekking company that specializes in trips to Bhutan, India, Nepal, and Tibet; offers specialized programs for women; publishes newsletter.

Indigenous World Tours PO Box 475, Ohsweken, Ontario, N0A 1M0, Canada; 519-445-0422, *www.indigenousworldtours.com*, *iwt@indigenousworldtours.com*. Indigenous World Tours is an Indigenous organization dedicated to providing authentic educational travel experiences for those who wish to meet and learn more about American Indians of the Western Hemisphere and about Native Hawaii.

International Bicycle Fund, 4887 Columbia Drive South, Seattle, WA 98108, USA; Tel/Fax: 206-767-0848, *www.ibike.org*, *ibike@ibike.org*. Promotes bicycle transport, economic development, international understanding, and safety education; newsletter; links with other auto-free and bicycling organizations around the world.

International Expeditions, One Environs Park, Helena, AL 35080, USA; 800-633-4734, Fax: 205-428-1714, *www.internationalexpeditions.com*, *nature@ietravel .com*. Nature travel stressing environmental awareness.

John Gray Sea Canoe Company, 124 Soil Yawarat Rd, Taladyai, Muang, Phuket 83000 Thailand; 66-76-254505-7, Fax: 66-76-226077-7, *www.johngray-seacanoe .com*, *info@johngray-seacanoe.*

Journeys International, 107 April Drive, Suite 3, Ann Arbor, MI 48103, USA; 734-665-4407, 800-255-8735, Fax: 734-665-2945, *www.journeys-intl.com*, *info@journeys-intl.com*. A well-established ecotour operator; guides are either natives or residents of the countries they visit; part of their profits supports environmental preservation.

Manaca Ecotravel, 3957 Pender Drive, Suite 102, Fairfax, VA 22030, USA; 866-962-3222 or 703-352-9533, *www.manaca.com*. Provides responsible travel that respects the environment and benefits the local community. Has ecotours and ecolodges where the visitors must take the responsible tourism pledge.

Marlene Ehrenberg Tourism, 2002 Colibri Award recipient for her work in Mexico, tel/fax in Mexico City: 011-52-5550-9080, *www.marlene366.tripod.com*, *marlene_ehrenberg@hotmail.com*. Specialized tours that focus on the ecology and culture of Mexico.

Mesoamerican Ecotourism Alliance/RARE, 1840 Wilson Boulevard, Suite 402, Arlington, VA 22201, USA; 703-522-5070, Fax: 703-522-5027, *www.rarecenter.org*, *jdion@rarecenter.org.* An alliance of organizations developing ecotourism projects in Central America supported by a US conservation organization called RARE.

Mexican Association of Adventure Travel and Ecotourism — AMTAVE (Asociación Méxicana de Turismo de Aventura y Ecoturismo), Camaron 32 SM 27, 77509 Cancún, Quintana Roo; 998-884-9214 and 800-509-7578, *www.amtave.com,* *info@amtave.com.* AMTAVE is a group of travel providers who work in the fields of ecotourism and adventure tourism. Useful website.

Mexican Cultural Adventures, 182-2496 E. Hastings Street, Vancouver, BC, Canada; 604-251-1425 *www.backcountrymexico.com, home@backcountrymexico.com.* This Canadian company focuses its operations in Oaxaca, taking travelers to a Mixtec mountain village and camping on tropical beaches. Learn from the local people about traditional crafts and plants.

Naestie Touristcenter, PO Box 18, 830 67 Valsjöbyn, Sweden; 46-645-320-57, Fax: 46-645-320-86, *www.itv.se/boreale/naestie_hotel.html.* Naestie tourist center is the first Sami-owned hotel in Sweden; the business is fully owned and managed by Indigenous personnel.

Native Tours, 6875 Highway 65 NE, Minneapolis, MN 55432, USA; 763-571-8184 or 866-404-9102, Fax: 763-571-7889. Provides native tours focusing on educating the public.

Oceanic Society Expeditions, Fort Mason Center, Building E, San Francisco, CA 94123, USA; 415-441-1106 or 800-326-7491, Fax: 415-474-3395, *www.oceanic-society.org.* Promotes environmental stewardship, education, and research through ecotourism.

RICANCIE — Red Indigena de Comunidades del Alto Napo para la Convivencia Intercultural y Ecoturismo, Avenida 15 de Noviembre 772, Tena, Ecuador; Tel/Fax: 593-6-887-953, *ricancie.nativeweb.org, ricancie@ecuanex.net.ec.* A network of ten Quichua communities in the Upper Napo valley who have established an ecotourism program based on traditional respect for their natural and cultural heritage, as an alternative way of developing their communities.

South American Explorer's Club (SAEC), 126 Indian Creek Road, Ithaca, NY 14850, USA; 607-277-0488, Fax: 607-277-6122, *www.samexplo.org,* *explorer@saexplorers.org.* Hiking club promotes responsible tourism.

Specialty Travel Index, 305 San Anselmo Avenue, Ste. 313, San Anselmo, CA 94960, USA; 415-459-4900 or 800-442-4922, Fax: 415-459-4974, *www.spectrav.com,* *info@specialtytravel.com.* Index of five hundred tour operators specializing in adventure and special-interest travel.

Tour de Cana, PO Box 7293, Philadelphia, PA 19101, USA; 215-222-1253, *tourdecana@aol.com.* An outgrowth of the organization Bikes Not Bombs, this group offers bike trekking with a social, cultural, and political spin.

Wilderness Travel, 1102 Ninth Street, Berkeley, CA 94710, USA; 800-368-2794 or 510-558-2488, Fax: 510-558-2489, *www.wildernesstravel.com,* *info@wildernesstravel.com.* Promotes cultural preservation and environmental protection; supports conservation, cultural, and development organizations.

Wildland Adventures, Inc., 3519 NE 155th Street, Seattle, WA 98155, USA; 206-365-0686 or 800-345-4453, Fax: 206-363-6615, *www.wildland.com,* *info@wildland.com.* Ecotour operator offers group travel, customized trips for independent travelers and families, rain forest workshops, and responsible trips like trail cleanups and community services. Contributes part of profits to conservation and community development at the local level.

Yukon River Tours, Native Heritage and Natural History, 214 Second Street, Fairbanks AK 99701, USA; 907-452-7162, *www.mosquitonet.com/~dlacey/yrt.html*, *dlacey@mosquitonet.com*. Educational ecotours; learn about Athabascan culture at a Native fish camp on the Yukon River.

Social and Environmental Justice Programs (Tours, Delegations, Volunteer Programs)

American Friends Service Committee, 1501 Cherry Street, Philadelphia, PA 19102, USA; 215-241-7000, *www.afsc.org*, *afscinfo@afsc.org*. Volunteer programs to community projects in Mexico and Cuba.

Bangladesh Workcamps Association, 289/2 Work Camps Road, North Shahjahanpur, Dhaka 17, Bangladesh; Fax: 882-86-3797. Links to short-term and medium-term volunteer work camp projects throughout Bangladesh.

Centro Felix Varela, Calle 5ta. #720 esq. 10, Vedado, Apartado Postal 4041, Plaza 10400 Ciudad de Havana, Cuba, 537-3377-31 or 537-3333-28, Fax: 537-3333-28, *www.cfvarela.org*, *cfvarela@cfv.org.cu*. Devoted to international peace and cooperation, ecologically responsible societies, seminars, exchanges, humanitarian donations, publications, video production, special reports.

Conflict Resolution Catalysts, PO Box 836, Montpelier, VT 05601, USA; 800-445-1165 or 802-229-1165, Fax: 802-229-1166, *www.crcvt.org*, *crc@sover.net*. Volunteers participate in conflict resolution programs in communities in countries like Bosnia-Herzegovina (works with the United Nations High Commissioner for Refugees). Helping children deal with trauma of war.

Cuba Information Project, 198 Broadway, Suite 800, New York, NY 10038, USA; 212-227-3422. Cosponsors social justice delegations.

Cultural Restoration Tourism Project (CRTP), Main Office, 410 Paloma Avenue, Pacifica, CA 94044, USA; 415-563-7221, *home.earthlink.net/~crtp*, *crtp@earthlink.net*. CRTP was established to restore temples and other beautiful and valuable artifacts throughout the world. Provides support to local communities using volunteers.

Earthstewards Network, PeaceTrees Vietnam PO Box 10697, Bainbridge Island, WA 98110, USA; 206-842-7986, Fax: 206-842-8918, *www.earthstewards.org*, *chuckm@peacetrees.vietnam.org*. PeaceTrees projects.

Earthwatch International, 3 Clock Tower Place, Suite 100, Box 75, Maynard, MA 01754, USA; 978-461-0081, 800-776-0188, Fax: 978-461-2332, *www.earthwatch.org*, *info@earthwatch.org*. Voluntary scientific international tours; magazine.

Ecotrackers Network Foundation, Av. Amazonas, N21–217, 2o piso, y Roca, Quito, Ecuador; (593-2) 2564-840, (593-2) 2561-620; *www.ecotrackers.com*. Volunteers live in a local community for a week or more, learn Spanish, help to preserve the culture and environment.

Ecumenical Program of Central America and the Caribbean (EPICA), 1470 Irving Street NW, Washington, DC 20010, USA; 202-332-0292, Fax: 202-332-1184, *epica@igc.apc.org*. A small press and solidarity group working on social justice issues, speaking tours, delegations.

Farm Helpers in New Zealand, 50 Bright Street, Eketahuna, New Zealand; 06-375-8955, *www.fhinz.co.nz*, *fhinz@xtra.co.nz*. Members link to farmers looking for helpers in exchange for room and board.

Foreign Placements, PO Box 912, Somerset West 7129, South Africa; 27-4457-7677. Volunteer programs in South Africa for those with medical and other skills.

Global Citizens Network, 130 N. Howell Street, St. Paul, MN 55104, USA; 651-644-0960 or 800-644-9292, *www.globalcitizens.org*, *gcn@mtn.org*. Volunteer programs to rural Kenya.

Leave No Trace, 2475 Broadway, Boulder, CO 80304, USA; 303-442-8222 or 800-332-4100, Fax: 303-442-8217, *www.lnt.org*. Teaches skills to hikers, backpackers, and horsepackers for protecting wilderness areas.

MADRE, 121 W. 27th Street, Room 301, New York, NY 10001; 212-627-0444, Fax: 212-675-3704, *www.madre.org*, *madre@igc.org*. An international women's human rights organization that works in partnership with women's community-based groups in conflict areas worldwide to address issues of health, education, economic development, and other human rights. Travels to different countries — "Voyages with a Mission."

Operations Crossroads Africa, 475 Riverside Drive, Suite 1366, New York, NY 10027, USA; 212-870-2106, Fax: 212-870-2644, *www.igc.org/oca*, *oca@igc.apc.org*. Projects in rural Africa staffed by self-financing volunteers.

Sacred Sites International Foundation, 1442A Walnut Street #330, Berkeley, CA 94709, USA; Tel/Fax: 510-525-1304, *www.sitesaver.org*, *sacredsites@aol.com*. Advocates the presentation of natural and built sacred places — a key to preserving traditional cultures and values of respecting the Earth.

Traveler's Earth Repair Network (TERN), PO Box 4469, Bellingham, WA 98227, USA; 360-738-4972, Fax: 360-671-9668, *www.geocities.com/rainforest/4663/ tern.html*, *tern@geocities.com*. Links travelers with people and organizations working in restoration, sustainable agriculture, and environmental issues; lists over one hundred countries.

Voluntarios Solidarios, 2017 Mission Street, #305, San Francisco, CA 94110, USA; 415-495-6334, Fax: 415-495-5628, *www.forusa.org/program/voluntaries.html*, *volfor@igc.org*. Places U.S. volunteers with Latin American and Caribbean peace and justice grassroots groups for service between three months and two years. Also sponsors occasional human rights and peace and justice delegations.

WWOOF (Working for Organic Growers), 19 Bradford Road, Lewes, Sussex BN7 1RB, UK. WWOOF, Mt. Murrindal Cooperative, Burchan, Victoria 3885, Australia; 61-5-155-0218, *www.wwoof.org*. Four hundred member farms and volunteer opportunities. Connects members with organic farmers throughout the world.

Human Rights and Social Justice Organizations (information only)

Akha Heritage Foundation, Akha University — Maesai; 386/3 Sailom Joi Rd, Maesai, Chiangrai, 57130 Thailand; *www.thailine.com/akha*, *akha@loxinfo.co.th*. Assists the Akha people in preserving their culture, language, and traditions.

Alaska Native Knowledge Network; *www.ankn.uaf.edu*. Resource for compiling and exchanging information related to Alaska Native knowledge systems and ways of knowing. It has been established to assist Native people, government agencies, educators, and the general public in gaining access to the knowledge base that Alaska Natives have acquired through cumulative experience over millennia.

Australia Burma Council, PO Box 2024, Queanbeyan NSW, Australia 2620; 616-297-7734, Fax: 616-297-7773, *azappia@spirit.com.au*. Opposes tourism to Burma under current oppressive government; publications available.

Australia West Papua Association, PO Box 65, Millers Point, NSW 2000, Australia, 552-6022 or 960-1698, Fax: 552-4588, *www.cs.utexas/users/cline/papua/core .html*. West Papua Action Kit: suggestions for action, resources, and maps on tourism, human rights, refugees, deforestation, mines, dams, and resistance movements.

Burma Action Group-UK, 3rd Floor Bickerton House, 25127 Bickerton Road, London, N19 5JT, 44-207-281-7377, Fax: 44-207-272-3559, *www.burmacampaign .org.uk*, *info@burmacampaign.org.uk*.

Forest Peoples Programme, 1c Fosseway Business Centre, Stratford Road, Moreton-in-Marsh, GL56 9NQ, UK; 44-01608-652893, Fax: 44-01608-652878, *forestpeoples.gn.apc.org*, *info@fppwrm@gn.apc.org*. Established to promote and protect the rights of forest people in their struggle to survive. The Forest Peoples Programme supports forest peoples' rights to determine their own futures, to control the use of their lands, and to carry out sustainable use of their resources.

Free-Tibet Campaign, 1 Rosoman Place, London EC1R 0JY, UK, 0870-770-0328 or 020-7833-9958, *www.freetibet.org*, *mail@freetibet.org*. Independent membership organization campaigning for the rights of Tibetan people. Publishes magazine; reports on tourism in Tibet.

International Campaign for Tibet, 1825 K Street, NW, Suite 520, Washington, DC 20006, USA; 202-785-1515, Fax: 202-785-4343, *www.savetibet.org*, *info@savetibet.org*. Publishes *On This Spot: An Unconventional Map and Guide to Lhasa*.

International Indian Treaty Council (IITC), 2390 Mission Street, Suite 301, San Francisco, CA 94110, USA; 415-641-4482, Fax: 415-641-1298, *www.treatycouncil.org*, *iitc@igc.org*. An organization of Indigenous Peoples from North, Central, and South America and the Pacific working for the Sovereignty and Self-Determination of Indigenous Peoples and the recognition and protection of Indigenous Rights, Traditional Cultures, and Sacred Lands. Seeks, promotes, and builds official participation of Indigenous Peoples in the United Nations and its specialized agencies, as well as other international forums.

International Network for Economic, Social and Cultural Rights (ESCR-net), 162 Montague Street, 2nd floor, Brooklyn, NY 11201, USA: 718-237-9145 ext. 12, Fax: 718-237-9147, *escr-net.org, escr-net@cesr.org*. Coalition of organizations and activists from around the world dedicated to advancing economic, social, and cultural rights.

L'auravetl'an Indigenous Information Center Russia, 103009, Moscow, Nikitskiy per., dom 4, office 406; 7-095-203-22-77 or 7-095-202-38-20, *www.indigenous.ru, iicl@orc.ru*. Aims to improve the abilities of Indigenous communities to fully participate in Russian multicultural society and diminish discrimination of Indigenous People. Center provides mechanism for Indigenous communities to speak out.

National Coalition Government of the Union of Burma (NCGUB), 1319 F Street NW, Suite 303, Washington, DC 20004, USA; 202-639-0639, Fax: 202-639-0638, *www.ncgub.net, ncgub@ncgub.net*. Works toward the restoration of democracy and human rights in Burma.

Open Society Institute-Burma Project, 400 W. 59th Street, New York, NY 10019, USA; 212-548-0632, Fax: 212-548-4655, *www.soros.org/burma, burma@sorosny.org*. Dedicated to increasing awareness of conditions in Burma. Provides information on an antitourism campaign.

World Neighbors, 1213-B York Street, San Francisco, CA 94110, USA; 415-648-9577, *www.wn.org, gbiggs@wn.org*. Provides long-term training to help impoverished communities of Asia, Africa, and Latin America. All of the self-help programs invest in local, Indigenous leadership and respect the dignity and ingenuity of all people. Six trips to visit villages where work is taking place are planned this year.

Short-Term Travel Study Programs

American University Study Tour, World Capitals Program, American University-Tenley Campus, 4400 Massachusetts Avenue NW, Washington, DC 20016, USA; 202-895-4900, 800-424-2600, Fax: 202-895-4960, *www.worldcapitals .american.edu, travel@american.edu*. Offers programs on both the United States and other countries on global policy issues.

Center for Global Education, Augsburg College, 2211 Riverside Avenue, Minneapolis, MN 55454, USA; 800-299-8889 or 612-330-1159, Fax: 612-330-1695, *www.augsburg.edu/global, globaled@augsburg.edu*. Organizes tours to the global South to learn about social and environmental issues.

Cross-Cultural Solutions, 47 Potter Avenue, New Rochelle, NY 10801, USA; 800-380-4777 or 914-632-0022, Fax: 914-632-8494, *www.crossculturalsolutions.org, info@crossculturalsolutions.org*. One of the leading international volunteer organizations in the United States and sends more than one thousand volunteers overseas every year.

Global Awareness Through Experience (GATE) 912 Mark Street, La Crosse, WI 54601, USA; 608-791-5283, *www.gate-travel.org, gate@fspa.org*. Student programs throughout the world.

Global Service Corps, 300 Broadway, Suite 28, San Francisco, CA 94133, USA; 415-788-3666 ext. 128, Fax: 415-788-7324, *www.globalservicecorps.org, gsc@igc.apc.org*. Service-learning and cultural immersion in Costa Rica, Tanzania, or Thailand. Live with a village family while assisting grassroots organizations on community service and development projects.

PlanetEdu, 1400 E. Southern Avenue, Suite B-108, Tempe, AZ 85282, USA; 800-433-9208, Fax: 480-505-2728, *www.PlanetEdu.com, info@PlanetEdu.com*. An international education search directory with information about study and work abroad programs.

School for Field Studies, 16 Broadway, Beverly, MA 01915, USA; 508-927-7777, *www.fieldstudies.org, admissions@fieldstudies.org*. International field studies and hands-on opportunities for high school and college students concerned about the environment.

School for International Training, PO Box 676, Kipling Road, Brattleboro, VT 05302, USA; 800-336-1616, Fax: 802-258-3500, *www.sit.edu, info@sit.edu*. The summer abroad training concentrates on experiential learning, homestays, intensive language instruction, and independent study projects.

University Research Expeditions Program (UREP), University of California-Berkeley, One Shields Avenue, Davis, CA 95616, USA; 530-757-3529 or 530-757-3537, *urep.ucdavis.edu, urep@ucdavis.edu*. Scientific, voluntary environmental travel study programs; participants assist researchers on programs such as tracking monkeys in the rain forests and pelicans in the Sea of Cortez; supports community-based ecotourism programs.

Tourism-Specific College and University Programs

Colorado State University, College of Natural Resources Recreation and Parks Association, 233 Forestry Building, Colorado State University, Fort Collins, CO 80523, USA; 970-491-6591, Fax: 970-491-2255, *www.cnr.colostate.edu/, ask_us_nrrt@cnr.colostate.edu*. Natural Resource Recreation and Tourism, one of seven programs in the United States that is both a comprehensive bachelor's, master's, and doctoral program and is accredited by the National Recreation and Parks Association.

Faulkner State Community College, Travel/Tourism Management, Baldwin County and Alabama Gulf Coast College, 3301 Gulf Shores Parkway, Bay Minette, AL 36507, USA; 334-986-3104, *www.faulkner.cc.al.us*. Undergraduate program in ecotourism.

George Washington University, Department of Tourism and Hospitality Management, 817 23rd Street NW, Bldg. K, Washington, DC 20052, USA; 202-994-7087, Fax: 202-994-1420, *www.gwutourism.org*. Graduate and undergraduate programs covering sustainability and ecotourism. Also has International Institute for Tourism Studies department.

Goddard College, 123 Pitkin Road, Plainfield, VT 05667, USA; 800-468-4888, *www.goddard.edu*. Travel study programs; individually designed programs allow students to take on critical tourism studies.

Griffith University Gold Coast, International Center for Ecotourism Research, PMB 50, Gold Coast 4215, Queensland, Australia; 61-75-948-668, Fax: 61-75-948-679, *www.gu.edu.au*. In-depth research programs on ecotourism, including environmental and cultural impacts, economic policies, and green behavior guidelines. Ecotourism studies.

Hocking College–School of Natural Resources, 3301 Hocking Parkway, Nelsonville, OH 45764, USA; 800-282-4163, Fax: 740-753-1452, *www.hocking.edu*. Focus on tourism that is environmentally sound, culturally sensitive, and economically sustainable.

HNB Garhwal University, Centre for Mountain Tourism and Hospitality Studies, Srinagar, Garhwal, India; Fax: 01388-52424, *bagri_sc@hotmail.com*. Produces the *Journal of Tourism* focusing on issues of mountain tourism.

Humber College, 205 Humber College Boulevard, Toronto, Ontario M9W 5L7, Canada; 416-675-3111, Fax: 416-675-2427, *www.humberc.on.ca*. School of Hospitality, Recreation, and Tourism, also offers Eco and Adventure Tourism postgraduate certificate.

Humboldt State University Office, of Extended Education, Arcata, CA 95521, USA; 707-826-3731, Fax: 707-826-5885, *www.humboldt.edu*. Ecotourism planning and management certificate program.

Institute of Eco-Tourism, Srinakkarinwirot University–Patumwan Campus, Henri-Dunant Road, Bangkok 10330, Thailand; 66-2-252-27044, Fax: 66-2-254-4599, *www.swu.ac.th/iet*, *ladawadee@hotmail.com*. Graduate programs and research opportunities.

Moffat Centre for Travel and Tourism Business Development, Glasgow Caledonian University, Caledonian Business School, Health Building, Cowcaddens Road, Glasgow G4 0BA, +44(0) 141 331 8400, Fax +44(0) 141 331 8411, *info@moffatcentre.com*, *www.moffatcentre.com/index.htm*. Professor John Lennon and his department offer opportunities to study dark tourism.

Native Education Centre, 285 East 5th Avenue, Vancouver, BC V5T 1H2, Canada; 604-874-3761, *www.necvancouver.org*. Tourism programs for the Aboriginal community include: First Host, a one-day workshop focusing on equality between host and guest, Sun Mask Tours, and Aboriginal Tourism Management.

Niagara College Canada, InfoCentre 300 Woodlawn Road, Welland, Ontario, Canada L3C 7L3; *www.niagarac.on.ca/*, *infocentre@niagarac.on.ca*. Tourism development, postgraduate, with emphasis on ecotourism, agritourism, adventure tourism, and cultural/heritage tourism.

North Carolina State, Sustainable Tourism Programs, Box 7344, Raleigh, NC 27695, USA; 919-515-2087, *www.ncsu.edu*. Undergraduate programs.

Paul Smith's College, Route 86 and 30, PO Box 265, Paul Smiths, NY 12970, USA; 518-327-6211 or 800-421-2605, Fax: 518-327-6016, *www.paulsmiths.edu/index.html*. In Forestry: Recreation, Adventure Travel, and Ecotourism.

Southwest Texas State University, Center for Nature and Heritage Tourism, Department of Geography, 601 University Drive, San Marcos, Texas 78666, USA; 512-245-2111, *www.geo.swt.edu/nht*, *as40550@swt.edu*. The mission of the Center for Nature and Heritage Tourism is to provide an interdisciplinary context for education and research in nature and heritage tourism planning, development, and management.

Texas A&M University, Department of Recreation, Park and Tourism Sciences, 2261 TAMU, College Station, TX 77843-2261, 979-845-5411, Fax: 979-845-0446, *www.http://rptsweb.tamu.edu/rpts*. The department's multidisciplinary and distinguished faculty has generated hundreds of books, scientific journal articles, and technical reports, and has provided intellectual leadership in recreation, park, and tourism sciences throughout the world.

Trent University, Department of Geography, Box 4800, Peterborough, Ontario, Canada, K9J 7B8; 705-748-1426, Fax: 705-748-1205, *www.trent.ca/geography*, *fhelleiner@trentu.ca*. Sustainable tourism studies.

University of Alaska–Fairbanks, School of Management, PO Box 756080, Fairbanks, AK 99775, USA; 907-474-7211, *www.som.uaf.edu*, *dean.som@uaf.edu*. Programs through the international tourism program and the Alaska Institute of Tourism.

University of Colorado at Boulder, Leeds School of Business, Center for Sustainable Tourism, Boulder, Colorado 80309, USA; 303-492-1411, *leeds.colorado.edu/tourism*, *jamie.walker@colorado.edu*. Provides a forum for the assessing of economic, social, cultural, and environmental implications of the tourism industry.

University of Hawaii at Manoa, 2444 Dole Street, Honolulu, HI 96822, USA; 808-956-8111, *www.uhm.hawaii.edu*, *info@uhm.hawaii.edu*. Tourism management, urban and regional land planning, other programs involving tourism research and studies.

University of New Hampshire, Department of Resource Economics and Development, 310 James Hall, Durham, NH 03824; 603-862-1234, *www.dred.unh.edu*, *info@dred.unh.edu*. Compiled report "University Based Education and Training Programs in Ecotourism or Nature-Based Tourism in the USA."

University of Oregon, Micronesia and South Pacific Program, 5244 University of Oregon, Eugene, OR 97403, USA; 541-346-3815, Fax: 541-346-2040, *www.uoregon.edu/~mspp*, *mspp@darkwing.uoregon.edu*. Program for sustainable communities studies and tourism development in Micronesia and the South Pacific.

University of Otago, New Zealand, Department of Tourism, 4th Floor, Commerce Building, Cnr Clyde and Union Streets, PO Box 56, Dunedin, New Zealand; 64-3-479-8520, Fax: 64-3-479-9034, *divcom.otago.ac.nz/tourism/index.html*, *tourism@otago.ac.nz*. Tourism research, undergraduate and graduate degrees. Hosted conference on "Ecotourism, Wilderness and Mountain Tourism: Issues, Strategies and Regional Development" in August 2002 as part of the UN International Year of Mountains and Ecotourism.

University of Strathclyde, 16 Richmond Street, Glasgow G1 1xQ, Scotland, UK; 44-141-552-4400, Fax: 44-141-552-0775, *www.strath.ac.uk*. The Scottish Hotel School has a program on Tourism in Developing Countries.

University of Surrey, Guildford, Surrey, GU2 7XH, UK; 44-0-1483-300800, Fax: 44-0-1483-300803, *www.surrey.ac.uk*, *information@surrey.ac.uk*. Has postgraduate program, Management Studies for the Service Sector, with some progressive professors specializing in tourism.

University of Vermont, School of Natural Resources, Burlington, VT 05405, USA; 802-656-4280, Fax: 802-656-8683, *www.snr.uvm.edu*. Recreation management, stressing the development of recreation and leisure opportunities integrated with the wise use and protection of natural resources.

University of Waikato, Private Bag 3105, Hamilton, New Zealand; 0800-WAIKATO or 64-7-838-4466, *www.waikato.ac.nz*. Tourism Studies providing skills in social and environmental analysis leading to an understanding of the impacts of tourism on natural environments and host communities.

University of Wisconsin-Stout, Hospitality and Tourism, Menomonie, WI 54751, USA; 715-232-2339, Fax: 715-232-3200, *www.uwstout.edu/chd/hosptour*, *clementsc@uwstout.edu*. Publishers of the *Annals of Tourism Research*.

U.S. Government Contacts

Designations to U.S. National Wilderness Preservation System require congressional approval, and agency management decisions involving public lands are open to public comment. For wilderness legislation updates, contact the Sierra Club Legislative Hotline: 202-675-2394 or *www.sierraclub.org*.

National Park Service Headquarters, 1849 C Street NW, Washington, DC 20240, USA; 202-208-6843, *www.nps.gov*. For information about national parks wilderness study area information, national parks, wildlife refuges, and Bureau of Land Management administrative decisions.

No Sweat, Department of Labor, Frances Perkins Building, 200 Constitution Avenue NW, Washington, DC 20210, USA; 866-4-USA-DOL or 877-889-5627, *www.dol.gov/dol/nosweat.htm*. Information about companies in the tourism industry that exploit laborers, strives to help end sweatshop conditions for American workers.

State Department, 2201 C Street NW, Washington, DC 20520, USA; 202-647-4000, *www.state.gov*.

United States Agency for International Development, Ronald Reagan Building, Washington, DC 20523, USA; 202-712-4810, Fax: 202-216-3524, *www.usaid.gov*.

United States Department of Commerce, 1401 Constitution Avenue NW, Washington, DC 20230, USA; Office of Travel and Tourism Industries: *tinet.ita.doc.gov*. Provide improved economic accountability on the impact of travel and tourism at the national, state, and local levels.

United States Forest Service, Cultural and Heritage Tourism, 324 25th Street, Ogden, UT 84401, USA; 801-625-5172, Fax: 801-625-5170. Contact for U.S. Forest Service ecotourism information, publications, planning.

United States Forest Service, Department of Agriculture, 201 14th Street SW, Washington, DC 20250, USA: 202-205-1661, *www.fs.fed.us*. Information about U.S. Forest Service wilderness study areas. Each state has designated tourism staff.

United States Department of the Interior, 1849 C Street, NW, Washington, DC 20240, USA; 202-208-3100, *www.doi.gov*. Protects and provides access to the nation's natural and cultural heritage while honoring Indian tribes and island communities. Administrative decisions affecting U.S. protected lands.

International Organization Contacts

Asian Pacific Economic Cooperation (APEC), 438 Alexandra Road, #14-00, Alexandra Point, Singapore 119958; 65-6276-1880, Fax: 65-6276-1775, *www.apecsec.org.sg, info@mail.apecsec.org.sg.* Primary regional vehicle for promoting open trade and economic cooperation.

Convention on Biological Diversity (CBD), World Trade Center, 393 St. Jacques Street, Office 300, Montreal, Quebec, H2Y 1N9, Canada; 514-288-2220, Fax: 514-288-6588, *www.biodiv.org, secretariat@biodiv.org.* A program of the UNEP, the CBD functions as the international body overseeing the conservation of biological diversity, with focus on genetic rights. Has a program on sustainable use and tourism.

Convention on International Trade in Endangered Species of Wild Fauna and Flora (CITES), CITES Secretariat, International Environment House, Chemin des Anémones, CH-1219 Châtelaine, Geneva, Switzerland; 4122-917-8139/40, Fax: 4122-797-3417, *www.cites.org, cites@unep.ch.* An international agreement that ensures that international trade in specimens of wild animals and plants does not threaten their survival.

Global Environment Facility (GEF), 1818 H Street NW, Washington DC 20433, USA; 202-473-0508, Fax: 202-522-3240, *www.gefweb.org, secretariatofgef@ worldbank.org.* Provides financial mechanism and international cooperation to assist developing countries in addressing environmental problems including: biodiversity loss, climate change, degradation of international waters, and ozone depletion.

International Union for Conservation of Nature and Natural Resources (IUCN), Rue Mauverney 28, Gland, 1196, Switzerland; 41-22-999-0000, Fax: 41-22-999-0002, *www.iucn.org, mail@hq.iucn.org.* This global coalition of experts distributes extensive information on conservation-related matters around the world.

National Center for Infectious Disease Control (CDC), Centers for Disease Control and Prevention, International Travel, 1600 Clifton Road NE, Mail Stop E03, Atlanta, GA 30333, USA: 800-311-3435 or 404-639-3311, *www.cdc.gov, info@cdc.gov.* Information on health and disease around the world.

Organization of American States (OAS), Headquarters: 17th Street and Constitution Ave NW, Washington DC 20006, USA; 202-458-3000, *www.oas.org.* An international body representing the Americas for the United Nations.

Organization for Economic Cooperation and Development (OECD), 2, rue Andre Pascal, F-75775, Paris Cedex 16, France; 33145-24-82-00, *www.oecd.org.* An international body of thirty member countries committed to democratic government and the market economy.

Pacific Asia Travel Association (PATA), Unit B1, 28th Floor, Sian Tower, 989 Rama I Road, Pathumwan, Bangkok, 10330 Thailand; 66-2-658-2000, Fax: 66-2-658-2010, *www.pata.org, patabkk@pata.th.com.* The recognized authority on

Pacific Asia travel and tourism, providing marketing, research, and educational opportunities to government tourist offices, airlines, hotels, travel agencies, tour operators, and related companies.

Sustainable Tourism Program, PO Box 777-1000, San José, Costa Rica, +506 223-1733, ext. 247, Fax: +506 258-2912, *info@turismo-sostenible.co.cr*. The C.S.T. Program was developed by the Department of Natural Resources of the Costa Rica Tourist Board and the Costa Rica National Accreditation Commission.

UNEP World Conservation Monitoring Centre, Information Office, UNEP-WCMC, 219 Huntingdon Road, Cambridge CB3 0DL, UK; 44-0-1223-277314 or 44-0-1223-277722, Fax: 44-0-1223-277136, *www.unep-wcmc.org*, *info@unep-wcmc.org*. Provides information for policy and action to conserve the living world, focusing on the relationship between trade and the environment. Has information and statistics on tourism.

United Nations Development Programme (UNDP), *www.undp.org*. The UN's global development network, focusing on democratic governance, poverty reduction, crisis prevention, energy and the environment, technology, and HIV/AIDS. Over one hundred offices located around the world, mostly in developing countries.

United Nations Division for Sustainable Development, 2 UN Plaza, Room DC2-2220, New York, NY 10017, USA; 212-963-0902, Fax: 212-963-4260, *www.un.org/esa/sustdev*, *dsd@un.org*. Division that oversees sustainable development, including Agenda 21, the Commission on Sustainable Development (CSB), and the World Summit on Sustainable Development (WSSD).

United Nations Economic and Social Council (ECOSOC), Division for ECOSOC Support and Coordination, Department of Economic and Social Affairs, 1 UN Plaza, Room DC1-1428, New York, NY 10017, USA; *www.un.org/esa/coordination/ecosoc*, *esa@un.org*. A leading body of the United Nations, ECOSOC is responsible for promoting higher standards of living, full employment, and economic and social progress. Responsible for some aspects of the WSSD.

United Nations Educational, Scientific, and Cultural Organization (UNESCO), 7, place de Fontenoy, 75352 Paris 07 SP, France; 331-45-68-1000, Fax: 33-1-45-67-1690, *www.unesco.org*. The United Nations branch for culture and sustainability contributes to peace and security in the world by promoting collaboration between countries.

United Nations Environment Programme, United Nations Avenue, Gigiri, PO Box 30552, Nairobi, Kenya; 254-2-621234, Fax: 254-2-624489, *www.unep.org*. Works to encourage sustainable development through sound environmental practices everywhere. The UN body overseeing the IYE.

World Bank, 1818 H Street NW, Washington DC 20433, USA; 202-473-1000, Fax: 202-477-6391, *www.worldbank.org*. Provides development assistance to countries, focusing on helping the poorest people and the poorest countries.

World Commission on Protected Areas (WCPA) and IUCN Program on Protected Areas, WCPA Chair, International Development and Conservation, World

Resources Institute, 10 G Street NE, Suite 800, Washington DC 20002; 202-729-7785, Fax: 202-729-7651, *wcpa.iucn.org, kenton@hardynet.com*. Promotes the international establishment and effective management of protected areas.

World Health Organization (WHO), Headquarters: Avenue Appai 20, 1211 Geneva 27, Switzerland; 004122-791-2121, Fax: 0041-22-791-3111, *www.who.int, info@who.int*. An international body under the United Nations that strives to attain the highest level of health for all people.

World Intellectual Property Organization (WIPO), 34, chemin des Colombettes, Geneva; 41-22-338-8181, *www.wipo.org, information.center@wipo.int*. An international organization dedicated to helping to ensure that the rights of creators and owners of intellectual property are protected worldwide.

World Tourism Organization (WTO), Capitán Haya 42, 28020 Madrid, Spain; 34-91-567-81-00, Fax: 34-91-571-37-33, *www.world-tourism.org, omt@world-tourism.org*. World tourism statistics, planning, policy, publications.

World Travel & Tourism Council, 1-2 Queen Victoria Terrace, Sovereign Court, London E1W 3HA, UK; 44-870-727-9882, Fax: 44-870-728-9882, *www.wttc.org, enquiries@wttc.org*. Council of travel industry CEOs; research, reports, publications.

Magazines, Newsletters, Journals, Surveys, and Travel Guides

Adventures in Nature: Travel Guide Series. John Muir Publications, PO Box 613, Santa Fe, NM 87504, USA; 505-982-4078.

Alaska Wilderness Recreation and Tourism Association Newsletter and Directory. Published by ARWTA, 2207 Spenard Road, Suite 201, Anchorage, AK 99503, USA: 907-258-3171, Fax: 907-258-3851, *www.awrta.org, info@awrta.org*. Updates on environmental issues related to tourism in Alaska; directory of ecotour operators.

Annals of Tourism Research. University of Wisconsin-Stout, Menomonie, WI 54751 USA; 715-232-2339, Fax: 715-232-3200, *jafari@uwstout.edu*. A leading scholarly journal in tourism.

Auto-Free Times. Alliance for a Paving Moratorium, Fossil Fuels Policy Action Institute, PO Box 4347, Arcata, CA 95518, USA: 707-826-7775, Fax: 707-822-7007, *www.culturalechange.org, info@culturalechange.org*. Dedicated to fighting road construction through revolutionary ecology and economics.

Broken Bud. 1765-D Le Roy, Berkeley, CA 94709, USA; *CRTourism@aol.com*. Newsletter of Center for Responsible Tourism, which is an advocacy for anti-prostitution tourism and child trafficking.

Contours: Concern for Tourism. Ecumenical Coalition on Third World Tourism, PO Box 35, Senanikhom, Bangkok 10902, Thailand; 66-2-939-7111, Fax: 66-2-939-7112, *Contours@ksc.net.th*. Quarterly magazine; news from developing countries.

Cultural Survival Quarterly. Cultural Survival, 215 Prospect Street, Cambridge, MA 02139, USA: 617-441-5407, Fax: 617-441-5417, *www.cs.org, dentremont@cs.org*.

Back issues include "Breaking Out of the Tourist Trap" 14 (1 and 2); ongoing coverage of tourism impacts.

E: The Environmental Magazine. Earth Action Network, 28 Knight Street, Norwalk, CT 06851, USA: 203-854-5559, Fax: 203-866-0602, *www.emagazine.com, info@emagazine.com.* Covers some environmental travel issues and ecotourism.

Earth Island Journal. Earth Island Institute, 300 Broadway, Suite 28, San Francisco, CA 94133, USA: 415-788-3666, Fax: 415-788-7324, *www.earthisland.org, info@earthisland.org.* Some environmental tourism issues.

The Ecologist. Hogarth House, PO Box 326, Sittingbourne, Kent ME9 8FA, UK; 44-0-1795-414-963, *www.theecologist.org, theecologist@thegalleon.co.uk.* Information on globalization issues, voices from the global South.

Frommer's Travel Guides. Macmillan Travel, 1633 Broadway, New York, NY 10019, USA; or Frommer's Travel Book Club, PO Box 473, Mt. Morris, IL 61054, USA; 815-734-1104. Travel guides.

Indigenous Affairs: The Indigenous World. Indigenous Affairs, International Work Group, Flolstroede 10, DK-1171 Copenhagen, Denmark; 45-3312-4724, Fax: 45-3314-7749. English and Spanish.

Indochina Spotlight: Tourism and Tourism-Related Developments in Cambodia, Laos, and Vietnam. ECTWT, PO Box 35, Senanikhom, Bangkok 10902, Thailand. Newspaper and magazine clippings.

In Focus. Tourism Concern, Stapleton House, 277-281 Holloway Road, London N7 8HN, UK; 44-171-753-3330, Fax: 44-171-753-3331, *www.tourismconcern .org, info@tourismconcern.org.* Magazine for Tourism Concern members and others.

The International Centre for Trade and Sustainable Development (ICTSD). 13, ch. des Anémones, 1219 Geneva, Switzerland; 41-22-917-8492; Fax: 917-8093, *www.ictsd.org, subscribe_biores@ictsd.ch.* ICTSD has a publication to the trade and sustainable development communities: *BRIDGES Trade BioRes — Trade and Biological Resources News Digest.* The publication is produced in collaboration with IUCN — The World Conservation Union, and its Commission on Environment, Economic and Social Policy (CEESP), in order to address the intersection of trade and biological resources. The issues will also be posted on the ICTSD website.

In These Times: The Alternative Newsmagazine. Institute for Public Affairs, 2040 N. Milwaukee Avenue, Chicago, IL 60647, USA; 773-772-0100, Fax: 773-772-4180, *www.inthesetimes.com, info@inthesetimes.com.* Independent progressive magazine with some articles on tourism.

Journal of Sustainable Tourism. Clevedon: Channel View Books/Multilingual Matters Ltd., Frankfort Lodge, annual.

Journal of Tourism. HNB Garhwal University, Centre for Mountain Tourism and Hospitality Studies, Srinagar, Garhwal, India; Fax: 01388-52424, *bagri_sc@hotmail.com.*

Ladakh Project Newsletter. ISEC, PO Box 9475, Berkeley, CA 94709, USA; 510-527-3873; in England, contact ISEC/Ladakh Project, 21 Victoria Square, Clifton, Bristol BS8 4ES, England.

Lonely Planet Guides. Lonely Planet Publications, PO Box 2001A, Berkeley, CA 94702, USA; 510-893-8555, Fax: 510-893-8563 or PO Box 617, Hawthorne, Vic 3122, Australia, *www.lonelyplanet.com, info@lonelyplanet.com.* For Lonely Planet travel guides.

MahilaWeb. Sancharika Samuha, PO Box 13293, Jawalakhel, Lalitpur, Nepal; 977-1-538549 or 546715, Fax: 977-1-547291, *www.mahilaweb.org, info@mahilaweb.org.* An electronic repository focusing on women and gender issues in Nepal.

Moon Travel Handbooks. Moon Travel Publications, PO Box 3040, Chico, CA 95927, USA; 800-345-5473, *www.moontravel.com.* Travel guides.

Multinational Monitor. PO Box 19405, Washington, DC 20036, USA; 202-387-8030, *www.multinational.com.* Monthly newsmagazine dedicated to tracking and exposing illegal, abusive, and deceptive activities of multinational corporations.

New Frontiers Newsletter. c/o Tourism Investigation and Monitoring Team, TERRA, 5th Floor, TVS Bldg., 409 Soi Rohitsook, Prachrat Bampen Road, Bangkok 10320, Thailand; 66-2-69-107-1820, Fax: 66-2-69-7910-714, *terraper@ksc.net.th.* Excellent monitoring of tourism in Mekong subregion.

New Internationalist. PO Box 1143, Lewiston, NY 14092, USA; 416-257-4626, *www.newinternationalist.org, info@newinternationalist.org.* Employee cooperative producing monthly magazine on Third World development; tourism issues included.

Newsletter of the Center for Responsible Tourism. PO Box 827, San Anselmo, CA 94979, USA; 415-258-6594, Fax: 415-454-2493. Tourism issues, articles, and poems from local people in destinations around the world; reviews new resources and books on tourism.

The Pacific Peoples' Partnership. 1921 Fernwood Road, Victoria BC, V8T 2Y6, Canada; 250-381-4131, *www.sppf.org, sppf@sppf.org.* Publishes *Tok Blong Pasifik — News and Views on the Pacific Islands* "Ecotourism: At What Price?" The issue has an article that focuses on the impact that the combination of globalization and tourism have on Indigenous Peoples. Other articles include *What Does Gender Have to Do with Ecotourism?* and *Ecotourism: Promoting Sustainable Livelihoods and Marine Conservation.*

Responsible Tourism: A Resource Guide. WorldViews and ECTWT, 462 19th Street, Oakland, CA 94612, USA; 510-835-4692, Fax: 510-835-3018. A compilation of resources on global tourism.

Samefolket. www.samefolket.se. A magazine published mostly in Sweden that covers political and cultural issues of the Sami, the Indigenous People of what is now areas of northern Norway, Sweden, Finland, and Russia.

Sierra Club Adventure Travel Guides. Sierra Club Books, 730 Polk Street, San Francisco, CA 94109, USA; 805-965-3452, *www.sierraclub.org.* For "Adventuring In..." travel guide series.

Survival for Tribal Peoples. Survival International, 11-15 Emerald Street, London WC1N 3QL, UK; 44-171-242-1441, *www.survivalinternational.org.* Newsletter for Survival International members.

Tranet (Transnational Network). PO Box 567, Rangeley, ME 04907, USA; 207-864-2252. Bimonthly newsletter by and for people participating in the social paradigm shift in all parts of the world. Numerous responsible tourism contacts, projects, ideas.

Transitions Abroad: The Guide to Learning, Living, and Working Overseas. Transitions Abroad, 18 Hulst Road, PO Box 344, Amherst, MA 01004, USA; 415-256-3414, *www.transitionsabroad.com.* An education-oriented travel magazine that pioneered socially and ecologically responsible tourism writing.

Voice of the Turtle Newsletter. Turtle Island Office, 4035 Ryan Road, Blue Mounds, WI 53517, USA; 608-767-3931, *beabriggs@aol.com.* From the organizers of the first bioregional gathering in the Americas in Mexico.

Audiovisuals

Bull Frog Films, PO Box 149, Oley, PA 19547, USA; 800-543-3764, *bullfrog@igc.apc .org.* Videos for rent or purchase include *Haida Gwaii — The Queen Charlotte Islands in the Web of Life,* produced by Barbara Barde, depicting tourism and Indigenous Peoples in Canada, and *Yosemite and the Fate of the Earth,* produced by the Yosemite Guardian Project of Earth Island Institute, depicting the impact of development around the world and its effect on wildlife.

Central Television Enterprises, Hesketh House, 43-45 Portman Square, London W1H 9FG, UK. Tourism films include *Thailand for Sale,* produced by David Jay and coproduced by Small World Productions.

Interlock Media/Environmental Media Unit, 607 Boylston Street, 4th Floor, Boston, MA 02116, USA; 617-236-4471, Fax: 617-236-4429, *intlock@ix.netcom.com.* Informational and training films and videos on Indigenous rights, environmental movements, domestic and Third World.

Ladakh Project, PO Box 9475, Berkeley, CA 94709, USA; 510-527-3873. *Ancient Futures: Learning from Ladakh* and *In Light of Reverence: Protecting America's Sacred Lands.* Available in several languages.

Living Media, produced by Peter Wirth and Chris Bolt, Write G/W Associates, 702 S. Beech, Syracuse, NY 13210, USA; 315-476-3396. This is a sixty-minute audiocassette tape designed to give people who travel to the Third World the skills and confidence to use the media to share that experience.

Native Solidarity News CKUT 90.3 FM, 3647 University, Montreal (Quebec), H3A 2B3 Canada; 514-486-0246, Fax: 514-398-8261, *nsn@tao.ca.* Native Solidarity News is a national radio service "in support of Indigenous peoples survival and dignity." The radio service has a new catalog out; included in it is the program, "Golf and Tourism Take on the World" (NSN 201, August 2000) with Deborah McLaren of Indigenous Tourism Rights International.

Planning an Excellent Adventure. Ecumenical Exchange Office. Worldwide Ministries Division, Presbyterian Distribution Service. 800-524-2612. Twenty-minute video offers a guide for groups planning trips.

Tourism Concern, Stapleton House, 277-281 Holloway Road, London N7 8HN, UK; 44-171-753-3330, Fax: 44-171-753-3331, *tourconcern@gn.apc.org.* Videos and films for rent or purchase include *Cannibal Tours* by Dennis O'Rourke (Australia, 1987); *Señor Turista,* by Gertrude Bohm (Germany/Peru, 1983/1985); *Our Man In . . . (Goa, Cuba, Kenya); Tourism in Zimbabwe; Tourism in Mountain Areas;* young people's programs. Many are also available on audiotape.

Books

Addo, Michael, ed. *Human Rights Standards and the Responsibility of Transnational Corporations*. The Hague: Kluwer Law International, 1999.

Agrawal, Arun, and Clark Gibson, eds. *Communities and the Environment: Ethnicity, Gender and the State in Community-Based Conservation*. Piscataway: Rutgers University Press, 2001.

Apostolopoulos, Yiorgos and Dennis Gayle, eds. *Island Tourism and Sustainable Development: Caribbean, Pacific and Mediterranean Experiences*. New York, Praeger Publishing Text, 2002.

———, Loukissas, Philippos, and Lila Leontidou, eds. *Mediterranean Tourism: Facets of Socioeconomic Development and Cultural Change*. London: Routledge, 2001.

Aronsson, Lars. *Development of Sustainable Tourism*. London: Continuum International Publishing Group, 2001.

Ashley, Caroline, Dilys Roe, and Harold Goodwin. *Pro-Poor Tourism Strategies: Making Tourism Work for the Poor*. Sterenage: International Institute for Environment and Development (IIED), 2001.

Ashton, Patricia, and Ray Ashton. *Ecotourism: Sustainable Nature and Conservation Based Tourism*. Melbourne: Krieger Publishing Company, 2002.

Badger, A., P. Barnett, L. Corbyn, and J. Keefe. *Trading Places: Tourism as Trade*. London: Tourism Concern, 1996.

Barry, Tom. *The Other Side of Paradise: Foreign Control in the Caribbean*. New York: Grove Press, 1984.

Beltran, Javier, and Adrian Phillips. *Indigenous and Traditional Peoples and Protected Areas: Principles, Guidelines and Case Studies*. Covelo: Island Press, 2000.

Benjamin, Medea, and Andrea Freedman. *Bridging the Global Gap*. Cabin John, Md.: Seven Locks Press, 1988.

Benz, Stephen. *Green Dreams: Travels in Central America*. Melbourne: Lonely Planet Publications, 1998.

Berkes, Fikret. *Sacred Ecology: Traditional Ecological Knowledge and Resource Management*. London: Taylor and Francis, 1999.

Bishop, Ryan, and Liilian Robinson. *Night Market: Sexual Cultures and the Thai Economic Miracle*. New York: Routledge, 1998.

Black, Maggie. *In the Twilight Zone: Child Workers in the Hotel, Tourism and Catering Industry*. Geneva: International Labor Organization, 1995.

Blackford, Mansel. *Fragile Paradise: The Impact of Tourism on Maui, 1959–2000*. Lawrence: University Press of Kansas, 2001.

Blake, Beatrice, and Anne Becher. *The New Key to Costa Rica*, 15th ed. Berkeley, Calif.: Ulysses Press, 2001.

Box, Ben, ed. *Footprint South America*. Bath, England: Footprint Handbooks, 2001.

Brandon, Katrina, Kent Redford, and Steven Sanderson, eds. *Parks in Peril: People, Politics, and Protected Areas*. Covelo, Calif.: Island Press, 1998.

Briassoulis, Helen, and Jan van der Straaten, eds. *Tourism and the Environment: Regional, Economic, Cultural and Policy Issues*. Dordrecht: Kluwer Academic Publishers, 2000.

Burns, Peter. *Tourism: A New Perspective.* Englewood Cliffs, N.J.: Prentice-Hall, 1995.

Butler, Richard, and Tom Hinch, eds. *Tourism and Indigenous Peoples.* London: Routledge, 1996.

Castaneda, Quetzil. *In the Museum of Maya Culture: Touring Chichen Itza.* Minneapolis: University of Minnesota Press, 1996.

Cater, Erlet, and Gwen Lowman, eds. *Ecotourism: A Sustainable Option?* New York: John Wiley and Sons, 1994.

Chambers, Erve. *Native Tours: The Anthropology of Travel and Tourism.* Prospect Heights, Ill.: Waveland Press, 1999.

————. *Tourism and Culture: An Applied Perspective.* Albany: State University of New York Press, 1997.

Chauhan, Surender. *Biodiversity, Biopiracy, and Biopolitics: The Global Perspective.* Delhi: Kalinga Publications, 2001.

Christian Aid. *Abuse of Innocence: Tourism and Child Prostitution in the Third World,* London: Christian Aid, 1995.

Chon, Kaye, ed. *Tourism in Southeast Asia.* New York: Haworth Hospitality Press, 2000.

Chopra, Suhita. *Tourism and Development in India.* New Delhi: Ashish Publishing House, 1996.

Clift, Stephen, and Simon Carter, eds. *Tourism and Sex: Cultural, Commerce, and Coercion.* London: Continuum International Publishing Group, 2000.

Cook-Lynn, Elizabeth. *Anti-Indianism in Modern American: A Voice from Tatekeya's Earth.* Champaign: University of Illinois Press, 2001.

Crouch, David. *Leisure/Tourism Geographies: Practices and Geographical Knowledge.* London: Routledge, 1999.

Danaher, Kevin. *Beyond Safaris: A Guide to Building People-to-People Ties with Africa.* Trenton, N.J.: Africa World Press, 1991.

Davidson, Julia. *Prostitution, Power and Freedom.* Ann Arbor: University of Michigan Press, 1999.

Davis, Susan. *Spectacular Nature: Corporate Culture and the Sea World Experience.* Berkeley: University of California Press, 1997.

de Kadt, Emanuel, ed. *Tourism: Passport to Development? Perspectives on the Social and Cultural Effects of Tourism in Developing Countries.* London: Oxford University Press, 1978.

Desmond, Jane. *Staging Tourism: Bodies on Display from Waikiki to Sea World.* Chicago: University of Chicago Press, 1999.

Duffy, Rosaleen. *A Trip Too Far: Ecotourism, Politics and Exploitation.* London: Earthscan Publications Ltd, 2002.

Eagles, Paul, and Per Nilsen, eds. *Ecotourism: An Annotated Bibliography for Planners and Managers.* 5th ed. Burlington, Vt.: The International Ecotourism Society, 2001.

Eber, Shirley, ed. *Beyond the Green Horizon: Principles for Sustainable Tourism.* London: Tourism Concern/World Wildlife Fund, 1992.

European Centre for Eco Agro Tourism. *Green Holiday Guides.* Amsterdam: European Centre for Eco Agro Tourism International, 2002.

Fennell, David. *Ecotourism: An Introduction.* London: Routledge, 1999.

Fillmore, Mary. *Suggested Guidelines for Assessment of the Impacts of Tourism on Women*. Bangalore: EQUATIONS, 1994.

Font, Xavier, and John Tribe, eds. *Forest Tourism and Recreation: Case Studies in Environmental Management*. New York, CABI Publishing, 2000.

———, John Tribe, and Richard Viskery, eds. *Environmental Management for Rural Tourism and Recreation*. London: Continuum International Publishing Group, 2000.

Forsyth, Tim. *Sustainable Tourism: Moving from Theory to Practice*. London: Tourism Concern and World Wildlife Fund for Nature, 1996.

Fossati, Amedeo, and Giorgio Panella, eds. *Tourism and Sustainable Economic Development*. Boston: Kluwer Academic, 2000.

France, Lesley, ed. *The Earthscan Reader in Sustainable Tourism*. London: Earthscan Publications Ltd, 1997.

Friar, William. *Adventures in Nature*. New York: Avalon, 2001.

Gandy, Matthew. *Concrete and Clay: Reworking Nature in New York City*. Cambridge, Mass.: MIT Press, 2002.

Garland, Alex. *The Beach*. New York: Riverhead Books, 1997.

Gathia, Joseph, and Justice Venkatachalian. *Child Prostitution in India*. New Delhi: APH Publishing Corporation, 1999.

Ghimire, Krishna. *The Native Tourist: Mass Tourism within Developing Countries*. London: Earthscan Publications Ltd, 2001.

Go, Frank, and Carson Jenkins. *Tourism and Economic Development in Asia and Australasia*. London: Pinter, 1998.

———, and Ray Pine. *Globalization Strategy in the Hotel Industry*. London: Routledge, 1995.

Gollin, Jim, and Ron Mader. *Honduras: Adventures in Nature*. Santa Fe, Calif.: John Muir Publications, 1997.

Graphic Arts. *Culture Shock!* series. Portland, Ore.: Graphic Arts Center Publishing, various years.

Green Tourism Association. *The Other Guide to Toronto: Opening the Door to Green Tourism*. Toronto: Green Tourism Association, 2000.

Grewal, Interpal. *Home and Harem: Nation, Gender, Empire and the Culture of Travel*. London: Continuum International Publishing Group, 1996.

Hall, Colin, and Stephen Page. *The Geography of Tourism and Recreation: Environment, Place and Space*. London: Routledge, 1999.

Hall, Michael, and Alan Lew, eds. *Sustainable Tourism: A Geographical Perspective*. Boston: Addison-Wesley Publishing Company, 1998.

———, and Stephen Page, eds. *Tourism and the Pacific: Issues and Cases*. London: Thomas Business Press, 1996.

Harrison, David, ed. *Tourism and the Less Developed Countries: Issues and Case Studies*. New York: CABI Publishing, 2001.

Harrison, Lynn, and Winston Husbands, eds. *Practicing Responsible Tourism: International Case Studies in Tourism Planning, Policy and Development*. New York: John Wiley and Sons, 1996.

Hawkins, Donald E., and J. P. Brent Ritchie, eds. *World Travel and Tourism Review: Indicators, Trends and Forecasts*. Wallingford, Oxford: CAB International, 1991.

Hitchcock, Michael, Victor T. King, and Michael J. G. Parnwell, eds. *Tourism in Southeast Asia*. London: Routledge, 1993.

Holden, Andrew. *Environment and Tourism*. London: Routledge, 2000.

Holing, Dwight. *Earthtrips: A Guide to Nature Travel on a Fragile Planet*. Los Angeles: Conservation International and Living Planet Press, 1991.

———, ed. *World Travel: A Guide to International Ecojourneys*. San Francisco: Nature Company-Time Life Books, 1996.

Holmes, David, ed. *Virtual Globalization: Virtual Spaces/Tourist Spaces*. London: Routledge, 2001.

Honey, Martha, ed. *Ecotourism and Certification: Setting Standard in Practice*. Covelo, Calif.: Island Press, 2002.

———. *Ecotourism and Sustainable Development: Who Owns Paradise?* Covelo, Calif.: Island Press, 1999.

———, and Abigail Rome. *Protecting Paradise: Certification Programs for Sustainable Tourism and Ecotourism*. Washington, D.C.: Institute for Policy Studies, 2001.

Hong, Evelyne. *See the Third World While It Lasts: The Social and Environmental Impact of Tourism*. Penang, Malaysia: Consumers' Association of Penang, 1985.

hooks, bell. *Black Looks: Race and Representation*. Boston: South End Press, 1992.

Hubbs, Clayton, and David Cline, ed. *Alternative Travel Director: The Complete Guide to Traveling, Studying and Living Overseas*. 7th ed. Amherst, Mass.: Transitions Abroad Publishing, 2002.

Hulme, David, and Marshall Murphree, eds. *African Wildlife and Livelihoods: The Promise and Performance of Community Conservation*. Oxford: Butterworth-Heinemann, 2001.

Hulme, Peter. *Remnants of Conquest: The Island Caribs and Their Visitors, 1877–1998*. Oxford: Oxford University Press, 2000.

Hunter, Colin. *Tourism and the Environment: A Sustainable Relationship?* London: Routledge, 1995.

Hutnyk, John. *Critique of Exotica: Music Politics and the Culture Industry*. London: Pluto Books, 2000.

Hviding, Edvard, and Tim Bayliss-Smith. *Islands of Rainforest: Agroforestry, Logging and Eco-tourism in Solomon Islands*. Aldershot, UK: Ashgate, 2000.

Inkpen, Gary. *Information Technology for Travel and Tourism*. London: Pitman Publishing, 1994.

International Society for Ecology and Culture (ISEC) and the Ladakh Project. *The Future of Progress: Reflections on Environment and Development*. Berkeley, Calif.: ISEC and the Ladakh Project, 1992.

Keller, Robert, and Michael Turek. *American Indians and National Parks*. Tucson: University of Arizona Press, 2001.

Kempadoo, Kamala, ed. *Sun, Sex and Gold: Tourism and Sex Work in the Caribbean*. Lanham, Md.: Rowman and Littlefield Publishing, 1999.

Kincaid, Jamaica. *A Small Place*. New York: PLUME/Penguin Books, 1988.

Kinnaird, Vivian, and Derek Hall, eds. *Tourism: A Gender Analysis*. New York: Wiley, 1994.

Kirshenblatt-Gimblett, Barbara. *Destination Culture: Tourism, Museums and Heritage*. Berkeley: University of California Press, 1998.

Kleymeyer, Charles David, ed. *Cultural Expression and Grassroots Development: Case Studies from Latin America and the Caribbean.* Boulder, Colo.: Lynne Rienner Publishers, 1994.

Krotz, Larry. *Tourists: How Our Fastest Growing Industry Is Changing the World.* New York: Faber and Faber, 1996.

Law, Chris. *Urban Tourism: The Visitor Economy and the Growth of Large Cities.* London: Continuum International Publishing Group, 2002.

Law, Lisa. *Sex Work in Southeast Asia: The Place of Desire in a Time of AIDS.* London: Routledge, 2000.

Lea, John. *Tourism and Development in the Third World.* London: Routledge, 1988.

Lennon, John, and Malcolm Foley. *Dark Tourism: The Attraction of Death and Disaster.* London: Continuum International Publishing Group, 2000.

Lew, Alan, and George Van Otten. *Tourism and Gaming on American Indian Lands.* Elmsford, N.Y.: Cognizant Communication Corporation, 1998.

Liu, Juanita. *Pacific Islands Ecotourism: A Public Policy and Planning Guide.* Honolulu: Pacific Business Center Program, University of Hawaii, 1994.

MacCannell, Dean, and Lucy Lippard. *The Tourist: A New Theory of the Leisure Class.* Berkeley: University of California Press, 1999.

Madeley, John. *Foreign Exploits: Transnationals and Tourism.* London: Catholic Institute for International Relations, 1995.

Mader, Ron. *Mexico: Adventures in Nature.* Santa Fe, Calif.: John Muir Publications, 1997.

Malet-Zadeh, Elizabeth, ed. *The Ecotourism Equation: Measuring the Impacts.* New Haven, Conn.: Yale University, 1996.

Mander, Jerry, and Edward Goldsmith, eds. *The Case against the Global Economy.* San Francisco: Sierra Club Books, 1996.

Mann, Mark, and Zainem Ibrahim. *The Good Alternative Travel Guide: Exciting Holidays for Responsible Travellers.* 2d ed. London: Earthscan Publications Ltd, 2002.

Mastny, Lisa, and Jane Peterson, ed. *Traveling Light: New Paths for International Tourism.* Washington, D.C.: Worldwatch Institute, 2001.

Mattson, Alexandra, Octavio Ruiz, and Meredith Sommers. *Buen Viaje: Mutually Beneficial Tourism.* Minneapolis: Resource Center of the Americas, 1999.

Mayo, C. M. *Sky over El Nido.* Athens: University of Georgia Press, 2002.

McCarthy, John. *Are Sweet Dreams Made of This? Tourism in Bali and Eastern Indonesia.* Northcote, Australia: Indonesian Resources and Information Program (IRIP), 1995.

McCool, Stephen, and Neil Moisey, eds. *Tourism, Recreation and Sustainability: Linking Culture and the Environment.* Oxfordshire: CABI Publishing, 2001.

McLaren, Deborah. *Rethinking Tourism and Ecotravel: The Paving of Paradise and What You Can Do to Stop It.* West Hartford, Conn.: Kumarian Press, 1998.

Meethan, Kevin. *Tourism in Global Society: Place, Culture, Consumption.* Basingstoke, UK: Palgrave, 2001.

Mehta, Hitesh, Ana Baez, and Paul O'Loughlin. *International Ecolodge Guidelines.* Burlington, Vt.: The International Ecotourism Society, 2002.

Meyer, Carter, and Diana Royer, eds. *Selling the Indian: Commercializing and Appropriating American Indian Cultures.* Tucson: University of Arizona Press, 2001.

Michaud, Jean, ed. *Turbulent Times and Enduring Peoples: Mountain Minorities in the South-East Asian Massif.* Richmond, UK: Curzon, 2000.

Mowforth, Martin, and Ian Munt. *Tourism and Sustainability: New Tourism in the Third World.* London: Routledge Books, 1998.

Naisbitt, John. *Global Paradox.* New York: Avon Books, 1994.

Nash, Dennis. *The Anthropology of Tourism.* Oxford: Pergamon Press, 1996.

Neale, Greg, and Trich Nicholson. *The Green Travel Guide.* London: Earthscan Publications Ltd, 1999.

Nelson, J. G., R. Butler, and G. Wall, eds. *Tourism and Sustainable Development: Monitoring, Planning and Managing.* Ontario: Department of Geography, University of Waterloo, 1993.

Norberg-Hodge, Helena. *Ancient Futures: Learning from Ladakh.* San Francisco: Sierra Club Books, 1991.

Oates, John. *Myth and Reality in the Rainforest: How Conservation Strategies Are Failing in West Africa.* Berkeley: University of California Press, 1999.

Oppermann, Martin, ed. *Sex Tourism and Prostitution: Aspects of Leisure, Recreation and Work.* Elmsford, N.Y.: Cognizant Communication Corporation, 1998.

Patterson, Carol. *The Business of Ecotourism: The Complete Guide for Nature and Culture-Based Tourism Operations.* Rhinelander, Wis.: Explorer's Guide Publishing, 1997.

Pattullo, Polly. *Last Resorts: The Cost of Tourism in the Caribbean.* London: Cassell, 1996.

Pearce, Douglas. *Tourism Today: A Geographical Analysis.* New York: Wiley, 1995.

———. *Tourist Development.* New York: Longman Scientific & Technical and Wiley, 1991.

———. *Tourist Organizations.* New York: Longman Scientific & Technical and Wiley, 1992.

Phillips, Ruth, and Christopher Steiner, eds. *Unpacking Culture: Art and Commodity in Colonial and Postcolonial Worlds.* Berkeley: University of California Press, 1999.

Pizam, Abraham, and Yoel Mansfeld, eds. *Tourism, Crime, and International Security Issues.* West Sussex, UK: Wiley, 1996.

Primack, Richard, and David Brey. *Timber, Tourists, and Temples: Conservation and Development in the Maya Forest of Belize, Guatemala, and Mexico.* Covelo, Calif.: Island Press, 1998.

Prentice, Richard. *Tourism and Heritage Attractions.* London: Routledge, 1993.

Reed, Ralph Thomas. *American Express: Its Origin and Growth.* New York: Newcomen Society in North America, 1952.

Richter, Linda K. *The Politics of Tourism in Asia.* Honolulu: University of Hawaii Press, 1989.

Robersons, Susan, ed. *Defining Travel: Diverse Visions.* Jackson: University Press of Mississippi, 2001.

Roberts, Lesley, and Derek Hall, eds. *Rural Tourism and Recreation: Principles to Practice.* Wallingford, Oxon, UK: CABI Publishing, 2001.

Robey, Tom. A *Gringo's Guide to Mexican White Water.* 2d ed. Santa Fe, Calif.: Sage Mesa Publications, 2001.

Robinson, Mike, and Priscilla Boniface, eds. *Tourism and Cultural Conflicts.* Wallingford, Oxon, UK: CABI Publishing, 1999.

Rogers, Paul, and John Aitchison. *Towards Sustainable Tourism in the Everest Region of Nepal.* Kathmandu: IUCN Nepal and ICPL, 1998.

Rossel, Pierre, ed. *Tourism: Manufacturing the Exotic.* Copenhagen: International Work Group for Indigenous Affairs, 1988.

Ryan, Chris, and Colin Hall. *Sex Tourism: Marginal People and Liminalities.* London: Routledge, 2001.

Scheyvans, Regina. *Tourism for Development: Empowering Communities.* Harlow: Prentice Hall — Pearson Education Limited, 2002.

Seabrook, Jeremy. *No Hiding Place: Child Sex Tourism and the Role of Extraterritorial Legislation.* London: Zed Books, 2000.

———. *Travels in the Skin Trade: Tourism and the Sex Industry.* 2d ed. London: Pluto Press, 2001.

Sears, John. *Sacred Places: American Tourist Attractions in the Nineteenth Century.* Amherst: University of Massachusetts Press, 1999.

Secor, R. J. *Mexico's Volcanoes: A Climbing Guide.* 3d ed. Seattle: The Mountaineers Books, 2001.

Selwyn, Tom, ed. *The Tourist Image: Myths and Myth Making in Tourism.* Chichester, UK: John Wiley and Sons, 1996.

Shaw, Gareth, and Allan Williams. *Critical Issues in Tourism: A Geographical Perspective.* 2d ed. Malden, Mass.: Blackwell Publishers, 2002.

———, and Allan Williams, eds. *The Rise and Fall of British Coastal Resorts: Cultural and Economic Perspectives.* London: Pinter, 1996.

———, and Allan Williams. *Tourism and Economic Development, European Experience.* 3d ed. New York: John Wiley and Sons, 1999.

Shiva, Vandana. *Biopiracy: The Plunder of Nature and Knowledge.* Cambridge, Mass.: South End Press, 1997.

Sindiga, Isaac. *Tourism and African Development: Change and Challenge of Tourism in Kenya.* Aldershot, UK: Ashgate, 1999.

Smith, Michael, and Thomas Bender, eds. *City and Nation: Rethinking Place and Identity.* New Brunswick, N.J.: Transaction Publishers, 2001.

Smith, Valene, ed. *Hosts and Guests: The Anthropology of Tourism.* Philadelphia: University of Pennsylvania Press, 1994.

———, and Maryann Brent, eds. *Hosts and Guest Revisited: Tourism Issues in the Twenty-first Century.* New York: Cognizant Communication Corporation, 2001.

———, and William R. Eadington, eds. *Tourism Alternatives: Potentials and Problems in the Development of Tourism.* Philadelphia: University of Pennsylvania Press, 1996.

South Pacific Peoples' Foundation. *Tourism: The Pacific Way.* Victoria, B.C., Canada: South Pacific Peoples' Foundation, 1994.

Spence, Mark. *Dispossessing the Wilderness: Indian Removal and the Making of the National Parks.* Oxford: Oxford University Press, 2000.

Stabler, M. J., ed. *Tourism and Sustainability: Principles to Practice.* Oxfordshire: CABI Publishing, 1997.

Stevens, Stan, ed. *Conservation Through Cultural Survival: Indigenous Peoples and Protected Areas.* Covelo, Calif.: Island Press, 1997.

Stonich, Susan. *The Other Side of Paradise.* New York: Cognizant Communication, 2000.

Swartbrooke, John. *Sustainable Tourism Management.* Wallingford, UK: CABI Publishing, 1999.

Sweeting, James, Aaron Bruner, and Amy Rosenfeld. *The Green Host Effect: An Integrated Tourism and Resort Development.* Washington, D.C.: Conservation International, 1999.

Taylor, Frank Fonda. *To Hell with Paradise: A History of the Jamaican Tourist Industry.* Pittsburgh: University of Pittsburgh Press, 1993.

Taylor, Lawrence, and Maeve Hickey. *Tunnel Kids.* Tucson: University of Arizona Press, 2001.

Theobald, William, ed. *Global Tourism.* Oxford: Butterworth-Heinemann, 1998.

Trask, Haunani Kay. *From a Native Daughter.* Monroe, Maine: Common Courage Press, 1990.

Truong, Thanh-Dam. *Sex, Money, and Morality: Prostitution and Tourism in Southeast Asia.* London: Zed Books, 1990.

Tuting, Ludmilla, and Kunda Dixint, eds. *Bikas-Binas Development: The Change in Life and Environment in the Himalayas.* Varanasi: Jauhari Printers, 1991.

United Nations Environmental Programme (UNEP). *Ecotourism: Principles, Practices and Policies for Sustainability.* Sterenage: UNEP, 2002.

Urry, John. *The Tourist Gaze: Leisure and Travel in Contemporary Societies.* Newbury Park, Calif.: Sage Publications, 1990.

———, ed. *Touring Cultures: Transformations of Travel and Theory.* London: Routledge, 1997.

Van den Berghe, Pierre. *Quest for the Other: Ethnic Tourism in San Cristobal, Mexico.* Seattle: University of Washington Press, 1994.

Van Harsell, Jan. *Tourism: An Exploration.* Englewood Cliffs, N.J.: National Publishers of the Black Hills and Prentice-Hall, 1982.

Vellas, François, and Lionel Bechard. *International Tourism: An Economic Perspective.* New York: St. Martin's Press, 1995.

Wahab, Salah, and John Pigram, eds. *Tourism, Development and Growth: The Challenge of Sustainability.* London: Routledge, 1997.

Wearing, Stephen. *Volunteer Tourism: Experiences That Make a Difference.* New York: CABI Publishing, 2001.

———, and John Neil. *Ecotourism: Impacts, Potentials and Possibilities.* Oxford: Butterworth-Heinemann, 1999.

Weaver, David. *Ecotourism.* New York: John Wiley and Sons, 2002.

———, ed. *The Encyclopedia of Ecotourism.* Wallingford, UK: CABI Publishing, 2001.

Wesche, Rolfe. *The Ecotourist's Guide to the Ecuadorian Amazon.* Quito, Ecuador: The Pan-American Center for Geographical Studies and Research, 1995.

———, and Andy Drumm. *Defending Our Rainforest: A Guide to Community-Based Ecotourism in the Ecuadorian Amazon.* Quito: Acción Amazoniz, 1999.

West, Patsy. *The Enduring Seminoles: From Alligator Wrestling to Ecotourism.* Gainesville: University of Florida Press, 1998.

Westerhausen, Klaus. *Beyond the Beach: An Ethnography of Modern Travellers in Asia.* Bangkok: White Lotus Press, 2002.

Wilson, Kemmons. *The Holiday Inn Story.* New York: Newcomen Society in North America, 1968.

World Bank and UNESCO. *Tourism: Passport to Development? Perspectives on the Social and Cultural Impacts of Tourism in Developing Countries.* London: Oxford University Press, 1979.

Wylie, Jerry. *Journey Through a Sea of Islands: A Review of Forest Tourism in Micronesia.* Ogden, Utah: USDA—Forest Service, 1994.

Young, Elspeth. *Third World in the First: Development and Indigenous Peoples.* London: Routledge, 1995.

Ziffer, Karen A. *Ecotourism: The Uneasy Alliance.* Washington, D.C.: Conservation International and Ernst & Young, 1989.

Zurich, David. *Hawaii Naturally: An Environmentally Oriented Guide to the Wonders and Pleasures of the Islands.* Berkeley, Calif.: Wilderness Press, 1990.

Guides for Students

Funding for U.S. Study, and Financial Resources for International Study: A Guide for U.S. Students and Professionals. IIE Books, PO Box 371, Annapolis Junction, MD 20701, USA.

A Guide to Israel Programs. World Zionist Organization, 110 E. 59th Street, 3rd Floor, New York, NY 10022, USA); 800-274-7723.

Multi-Cultural Tourism Development Workbook. Western Entrepreneurial Network, Colorado Center for Community Development, University of Colorado at Denver, PO Box 173364, Campus Box 128, Denver, CO 80217, USA; Indicate specialized area: African American, Asian American, Hispanic American, Native American; each comes with video case study.

Opportunities in Africa. Interbook, 130 Cedar Street, New York, NY 10006, USA.

Routledge Introductions to Development. John Bale and Dave Drakakis-Smith, eds. Routledge, 11 New Fetter Lane, London 4P 433, UK, or Routledge, Chapman and Hall, Inc., 29 W. 35th Street, New York, NY 10001, USA. Series of introductory books for students includes *Tourism and Development in the Third World* by John Lea.

Writing Your Dissertation on Sustainable Tourism. Tourism Concern, Stapleton House, 277-281 Holloway Road, London N7 8HN, UK; 44-171-753-3330, Fax 44-171-753-3331, *tourconcern@gn.apc.org.*

Helpful Websites

about.com. A broad US "portal" website with a good ecotourism section.

www.c-e-r-t.org. Center for Environmentally Responsible Tourism (CERT). Runs ecotours and has awards for tours operators that are working towards high environmental standards.

www.teleprot.com/~earthwyz. Earthwise Journeys. A website that lists responsible tour operators and "alternatives to mass tourism."

www.bikefed.org/economic_impact.htm. The Economic Benefits of Bicycle- and Pedestrian-Based Tourism. Links and information about bike tourism.

public-www.pi.se/%7Eorbit/eco.html. Eco-Orbit. Provides information and debate on ecotourism and sustainable development.

www.bigvolcano.com.au/ercentre/ercpage.htm. Ecotourism Resource Centre. An Australian ecotourism website with useful links.

csf.colorado.edu/mail/elan. Environment and Latin American Network. Online discussion on tourism and environmental impact in Latin America.

www.green-travel.com. Green-Travel. A website with information on ecotourism and online discussions.

www.mtnforum.org. The Mountain Forum. Promotes global action toward equitable and ecologically sustainable mountain development, online library.

www.icimod.org.sg/focus/tourism/tourlinks.htm. Mountain Tourism. Provides links to organizations and information on mountain tourism.

www.nativehawaiians.com. Native Hawaiians. A website where aboriginal people seek to protect their unique status as the Indigenous People of Hawaii.

www.nativeweb.org. Native Web. An international, nonprofit, educational organization dedicated to using telecommunications including computer technology and the Internet to disseminate information from and about Indigenous nations, peoples, and organizations around the world; to foster communication between native and non-native peoples.

www.nationalgeographic.com/travel/sustainable/index.html. National Geographic Sustainable Tourism Resource Center. Information about sustainable tourism with great links.

www.oneworld.org/news/world/tourism.html. One World Partnership. Information about tourism around the world from organizations working for social justice.

www.planeta.com. Planeta.com. A website on ecotourism in Latin America maintained by Ron Mader (*ron@planeta.com*).

www.hasbrouck.org/. The Practical Nomad. Travel Advice

www.responsibletravel.com. Responsible Travel. A website featuring international vacations that are sustainable and responsible.

www.transitionsabroad.com/listings/travel/responsible/resources.shtml. Responsible Travel from Transitions Abroad. Links to information on responsible travel.

www.for.nau.edu/geography/igust. Study Group on Sustainable Tourism. Discussion on tourism issues and tourism newsletters.

www.dkglobal.org/string. Sustainable Tourism Research Interest Group (STRING). A website that provides tourism researchers with a comprehensive collection of Internet resources relevant to sustainable tourism.

www.msue.msu.edu/msue/imp/modtd/mastertd.html. Michigan State University's Tourism Database. Comprehensive information on tourism.

webhome.idirect.com/~tourism/index.html. Tourism Information Network. A comprehensive directory of links to responsible tourism and aboriginal tourism organizations.

www.waksberg.com/research.htm. Tourism Research Links. Site for tourism researchers, consultants, and managers lists links to tourism schools, journals, and research institutes.

x.webring.com/webring?ring=tourism13;list. Tourism Research Webring. Links tourism research websites.

tii-kokopellispirit.org. Turtle Island Institute. Designs and disseminates educational programs focused on sustainable development techniques developed in cooperation with representatives of Indigenous cultures who can impart ancient knowledge with which to combine alternative technologies. Also many links to ecotravel education and volunteer opportunities.

www.igc.org/worldviews. WorldViews. A website that provides information and educational resource materials on issues of peace and justice in world affairs.

Contributors

David Barkin has been a Professor of Economics at the Xochimilco Campus of the Universidad Autónoma Metropolitana in México City since 1975. He received his doctorate in economics from Yale University and was awarded the National Prize in Political Economics in 1979 for his analysis of inflation in Mexico. He is a member of the Mexican Academy of Sciences and of the National Research Council. In 1974, he was a founding member of the Ecodevelopment Center. His most recent books include: *Wealth, Poverty, and Sustainable Development* and *Innovaciones Mexicanas en el Manejo del Agua*. He is interested in the process of unequal development that creates profound imbalances throughout society and promotes environmental degradation. His recent research focuses on the implementation of alternative strategies for the sustainable management of resources. Much of his work is conducted in collaboration with local communities and regional citizens' groups. He can be contacted at: *barkin@cueyatl.uam.mx*.

Chris Beck is owner and principal of Christopher Beck & Associates, an Anchorage-based community and tourism planning firm. He has worked on tourism issues all over Alaska, specializing in managing tourism growth in small towns.

Charles R. de Burlo is a tourism researcher and consultant with a specialization in Indigenous tourism and the Pacific Islands. He teaches in tourism, geography, and anthropology at the University of Vermont.

Cynthia Harrison recently graduated from Macalester College in St. Paul, Minnesota, with a BA in Environmental Studies. She is the Program Administrator at Indigenous Tourism Rights International, focusing on international policy and administrative support. She provided research and editing.

Norbert Hohl is a development consultant with a strong interest in community and tourism development as they relate to human rights issues in general, and Indigenous groups in particular. He lives in Australia.

Martha Honey is the director of the International Ecotourism Society (TIES) and Center for Ecotourism and Sustainable Development (a joint project for the Institute for Policy Studies and Stanford University). She has written and spoken widely on ecotourism as a tool for development and conservation and on certification, including *Ecotourism and Certification: Setting Standards in Practice* (2002), *Ecotourism and Sustainable Development: Who Owns Paradise?* (1999), and *Protecting Paradise: Certification Programs for Sustainable Tourism and Ecotourism* (2001, with Abigail Rome). For twenty years Martha worked as a journalist overseas, based first in Tanzania and then in Costa Rica. She reported for BBC, CBC, National Public Radio, the *Washington Post*, the *New York Times*, the *Guardian* (London), and other news media. She holds a B.A. in history from Oberlin College, an M.A. in African American Studies from Syracuse University, and a Ph.D. in African History from the University of Dar es Salaam. She is a fellow at the Institute for Policy Studies.

Ron Mader is a journalist based in Oaxaca, Mexico, where he directs the Planeta.com website *www.planeta.com*, which he created in 1994 to focus on environmental news, travel, and ecotourism. He is the author of the guidebook *Mexico: Adventures in Nature* (John Muir Publications, 1998) and *Exploring Ecotourism Resource Guide* (Planeta.com, 2002). In April 2000, Ron was named a finalist from Conservation International in its first "Ecotourism Excellence" competition for "commitment and leadership which has made a significant contribution to biodiversity conservation and to the protection of our planet's natural heritage."

Kaleo Patterson is a kanaka maoli whose taro roots struggles include evictions, protecting sacred sites, demilitarization, and sovereignty. As a kahu ordained in the United Church of Christ, Patterson is committed to the transformation of church in society in and through the Hawaiian sovereignty movement. He carried a key role in calling the "missionaries" church to initiate an Apology and process of Redress for the church's role in the 1893 overthrow of the Hawaiian nation.

Patterson has served churches in Maine and Hawai'i and is currently on the pastoral team of Kaumakapili Church, one of the earlist Christian churches formed among native Hawaiians. He directs the Hawaii Ecumenical Coalition, the only church-related na kanaka maoli justice initiative. Patterson serves on the Native American Legal Rights Fund Board of Directors.

Anita Pleumarom is a geographer and political scientist by training, and presently coordinates the Bangkok-based Tourism Investigation & Monitoring Team (tim-team). She is the editor of *New Frontiers — Briefing on Tourism, Development and Environment in the Mekong Subregion*. She has also published in Thailand and internationally a number of articles on the critical issues of Third World tourism, sustainable and ecotourism, and golf resort developments.

Nina Rao is the Southern co-chair of the NGO Tourism Caucus at the UN Commission for Sustainable Development (CSD); Member of the Board, EQUATIONS: Equitable Tourism Options, Bangalore; Head, Department of Tourism, College of Vocational Studies, University of Delhi; member, PATA Environment Committee, India.

Crescencio Resendiz-Hernandez is a Tenek (Maya) Indigenous person by birth, born and raised in an Indigenous agricultural community in Mexico. Through the auspices of Las Cuatro Flechas of Mexico, A.C. (Four Arrows), a nonprofit organization composed of Indigenous Peoples of Guatemala, Mexico, Canada, and the United States, he completed degrees in Biology and Geography from Carleton University in Ottawa, Canada. He is a lifetime member of "Las Cuatro Flechas de México, A.C.," and a serving member of its Board of Trustees since 1992. Crescencio is Biodiversity Specialist and Community Outreach Coordinator at Indigenous Tourism Rights International and monitors international biodiversity and tourism policies.

Luis A. Vivanco holds a Ph.D. from Princeton University in Cultural Anthropology, and teaches at the University of Vermont. He does ethnographic research on the cultural politics of environmentalism and ecotourism in Costa Rica and Oaxaca, Mexico.

Sally Weleczki-Cmiel is an artist and photographer who resides in Minnesota. She provided her amazing research and editing skills.

Index

211

About the Author

Deborah McLaren is the Director of Indigenous Tourism Rights International, a nonprofit education and networking project that supports Indigenous self-development, as well as a columnist who writes about environmentally and socially responsible tourism. Ms. McLaren earned her master's degree in social ecology from Goddard College. She has lived and worked throughout Asia and the Americas and resides in Minnesota.

Currently she is organizing educational exchanges between Indigenous Peoples to work together on tourism issues (such as the International Forum on Indigenous Tourism in Oaxaca, Mexico), designing educational programs that integrate Indigenous science and wisdom, and recruiting Indigenous Peoples and others to work on international tourism policy and research.

© Sally Weleczki Cmiel

Also from Kumarian Press...

Global Issues

Going Global: Transforming Relief and Development NGOs
Marc Lindenberg and Coralie Bryant

Inequity in the Global Village: Recycled Rhetoric and Disposable People
Jan Knippers Black

Running Out of Control: Dilemmas of Globalization
R. Alan Hedley

Sustainable Livelihoods: Building on the Wealth of the Poor
Kristin Helmore and Naresh Singh

Trapped: Modern-Day Slavery in the Brazilian Amazon
Binka Le Breton

Where Corruption Lives
Edited by Gerald E. Caiden, O.P. Dwivedi and Joseph Jabbra

*Conflict Resolution, Environment, Gender Studies, Globalization,
International Development, Microfinance, Political Economy*

Advocacy for Social Justice: A Global Action and Reflection Guide
David Cohen, Rosa de la Vega, Gabrielle Watson for Oxfam America and the Advocacy Institute

Better Governance and Public Policy
Capacity Building and Democratic Renewal in Africa
Edited by Dele Olowu and Soumana Sako

Bringing the Food Economy Home: Local Alternatives to Global Agribusiness
Helena Norberg-Hodge, Todd Merrifield and Steven Gorelick

Confronting Globalization
Economic Integration and Popular Resistance in Mexico
Edited by Timothy A. Wise, Hilda Salazar and Laura Carlsen

The Humanitarian Enterprise: Dilemmas and Discoveries
Larry Minear

Pathways Out of Poverty: Innovations in Microfinance for the Poorest Families
Edited by Sam Daley-Harris

Protecting the Future: HIV Prevention, Care and Support Among Displaced
and War-Affected Populations
Wendy Holmes for The International Rescue Committee

Visit Kumarian Press at **www.kpbooks.com** or
call **toll-free 800.289.2664** for a complete catalog.

Kumarian Press, located in Bloomfield, Connecticut, is a forward-looking, scholarly press that promotes active international engagement and an awareness of global connectedness.